Greenhill Books

MILITARY MEMOIRS OF MARLBOROUGH'S CAMPAIGNS, 1702–1712

MILITARY MEMOIRS OF MARLBOROUGH'S CAMPAIGNS, 1702–1712

by Captain Robert Parker, Royal Regiment of Foot of Ireland,
and the Comte de Mérode-Westerloo, Field Marshal of the
Holy Roman Empire

Edited by David Chandler

Greenhill Books, London
Stackpole Books, Pennsylvania

#38948374

Greenhill Books

This edition of *Military Memoirs of Marlborough's Campaigns,
1702–1712* first published 1998 by Greenhill Books,
Lionel Leventhal Limited, Park House, 1 Russell Gardens,
London NW11 9NN
and
Stackpole Books, 5067 Ritter Road, Mechanicsburg, PA 17055, USA

English translation of extracts from *Mémoires du Feld-Maréchal
Comte de Mérode-Westerloo* and
Introduction © David Chandler, 1968
© Longmans, Green and Co Ltd, 1968
This edition © Lionel Leventhal Limited, 1998

British Library Cataloguing in Publication Data
Military memoirs of Marlborough's campaigns, 1702–1712
1. Parker, Robert – Diaries 2. Mérode-Westerloo, Comte de – Diaries
3. Marlborough, John Churchill, Duke of – Military leadership 4.
Spanish Succession, War of, 1701–1714 – Personal narratives,
French 6. Great Britain – History, Military – 1603–1714
I. Title II. Mérode-Westerloo, Comte de III. Chandler, David, 1934–
940.2'526

ISBN 1-85367-330-7

Library of Congress Catalog Card Number: 98-19844

Publishing History
Military Memoirs of Marlborough's Campaigns, 1702–1712 was
first published as *Robert Parker and Comte de Mérode-Westerloo:
The Marlborough Wars* in 1968 (Longmans, London), and is now
reproduced complete and unabridged.

Printed in Great Britain

Contents

Plates

Maps

Captain Robert Parker

Comte de Mérode-Westerloo

Introduction

The War of the Spanish Succession (1701–13) holds a special place in the annals of European armies. The protracted struggle produced several Great Captains—John Churchill, first Duke of Marlborough, Prince Eugène of Savoy and the French Marshal, Villars, and their respective martial achievements still exert a strong fascination. Contemporary chroniclers and later historians have drawn very different pictures of the war, and national bias has frequently coloured both their methods of approaching the subject and the conclusions they draw from it. English historians, for instance, generally conclude that the Grand Alliance 'won the war but lost the peace'—and in their military studies tend to devote most of their attention to the first eight years of conflict, which include Marlborough's quartet of great battles. French analysts, on the other hand, believe their armies contributed very significantly to the favourable peace gained in 1713–14, and tend to concentrate on the events of the last years of the war, when Villars indubitably gained a measure of ascendancy over his opponents which dates from the battle of Denain if not earlier. Dutch and Austrian historians similarly see certain aspects of the struggle from very differing points of view. As Professor Geyl remarked, 'History is indeed an argument without end'[1]—and few would deny that this constitutes one of the subject's great fascinations, as well as one of its most baffling features.

In any attempt to resolve historical enigmas it is often useful to turn to the recorded impressions of contemporaries. Although their writings may contain hosts of inaccuracies, and their conclusions be the product of strong and often irrational prejudices, such sources perform several important services. First, they reveal how the conduct of affairs appeared to at least a section of the literate public at the time. Secondly, many memoirs contain fascinating vignettes and points of detail which would otherwise have become completely lost with the passage of time—or at the very least obscured amongst the descriptions of the greater events that surrounded them. Yet a number of such small points, culled from different sources and carefully compared, can quite often throw no inconsiderable light on

[1] Pieter Geyl, *Napoleon* (London, 1946), p. 16.

greater historical questions. Thirdly, any study of past generations would be incomparably duller and less complete without the re-miniscences—however biased and inaccurate—of the men, both humble and great, who lived through the events they describe. They supply the human touch, the eyewitness impression, and record the pulse of the time, thus providing the flesh and blood of History.

Two contemporaries who throw a considerable amount of light on the day-to-day conduct of Marlborough's most important cam-paigns are Captain Robert Parker of the Royal Regiment of Foot of Ireland (whose *Memoirs of the most Remarkable Military Transactions, From the Year 1683 to 1718* were published in Dublin (1746) and London (1747) some time after his death) and Eugène-Jean-Philippe, Count of Mérode-Westerloo (whose two-volume *Mémoires* were first published in Belgium by his great-grandson in 1840). Parker's writings have been relatively well known for some time, but do not appear to have been republished in even an edited form since the eighteenth century, although short passages have been incorporated in many learned works. It is hoped, therefore, that the inclusion of those parts relating to the years 1701–13 in this present volume will facilitate a wider appreciation of his literary efforts. The recollections of the Count of Mérode-Westerloo, on the other hand, are hardly known at all outside Belgium. Apart from a few brief passages relating to the battle of Blenheim included in Winston Churchill's great study of his distinguished ancestor,[1] he does not appear to have been much used in this country, so it is hoped that this new translation of those chapters of his *Mémoires* relating to the campaigns in Flanders, along the Danube in 1704, and the Imperial coronation of 1711, will intro-duce his lively writings to a new public.

The greatest problem facing an editor making a selection from such works is deciding what to include and what to leave out. In the end, it was determined to concentrate on those parts of Mérode-Westerloo's recollections which bear directly upon Parker's narrative; placed in juxtaposition, their individual treatments of the same events give their subjects greater depth and interest.

In almost every respect our two authors present striking contrasts. Robert Parker's obscure Irish origins could scarcely have been more different from the Count's distinguished ancestry. Their respective careers[2] led the former to the relatively humble rank of Captain of

1 W. S. Churchill, *Marlborough, his Life and Times* (London, 1947).

2 See biographical chapters, pp. 5 and 139 below.

Grenadiers, while the latter eventually became a Field-Marshal of the Holy Roman Empire and for a period Vice-President of the *Hofkriegsrat* or Imperial Council of War.

Their characters, as revealed by their writings, are similarly poles apart. 'The estimable Parker' (as Churchill has dubbed him) reveals himself as a solid, sober and reliable soldier whose whole life from 1689 to 1718 was intimately bound up with his regimental family. He was certainly no sycophant: in an age when almost all military preferment was attained through purchase or patronage, he refused to seek the favours of his companion of boyhood days, James Butler, later Duke of Ormonde and (from 1712) Captain-General, whom he despised as a soldier. Nor, as he himself admits, had he any particular reason to be personally beholden to the great Duke of Marlborough, who on one occasion awarded a coveted and deserved promotion to another officer for private reasons.[1] Yet Parker was not the kind of man to bear a grudge, and his genuine admiration for Marlborough shows in practically every page of his narrative and from time to time almost amounts to uncritical hero-worship. From first to last Parker gives us the impression of a highly competent professional soldier of modest and unpretentious character—although his writings pose one serious problem which will be discussed below.

When we turn to consider the Count of Mérode-Westerloo a very different type of personality confronts us, full of baffling and yet often endearing contradictions. Brave to the point of folly, the Count was also of the most irascible temper, touchy pride and overbearing arrogance—characteristics which continually landed him in trouble of one sort or another throughout his life. A stickler for the last detail of the deadening etiquette so dear to his snobbish heart, and firmly convinced of his superb talents as courtier, landowner and soldier, he bore lasting jealous grudges against the men whom he considered had ruined his military career—namely the Duke of Marlborough and Prince Eugène—and lost no opportunity to besmirch their reputations, however unjustly, in his writings. As a commander, the Count has been well described as 'the hero of skirmishes'[2] and it is doubtful—despite his claims—whether he possessed sufficient cool judgement to merit his appointment to posts of the highest responsibility.

[1] See below, p. 115.

[2] E. von Elewyck, 'Le Feld-Maréchal, Comte de Mérode-Westerloo'—article in the *Revue de Belges*, November 1876, p. 300.

There is little evidence to show that the objects of his wrath prosecuted any sort of vendetta against him. Although one stiff letter of
reprimand from Marlborough, dated 26 August 1708, relating to the
Count's duel with Pascale, has survived (see p. 210 n. below), another
letter written to Prince Eugène and dated Antwerp, 4 November
1711, would seem to show that the Duke valued our hero quite
highly. 'I find here M. the Marquis de Westerloo', he writes, 'on the
point of departing to join the Emperor, and he will of course be in as
close proximity to you as to him. He has communicated his views to
me, and I can only applaud them. We could certainly wish that there
were more of these gentlemen endowed with the same zeal and un-
selfishness for the cause of His Imperial Majesty. If that were the case
it is certain that affairs would follow a very different course and
whatever the appearances we would not be at such pains as he is at
this present time to find funds for the troops' bread and forage. I dare
flatter myself that Your Highness will extend your friendship to him,
and support him in his business.'[1] Of course, the great Duke could
have been writing with his tongue in his cheek—and his boundless
urbanity might have led him to conceal his innermost thoughts—but
this is somewhat improbable.

Always spoiling for a fight though he was (he once organized the
rescue by force of arms of a fellow member of the Order of the Golden
Fleece imprisoned for debt), the Count was nevertheless a great lover
of home, and certainly lavished much attention on repairing and
improving his war-ravished estates. By the lights of the time he was a
loyal husband and devoted father, scorning, he says, wine, gambling
and dalliance; but on the other hand he was perfectly prepared to
desert the cause of King Philip V of Spain in mid-war to avenge an
imagined slight when a rival nobleman secured a desired promotion
in his stead, and transfer his services to the Habsburg claimant, Charles
III, with never a flicker of conscience. The ruination of his estates and
the heavy expenses of his active soldiering years left him saddled for
life with heavy debts and almost continuous lawsuits, and these difficulties dominated his later years and doubtless account for some of the
acerbity he displays in his writings. At the same time it must be
admitted that he displayed a notable degree of resilience in time of
trouble—if we are to give full credence to his tale of tribulation.

These great contrasts in background and temperament are not

---

[1] *The Letters and Dispatches of John Churchill*, vol. V, p. 561. See also p. 218 below for the
circumstances behind the Count's journey.

unnaturally reflected in the respective ways each writer tackled his subject. Of the two, the Count undoubtedly makes the livelier reading. Robert Parker was concerned to provide an exact and private chronicle of the wars in which he served, hoping thereby to record his high opinion of King William III and Marlborough, and at the same time to expose the vices of lesser men—Ormonde in particular—who ultimately ruined their military achievements. As a result the greater part of his space is taken up with a factual, chronological narrative, enlivened by occasional flashes of personal experience and anecdote. Mérode-Westerloo, on the other hand, wrote with very different intentions in mind; his main purpose was to produce an *apologia pro vita sua*—or vindication of his career—for the instruction of his heirs and the edification of his Flemish peers. His avowed ambition in life was 'to leave some sort of memory behind me'—and he hoped that his Memoirs would explain away the many disappointments of a very chequered career by displaying how hardly he had been done by. He pursued the shades of his former commanders-in-chief with a venomous pen, and yet even his limitless sense of grievance and jealousy, his very vindictiveness and persecution-mania, contribute to the interest of his work to a very real extent; for his determination to justify the parts he played in the stirring events that befell his country have caused him to recall the very least detail of the most exciting moments of his active career. As a result many of his descriptive passages— whether dealing with the battles in which he fought (which included Eckeren, Blenheim, Ramillies and Oudenarde), his duels or the Emperor's coronation—leap to life, and the reader is able to enter for a brief moment into the atmosphere of the early eighteenth century. This life-giving quality is the Count's most notable attribute as a writer, and goes a long way to excuse his inaccuracies as an historian and even his occasional deliberate distortion of the facts.

In conclusion, we must consider the reliability of these two soldier-authors, and try to assess their respective contributions to the history of their period. Generally speaking, Parker is the more reliable witness to his age. What his prose tends to lack in liveliness it makes up for in general accuracy and comprehensiveness, although some of his dates are wrong. In one respect, however, he poses posterity with a problem, for the genuine originality of his work has been questioned by at least one notable historian—the late C. T. Atkinson.[1] The 18th Foot

---

[1] *Marlborough and the Rise of the British Army* (London, 1924), p. ix.

of this period was remarkable in that it produced no less than four soldier-historians, all of whose writings have survived. Two of these—Brigadier-General Robert Sterne[1] and Sergeant John Millner[2]—wrote in very distinctive styles, and are completely free from any implication of collusion. This cannot be said, however, of the remaining pair—namely Brigadier-General Richard Kane and our Captain Robert Parker. Any comparison of their historical writings reveals long passages which are very similar in content and overall presentation, although in points of detail they frequently differ.[3] This similarity is altogether too extensive to be deemed wholly coincidental. The problem is, therefore, to determine who copied whom—or to establish some other convincing reason for the closeness of their respective texts.

It is impossible to reach a firm conclusion from the available evidence. Both authors were published after their deaths by relatives or friends—and neither seems to have had any other motive in putting quill to paper than a desire to inform a circle of their friends of the events they participated in during their lifetimes. So far as can be determined, Parker's volume was only published twice—namely in Dublin (1746) and in London the year following. Kane's work, on the other hand, saw at least three impressions—in 1745, 1747 and 1757,

[1] Copiously quoted by R. Cannon, *Historical Records of the British Army* (London, 1835); this official historian of the Royal Regiment of Ireland states that the Sterne (or Stearne) manuscript is in the British Museum. The present editor has not yet managed to bring the original to light.

[2] Sgt John Millner, *A Compendious Journal of all the Marches, famous Battles and Sieges of the Confederate Allies in their late war* (London, 1733).

[3] Compare the following brief extracts:

'It was on the 9th of September we pitched our camp at Dundalk; and the Duke finding it to be a strong situation, with a commodious haven for shipping, whereby he might be supplied with all necessaries from England; and knowing that the enemy were already more than double his number; he resolved not to advance further, but to maintain this post the remaining part of the campaign.' (Parker (1747), p. 16.)

'It was on the 9th of September when we came to Dundalk, which the Duke finding it to be a strong Pass, with a pretty good Haven for small ships to bring him Necessaries from England, and the Newry-Mountains just in his Rear, which secured him behind, and kept open a communication with the North, where he proposed to take up his Winter-Quarters, and be supplied from thence with fresh provisions; whereupon he resolved to advance no further, but fix here for the remaining Part of the Campaign.' (Kane, *Campaigns of King William and Queen Anne, From 1689 to 1712* (1745), p. 2.)

Despite the different phrases incorporated in the middle of this passage, the basic similarity is clear. Many similar instances might be cited.

the last clearly labelled as a second edition, being embellished with considerable additions of textual matter by an unknown 'impartial hand', and admitting on the title-page that the main text has been 'improved from the late Earl of Craufurd's and Colonel Dunbar's copies, taken from General Kane's own writings'.[1] Perhaps the facts that Richard Kane was in acting command of the Regiment at Malplaquet, and went on to become a General Officer and Governor of Minorca may strengthen his claim to be the original author in the eyes of some readers, but really his comparatively distinguished career proves nothing in this context of disputed authorship, nor does the fact that his published work appeared first have much significance, as both men wrote a considerable number of years earlier. In defence of Robert Parker's claim to originality, on the other hand, it can be shown that his version is considerably longer than Kane's incorporating much more anecdotal and personal material (including several details of Kane's own activities—none of which are given in the Brigadier-General's version), and Parker specifically mentions that he kept a journal from 1689 onwards,[2] whilst on the very first page of his text our Captain also states that 'the following sheets are a collection made from several hints, which were entered down regularly as the facts happened'.[3] Parker's son, in the Publisher's Preface, specifically claims that 'the following Memoirs were not wrote with a view of making them publick', and goes on to avow that the manuscript 'fell into my hands on the death of the author. I communicated it to some of my friends, of whose judgement I have a high opinion; and it is by their advice I offer it to the publick'.[4] The 1747 edition of Kane, moreover, contains a curious sentence in its Preface which hints that there was some controversy over this authorship issue at the time: 'This book was copied from a manuscript in General Kane's own writing, which can easily be made appear when required',[5] and the Preface writer is eager to establish himself (although anonymously) as 'an officer who was intimate with him [*General Kane*] and has seen it in his own writing'. Perhaps it may be felt that this gentleman 'doth protest too much'!

[1] Title page of Kane's 1757 edition; British Museum 6586/58/d/20.

[2] Parker (1747), p. 12.

[3] Ibid., p. 1.

[4] Ibid., p. 1.

[5] Kane (1747), p. 4.

Thus the evidence concerning Parker's originality is, to say the least, conflicting. Two possible answers to the problem may be cautiously entertained. It is arguable that Parker's son pirated General Kane's book on its first publication in 1745, reworded the greater part of it, and added parts of his father's anecdotes and personal history to make up the length of the volume, subsequently publishing it as all Captain Parker's own work. Such a solution, however, is rather far-fetched—for the volume gives no impression of being a crude hotch-potch of information drawn from two sources. Or, secondly, we can accept Winston Churchill's conclusion that both Parker and Kane worked from a third source,[1] possibly some sort of rudimentary war diary kept by the Royal Regiment of Ireland, and to which both contributed at different times, and subsequently had full access to in the years following the conclusion of the war they both participated in. We know from a letter written by Parker from Dublin in 1708[2] that he was on good terms with 'the Major' (at that time Brevet-Lieutenant-Colonel Kane) and was in correspondence with him during the Captain's secondment to Ireland, and there is consequently no valid reason for doubting this more charitable hypothesis. So although it is not possible to pronounce on the problem with any certainty, posterity can certainly afford to give Parker the benefit of the doubt without in any way imputing anything dishonourable to the worthy Richard Kane, his brother officer and fellow author.

As for the overall value of Parker's published volume, we need only once again quote Churchill's opinion: 'If we had to choose one single record of Marlborough's Campaigns and of his personality, we might well be content with the journals of this marching captain, whose grasp not only of the war, but of the great causes which stirred the world, so far exceeded his station. The testimony of ordinary regimental officers is often a truer guide to the qualities of generals than the inscriptions on their own monuments.'[3]

Fortunately no such question of authenticity overhangs the work of the Count of Mérode-Westerloo; his writings are indubitably his own work. Any reservations concerning the reliability of his *Mémoires* must stem from what they contain rather than from what pen they came. As has already been mentioned, the Count writes from a very

---

[1] Churchill (1947), Book One, p. 489.

[2] See below, p.8.

[3] Churchill (1947), Book One, p. 490.

biased point of view, and consequently his narration of facts and the opinions he expresses need to be treated with great care. The unsympathetic pictures he deliberately paints of the 'Twin Generals'—Marlborough and Eugène—are to a large degree inaccurate and unjustifiable—being the product of jealousy and pique. Resentful that he was never in a position to share their gilded laurels, Mérode-Westerloo seems determined to destroy the reputations of the two greatest soldiers of his generation. Yet even in so doing he is indirectly of value to us, for he can be said to represent 'the Devil's Advocate'; by giving the worst possible impression of the two soldiers, he acts as a valuable corrective to the equally extreme portraits drawn by Marlborough's many adulators—amongst whose number we must in all fairness place both Parker and Kane. Somewhere between the two attitudes represented by these extracts, therefore, the truth most probably lies. Thus each writer has made his own valuable contribution to the military history of the early eighteenth century; and in the last analysis it must be left to the individual reader to evaluate the divergent opinions these two veterans express and the contemporary points of view they represent.

DAVID CHANDLER

Acknowledgements

I am grateful to the Editor of the *Journal of the Society for Army Historical Research* for permission to reproduce my translation of Mérode-Westerloo's account of the battle of Blenheim, and to Dr J. L. Charles of *l'Ecole Royale Militaire*, Brussels, for providing me with copies of certain documents and pictures.

I am also indebted to Baron d'Anethan, *Conservateur* of the *Bureau d'Iconographie, l'Association de la Noblesse du Royaume de Belgique*, for permission to reproduce the portrait of the Count of Mérode-Westerloo. The Director of the National Army Museum, Sandhurst, was kind enough to provide me with a photograph of the portrait reputed to be of Captain Robert Parker, which is reproduced here by courtesy of Mrs Georgina Garde-Browne.

Lastly, I owe a debt of gratitude to my wife for her invaluable assistance in compiling the Index.

D.G.C.

Chronological Table

THE MAIN EVENTS IN FLANDERS

This table relates mainly to the happenings in the Spanish Netherlands, the United Provinces and North-East France; selected events of
great significance that took place outside this area—and exerted a
notable influence on the theatre—are included in italics. All dates are
New Style. See Editor's Note p. 3 and footnote p. 14.

1700

1 Nov.   *Death of King Charles II of Spain*

16 Nov.   *Louis XIV recognizes grandson, Philip of Anjou, as new King of Spain. England and the United Provinces eventually follow suit*

1701

Feb.   French troops occupy Spanish Netherlands' fortresses

9 July   *First action of war in Italy between Franco-Spanish and Austrian forces—the battle of Carpi*

8 Aug.   Marlborough appointed to command all troops in the English pay in Holland

7 Sept.   England, United Provinces and Austria conclude the Grand Alliance

17 Sept.   *Louis XIV recognizes the Old Pretender as rightful King of England*

1702

19 Mar.   *Death of William III and accession of Queen Anne*

15 May   The Grand Alliance formally declares war on France

18 Apr.–
15 June   Dutch besiege and capture Kaiserworth[1]

11 June   French defeat Dutch at action of Nijmegen

1 July   Marlborough assumes command as Allied Captain-General in the Netherlands region

31 July–
23 Aug.   Abortive Allied operations around the Heaths of Peer

29 Aug.–
25 Sept.   Allies besiege and capture Venlo

29 Sept.–
7 Oct.   Allies besiege and capture Ruremonde

Sept.   *Bavaria and Liège join Franco-Spanish Alliance*

23 Oct.   *Allies storm Liège*

1703

27 Apr.–
15 May   Allies besiege and take Bonn

27 June   Allies defeat French at action of Steckene

30 June   French defeat the Dutch at battle of Eckeren

14–26 Aug.   Allies besiege and take Huy

10–27 Sept.   Allies besiege and take Limburg

[1] For more details concerning the sieges undertaken in Flanders see Appendix II, p. 242–3.

Nov.	Savoy joins the Grand Alliance		Sept.	Lord Peterborough's Allied force reaches Spain
May and Dec.	Portugal joins the Grand Alliance—the two Methuen Treaties		23–29 Oct.	Allies besiege and capture Sand Vliet (or Santoliet)

1704

Little activity in the Netherlands area
Failure of first Allied
May — invasion of Spain from Portugal
20 May — Marlborough marches from Bedburg for the Danube
2 July — *The storm of the Schellenberg and capture of Donauwörth*
6 Aug. — *The Allies capture Gibraltar*
11–21 Aug. — *Baden besieges and takes Ingolstadt*
13 Aug. — *The Allies win the battle of Blenheim*
24 Oct.–28 Nov. — *Allies besiege and take Landau*
29 Oct. — Allies occupy Trèves
4 Nov.–20 Dec. — Allies besiege and capture Trarbach

1705

5 May — *Death of Emperor Leopold I and succession of Joseph I*
28 May–10 June — French besiege and capture Huy
6–11 July — Allies besiege and re-capture Huy
17/18 July — Allies pass the lines of Brabant and win the action of Elixheim (or Wanghé)
18 Aug. — Dutch thwart Marlborough's desire to fight near Waterloo
29 Aug.–6 Sept. — Allies besiege and capture Léau

1706

23 May — Allies win the battle of Ramillies
25 May — Allies occupy Louvain
28 May — French abandon Brussels
1–3 June — Ghent, Oudenarde and Bruges capitulate to the Allies
17 June — Antwerp capitulates to the Allies
19 June–9 July — Allies besiege and capture Ostend
22 July–22 Aug. — Allies besiege and capture Menin
27 Aug.–9 Sept. — Allies besiege and capture Dendermonde
7 Sept. — *Imperialists win the battle of Turin*
16 Sept.–1 Oct. — Allies besiege and capture Ath

1707

13 Mar. — *Austro-French treaty neutralizes North Italy*
25 Apr. — *French defeat Allies at the battle of Almanza in Spain*
27 April — *Marlborough visits Charles XII of Sweden at Altranstadt*
22 May — *French under Villars storm the lines of Stollhofen*
30 May — Dutch veto Marlborough's proposal to fight at Terbank
26 July–22 Aug. — *Imperialists besiege but fail to take Toulon*

1708

5 July — French surprise and capture Bruges
5–7 July — French take possession of Ghent

11 July	Allies win the battle of Oudenarde
12 Aug.–10 Dec.	Allies besiege and capture Lille. (N.B.—Town capitulated on 22 October)
28 Sept.	Allies win battle of Wynendael
14 Nov.	French storm and capture Hondschoote
22–27 Nov.	French bombard Brussels
18 Dec.–2 Jan. '09	Allies besiege and recapture Ghent; French abandon Bruges

1709

27 June–3 Sept.	Allies besiege and capture Tournai
9 Sept.–20 Oct.	Allies besiege and capture Mons
11 Sept.	Allies win battle of Malplaquet
29 Oct.	Anglo-Dutch First Barrier Treaty

1710

Mar.–July	Abortive peace negotiations at Gertruydenberg
23 Apr.–25 June	Allies besiege and capture Douai
15 July–28 Aug.	Allies besiege and capture Béthune
19 Aug.	*Fall of Godolphin; new ministry in Great Britain*
5–29 Sept.	Allies besiege and capture St Venant
12 Sept.–8 Nov.	Allies besiege and capture Aire
9–10 Dec.	*French defeat Allies at Brihuega and Villaviciosa in Spain*

1711

17 Apr.	*Death of Emperor Joseph I and Succession of Charles VI*
1 May	*End of the Hungarian Revolt*
6 July	Allies capture Arleux

23 July	French recapture and raze Arleux
4–7 Aug.	Allied passage of the lines of *Ne Plus Ultra* and associated operations
9 Aug.–14 Sept.	Allied siege and capture of Bouchain
8 Oct.	*Secret Anglo-French Articles of London*

1712

10 Jan.	Marlborough removed from all offices; Ormonde becomes Captain-General in his place
29 Jan.	Congress of Utrecht meets
8 June–4 July	Allies besiege and capture Le Quesnoy
16 July	British native troops withdraw from struggle
17 July–2 Aug.	Imperialists and Dutch besiege Landrécies unsuccessfully
19 July	French hand over Dunkirk to British forces as a surety
24 July	French win the battle of Denain
25–30 July	French besiege and capture Marchiennes
14 Aug.–8 Sept.	French besiege and recapture Douai
8 Sept.–3 Oct.	French besiege and recapture Le Quesnoy
1–19 Oct.	French besiege and recapture Bouchain
8 Oct.	Preliminaries of Peace signed between England and France

1713

30 Jan.	Second Anglo-Dutch Barrier Treaty
11 Apr.	France, England, United Provinces, Portugal, Savoy and Prussia sign the Peace of Utrecht

13 July	*Anglo-Spanish treaty of peace*	7 Sept.	*Peace of Baden between France and the Empire*

1714

6 Mar.	*Peace of Rastadt between France and Austria*		**1715**
26 June	*Peace between Spain and the United Provinces*	6 Feb.	*Peace between Spain and Portugal*
31 July	*Death of Queen Anne and succession of George I*	1 Sept.	*Death of Louis XIV; succession of Louis XV under Regency*
17 Aug.	*Marlborough reappointed Captain-General, etc.*	15 Nov.	France, the Empire and the United Provinces sign the Barrier Treaty

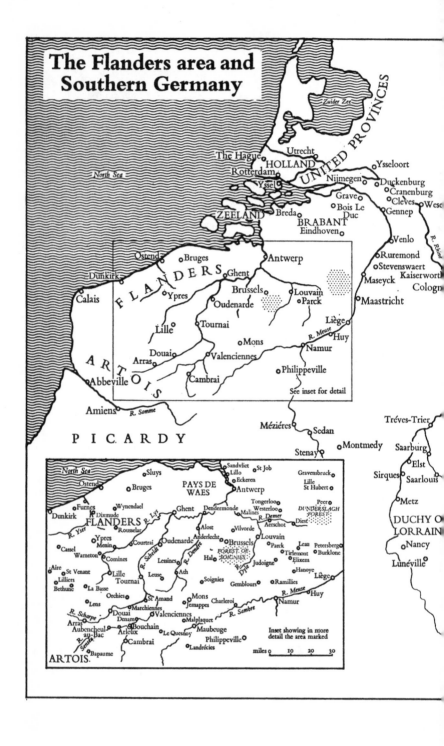

The Flanders area and Southern Germany

Zuider Zee

North Sea

UNITED PROVINCES

Utrecht
The Hague
HOLLAND
Rotterdam
Yssel
ZEELAND
Breda
BRABANT
Eindhoven

Ysseloort
Nijmegen
Grave
Bois Le
Duc
Gennep
Duckenburg
Cranenburg
Cleves
Wese

Ostend
Bruges
Ghent
Antwerp
Ruremond
Stevenswaert
Maseyck
Kaiserwort
R. Rhine

Dunkirk
FLANDERS
Ypres
Brussels
Oudenarde
Louvain
Parck
Maastricht
Colognᵉ

Calais
Lille
Tournai
Mons
Liège
Huy
R. Meuse

ARTOIS
Douai
Arras
Valenciennes
Namur

Abbeville
Cambrai
Philippeville

See inset for detail

Amiens
R. Somme

PICARDY
Méziéres
Sedan
Montmedy
Stenay

Tréves-Trier
Saarburg
Elst
Sirques
Saarlouis
Metz

DUCHY Oⁱ
LORRAINᵉ
Nancy
Lunéville

Inset

North Sea
Ostend
Sluys
Bruges
PAYS DE
WAES
Furnes
Wyncndael
Dixmude
FLANDERS
Rousselar
Ghent
Dendermonde
Sandvliet
Lillo
Eckeren
St Job
Antwerp
Gravensbruck
Lille
St Hubert
Tongerloo
Westerloo
Malines
R. Demer
Aerschot
Diest
Peer
D'UNDERSLAGH
FOREST.
R. Lys
Vilvorde
Cassel
Ypres
Menin
Warneton
Comines
Courtrai
R. Scheldt
Oudenarde
R. Dender
Anderlecht
Alost
Brussels
Louvain
Parck
Leau
Tirlemont
Elixem
Petersberg
Burklone
Aire
St Venant
Lilliers
Bethune
La Basse
Lille
Tournai
Leuse
Lessines
Hal
FOREST OF
SOIGNIES
R. Dyle
Judoigne
Hanoye
Liège
Orchies
St Amand
Marchiennes
Ath
Soignies
Gemblours
Ramillies
R. Meuse
Huy
Lens
Douai
Denam
Valenciennes
Mons
Charleroi
Namur
Jemappes
R. Sambre
Arras
Aubencheul
au-Bac
R. Scarpe
Bouchain
Arleux
Le Quesnoy
Malplaquet
Maubeuge
Philippeville
R. Scarpe
Bapaume
Cambrai
Landrécies
ARTOIS

Inset showing in more
detail the area marked

miles 0 10 20 30

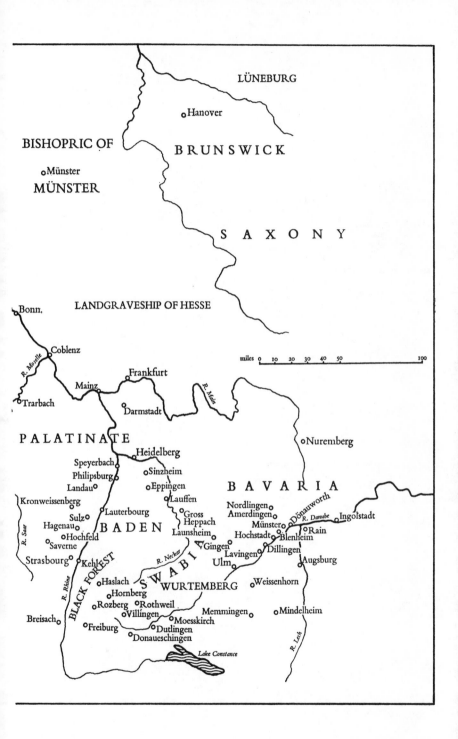

Robert Parker

Edited extracts from:

Memoirs of the Most Remarkable Military Transactions from
the Year 1683 to 1718
—containing a more Particular Account than ever yet published of
the several battles, sieges, etc, in Ireland and Flanders during the
Reigns of K. William and Q. Anne.
by Captain Robert Parker,
late of the Royal Regiment of Foot in Ireland,
who was an eyewitness to most of them.
First published by his Son.

The extracts that follow comprise pp. 68–224 of the original work
(1747 edition), suitably annotated, and relate to the years 1701 to 1713,
the period of the War of the Spanish Succession. Chapter headings
have been inserted where necessary.

Editor's Note

The following points should be noted concerning dating throughout. 'Old Style' dating, as used in England at the time, differed by eleven days from 'New Style', which was widely employed on the Continent. Parker employed 'Old Style' throughout, and in consequence the editor has added the N.S. date in parentheses wherever necessary.

Occasionally Parker mistakes certain dates. Where this is the case, footnotes have been added to point out major errors, but when the discrepancy is only slight the necessary adjustment has been made to the N.S. date preceded by the words '*in fact*'.

It has often been difficult to reconcile contemporary dates regarding the opening and ending of sieges. Different authors employed different conventions: some, for example, dated the opening of a siege from the investment of the town; others, from the opening of the trenches; similarly, the close of a siege is variously recorded as the date on which the defending commander agreed to surrender, or the date on which the garrison actually marched out. To achieve a measure of uniformity, the editor has, as a general rule, accepted the dates used by the late C. T. Atkinson.[1]

[1] *Marlborough and the Rise of the British Army;* 'Marlborough's Sieges'. (*See Bibliography*.)

The Career of Captain
Robert Parker

Robert Parker was born in Ireland some time between 1665 and 1668. Of his antecedents we know but little; his father owned a small 'concern of his own' near Kilkenny (southern central Ireland) and was probably a 'plantation Irish' or Protestant settler. His son was brought up to abhor Popery, and provided with as good an education as was possible, in the hope that one day he, too, would enter 'country business', as Parker calls it. From a very tender age, however, the young Robert had other inclinations. When James Butler[1]—grandson of the Lord Lieutenant of Ireland—raised a company of thirty Protestant schoolboys, Parker was one of the keenest recuits to handle a wooden musket. 'From this trifling circumstance', he reminisced years later, 'I was induced to entertain a high opinion of a military life.'

In most respects Parker seems to have been an indifferent scholar. In October 1683, when, as he puts it, 'it now appeared that very little was to be expected from me in the way of learning', he ran away from home and enlisted as a private soldier in Captain Frederick Hamilton's independent company which eventually became incorporated in Lord Mountjoy's Regiment.

Parker's early experience of soldiering proved of short duration. When, early in 1687, King James II began packing his army with Catholic officers both Parker and his company commander found themselves disbanded. Shortly after he had returned somewhat disconsolately home both his parents died, and this, in due course, helped their second son to resume the career of his choice. He was able to sell his portion of the family inheritance to an elder brother, and this provided him with funds for a proposed journey to the United Provinces to enlist under William of Orange. In fact, he travelled no farther than London, for upheavals of a great moment were clearly imminent, and shortly after the 'Glorious Revolution' a chance encounter in the Park with his old company commander—the newly promoted Major Hamilton—led to an invitation to join Lord Forbes's

[1] Later the Duke of Ormonde, who succeeded to the command of the British forces in Flanders upon the disgrace of the Duke of Marlborough in 1712.

Regiment (later the Royal Regiment of Ireland or 18th Foot) in March 1689. His mind was soon made up, and he found himself sent to Chester, where he seems to have found his basic training somewhat trying, for he recalls that he pondered the prospects of a military career with some hesitation: 'I then began to reflect on the circumstances of life I was in, and that carrying a brown musket was but a melancholy prospect.' However, he also started to keep his journal —a circumstance for which posterity is considerably indebted.

Once the 'Glorious Revolution' had been consolidated in England, Parker's Regiment—now commanded by Edward, Earl of Meath— joined the Duke of Schomberg's army in Ireland. There he took part in various minor operations against the Jacobites, but the campaign of 1689 was most famous for its dreadful weather, which laid low the English army with 'a violent lax' which killed many, reducing some regiments to a mere sixty men with the colours.

After King William had come in person to join his forces in Ireland, Parker carried his musket at the Boyne (1 July 1690), the first siege of Limerick, and at the siege of Athlone in 1691 he volunteered for a storming party. He lived to regret his zeal. 'Here I had a narrow escape of my life,' he recalled; 'a stone which had been thrown from the top of the castle as I passed under it, fell on my shoulder, the effects of which I feel to this day on every change of weather. This indeed I deserved for being so foolhardy as to put myself on this command when it was not my turn; but it was a warning to me ever after. It is an old maxim in war, that he who goes so far as he is commanded is a good man, but he that goes farther is a fool'.[1] Parker was clearly becoming something of an 'old soldier'! Some time before the siege of Athlone, William III had handed over command to Generals Ginkel and the Earl of Marlborough, and it was under them that Parker fought at Aughrim (12 July) and the second siege of Limerick. Thereafter the Irish war was all but over, and soon the greater part of the army was embarking at Waterford for Bristol.

The year 1692 found Meath's Regiment taking part in the abortive 'descent upon France', which led to Marlborough being accused of betraying the plan to the enemy—'a groundless report' in Parker's opinion. The remainder of the year contained a brief visit of the Regiment to Furnes and Dixmude before returning to England, where, in December, Parker's old patron Frederick Hamilton took over command from the Earl of Meath. More sea service followed in

[1] Parker, p. 34.

1693, Parker serving aboard the Fleet as a marine, but by late September he once again had his feet on terra firma at Portsmouth. The end of the year, however, at last found him in Flanders—'the Cockpit of Europe'.

By 1694 the Nine Years War (or War of the League of Augsburg) was well over half-way through, but our chronicler was in time to serve at the great siege of Namur (1695), King William's greatest military achievement. Hamilton's Regiment took part in the bloody storm of the *Terra-Nova* breach, losing in this single action a total of 291 casualties, including twelve officers killed and a further fourteen wounded. Parker was amongst these last. 'At this attack I received a shot in my right shoulder: the bullet was cut in two by the bone (or perhaps there were a brace of balls), for one part went quite through, and the other was taken out ten weeks after.'[1] His wound proved extremely troublesome, and, as Parker records, 'I was thirty weeks under cure.' However, he was able to draw some consolation from the fact that this gory action had earned distinction for his Regiment and promotion for himself; in recognition of the unit's valour at Namur, King William conferred upon it the title of 'the Royal Regiment of Foot of Ireland'; and Colonel Hamilton soon after appointed Parker the regimental Colour-Ensign (16 December 1695).

After further somewhat ineffectual campaigns, William, the Holy Roman Emperor and 'Old Lewis' were more than ready to conclude the Peace of Ryswick (September 1697). The army was immediately drastically cut back, Parker's Regiment being reduced from thirteen to three companies, each containing a mere two sergeants, two corporals, one drummer, and thirty-four privates. Rather less exciting years of garrison duty at Cork, Waterford, Dublin and Charlesfont followed, but this period of peacetime soldiering also saw Parker's marriage in June 1698.

The years of inaction abruptly ended with the outbreak of the War of Spanish Succession. Very soon Hamilton's Foot was on its way back to Flanders along with eleven more regiments. In the period of rapid expansion that followed Parker was promoted lieutenant (1702). As Parker's account of the events that took place between 1701 and 1713 forms the main part of this book, there is only need here to throw a trifle more light on the two-year period he spent on extra-regimental employment as a tactical instructor in Ireland, which began in August 1708, shortly after the battle of Oudenarde. This

[1] Parker, p. 56.

ROBERT PARKER

resulted in his missing the long-drawn-out siege of Lille, and the
battle of Malplaquet the following year. A letter survives written by
Parker to his Colonel Commanding (Robert Sterne) from Dublin and
dated 13 September 1708. From it we can deduce that Parker found
his training duties somewhat uncongenial, and that his heart was still
in Flanders.

'I do assure you that I am in no small pain for you and all my other
friends before Lille', he writes. "Tis a hard case that our poor Regiment must be always pick'd upon [for] all extraordinary commands.
May God Almighty preserve you all and bring you safe off. . . .

'I have been labouring hard with ye two regiments here in town in
showing them and ye Adjutants our firings [*see pp. 88–9 and 236 below*].
The general [*doubtless Lieutenant-General Ingoldsby, who had selected
Parker for this task*] is come from his progress and will see this regiment
perform in a day or two, after which I shall be going to Cork. . . .
There is no likelihood of having anything done for me on this side
that would be worth my acceptance, and indeed I am very loth to
quit ye ould Regiment that I have served so long in. Therefore, Sir,
I must desire you and all my worthy friends that if anything happen
in ye Regiment that I may not suffer being employed where I am, for
I assure you that I have had a great deal of trouble and have been at a
great expense since I left you. Pray make my services acceptable to my
good friend ye Major [*Brevet-Lieutenant-Colonel Richard Kane*[1]] (tell
him I answered his from Audenarde) and all ye worthys of ye
Regiment.'

The slightly lugubrious tone of the letter ends with a somewhat
gayer postscript: 'I have drank a hearty bottle with your ould friend
Mrs Rorke, where your health was not wanting. She is a widow and
resolves to continue so till you come over.'[2] Clearly a soldier's red
coat, particularly a bachelor—or widower—Colonel's, could cause a
lady's heart to flutter in the early years of the eighteenth century!

Parker's employment in Ireland seems to have ended some time in
the year 1710. His service had clearly been appreciated, for he was
awarded a bounty of £200—no inconsiderable sum at the time.
Nevertheless, we gain the impression that he was more than happy to

[1] Although he had been promoted brevet-lieutenant-colonel on 1 January 1706, Richard
Kane was still serving as major of the 18th Foot, even as late as Malplaquet—where he
was in temporary command of the Regiment in the colonel's absence. See C. Dalton,
English Army Lists and Commission Registers 1661–1714, vol 6, p. 335.

[2] British Museum, Add. MSS 23,642 f. 35.

rejoin his Regiment. Thereafter he remained in Flanders for the duration of the war.

The year 1713 saw the establishment of peace between England and France, and once again most of the army was disbanded and sent home, but the Royal Regiment of Ireland, together with Webb's Regiment, the 8th or King's Regiment (Liverpool), remained in the Spanish Netherlands as the garrison of Ghent. Much of this time was taken up with wrangles about regimental precedence, a truly vital matter for the officers concerned, as seniority of numbering determined which regiments were retained and which disbanded. Parker was sent over to England to further his Regiment's claims, but in his opinion his unit received a hard bargain when it eventually was confirmed as the 18th Foot.

On one occasion in 1714 Captain Robert Parker caught a last glimpse of his former Commander-in-Chief, the great Duke of Marlborough, as he travelled back towards England from exile as Queen Anne's death approached. 'On hearing that the Duke was to pass that way, all the officers of both regiments went without Antwerp port [*gate*] and drew up in two lines to pay him our compliments and show the respect we still retained for his Grace. He and his Duchess came up to us on horseback; they stopped and talked to us of indifferent matters about half an hour, then seeming very well pleased with the compliment we had paid them, they returned us thanks and proceeded directly through Ghent to Ostend.'[1]

In due course the Royal Irish followed Marlborough back to England, and after taking part in repressing the Jacobite revolt of 1715, found themselves billeted at Oxford (April 1716). Here there was soon trouble with the turbulent High Tory undergraduates of the University, who were always spoiling for a fight, but on this occasion they received rather more than they had bargained for from the tough Irish veterans. 'Upon this they [*the troops*] had orders to leave their swords and bayonets in their quarters, every man to provide himself with a good cudgel, to walk the streets not less than four or five in company, especially at night, and in case they were assaulted, to defend themselves. This soon made that matter easy, and the scholars were never before known to keep so close to their Colleges.'[2] This did not, however, prevent them from doing £500 worth of damage on

[1] Parker, p. 254.

[2] Ibid., p. 272.

the Prince of Wales's birthday. The Vice-Chancellor and Mayor tried, of course, to blame the 'licentious and brutal soldiery' for these excesses, but in the end the House of Lords absolved the Regiment from all responsibility.

Parker's days of active soldiering were now drawing to their close. In November 1717 he decided to sell his company when King George I—as a preliminary to further drastic military reductions—gave formal leave for any officer to dispose of his commission if he so wished. 'As I had spent my youth in the service of my country, and had also a family to take care of, I thought it advisable to lay hold of this opportunity; and accordingly, in April 1718, I resigned my Commission to a nephew of my very good friend and benefactor, Lt General Frederick Hamilton, he paying me a valuable consideration for it.'[1]

Here we begin to lose sight of the estimable Parker. It is known that he settled near Cork, but the rest of his life—and even the date of his death—are shrouded in the pall of anonymity cast by more than two centuries of history. It is certain that his 'Recollections' were not published in his own lifetime, and that their appearance in print was deliberately delayed by his son for obvious reasons until after the death of his *bête noire*, the Duke of Ormonde, in 1745. Nevertheless, Parker's spirit burns brightly on through his writings, and posterity has a considerable debt of gratitude to pay to the memory of the valiant Robert Parker Esquire, some time Captain of Grenadiers in the Royal Regiment of Foot of Ireland, and self-appointed Chronicler of the British Army.[2]

[1] Ibid., pp. 274-5.

[2] *Summary of Robert Parker's Promotions* (taken from his own writings, and Dalton, *English Army Lists*, vol. V, Pt II, p. 55, n. 15).
First Enlisted in Frederick Hamilton's Independent Company (later Lord Mountjoy's Regiment of Foot)—October 1683.
Re-enlisted in Lord Forbes's Regiment of Foot (later the Earl of Meath's)—March 1689.
Commission of Ensign in the Royal Regiment of Foot of Ireland (formerly in the Earl of Meath's)—16 December 1695.
Lieutenant in the above Regiment—1702.
Adjutant of the above Regiment—before 1706.
Captain-Lieutenant in the above Regiment—1 May 1706.
Captain of Grenadiers in the above Regiment—11 September 1708 (probably held for some time previous in an acting capacity).

I

The Origins of the War

On the fatal eighth of March following [*19 March 1702*], died the great King William,[1] whose name ought to be written in our British annals, in letters of gold. A prince whom Providence had raised up, not only to restore and support our Religion and Liberties in particular; but also to check the pride and ambition of Lewis the Fourteenth, who had combined with King James to enslave all Europe. And indeed, considering the infinite hazards and difficulties he passed through, even from his cradle, the plots that had been made against his sacred life, both at home and abroad, and the infinite dangers he was exposed to in the field; he seems, all along, to have been the care of a special and peculiar Providence, which had determined to preserve him, until he had affected the great and glorious work that had been allotted him. It was singularly providential in particular, that his life was preserved until he had formed a second Grand Alliance[2] against that aspiring monarch, who, contrary to the sacred ties of treaties, had placed his grandson Philip on the Spanish throne; by which accession of power, he was in a fairer way than ever, of accomplishing his long-projected scheme of universal monarchy.

When he found himself in a declining state of health, and was sensible of his approaching death, he well knowing, as has been said, the capacity of the man, placed the Earl of Marlborough at the head of the British affairs, made him general of his forces, and let him into the whole affair of the Confederacy. But would you know the heart and

[1] For simple biographical details of William III and other prominent personages mentioned in these extracts, consult the alphabetical Biographical Notes commencing on p. 244 below.

[2] The first Grand Alliance had been formed to oppose Louis XIV during the Nine Years War (1688–97), often alternatively known as the War of the League of Augsburg.

The original members of the second (signed in its final form on 7 September 1701) were England, the United Provinces and Austria. Brandenburg-Prussia, Hesse and various other minor German states of the Holy Roman Empire became associated during the winter of 1701–2. War was formally declared on 15 May 1702, but hostilities between Austria and France had already broken out the previous year in North Italy (see Chronological Table, p. xxi above). In 1703 Portugal and Savoy also joined the Alliance.

soul of that great man, read it in his last memorable speech to the British Parliament, (dictated by himself, as were all his speeches) when he had put everything in a right channel for carrying on the war.

'My Lords and Gentlemen,

'I promise myself you are met together full of the just sense of the common danger of Europe, and that resentment of the late proceedings of the French King, which has been so fully and universally expressed in the loyal and seasonable Addresses of my people.

'The owning and setting up the pretended Prince of Wales[1] for King of England, is not only the highest indignity offered to me and the whole nation, but does so nearly concern every man, who has a regard for the Protestant religion, or the present and future quiet and happiness of your country, that I need not press you to lay it seriously to heart, and to consider what further effectual means may be used, for securing the succession of the Crown in the Protestant line, and extinguishing the hopes of all Pretenders, and their open or secret abettors.

'By the French King's placing his grandson on the throne of Spain, he is in a condition to oppress the rest of Europe, unless speedy and effectual measures be taken. Under this pretence he is become the real master of the whole Spanish Monarchy; he has made it to be entirely depending on France, and disposes of it as of his own dominions; and by that means he has surrounded his neighbours in such a manner, that though the name of peace may be said to continue, yet they are put to the expense and inconveniences of war. This must affect England in the nearest and most sensible manner, in respect to our trade which will soon become precarious in all the valuable branches of it; in respect to our peace and safety at home, which we cannot hope should long continue; and in respect to that part which England ought to have, in the preservation of the liberty of Europe.

'In order to obviate the general calamity with which the rest of Christendom is threatened by this exorbitant power of France, I have concluded several alliances, according to encouragement given me by both Houses of Parliament; which I will direct shall be laid before you, and which I do not doubt you will enable me to make good. There are some other treaties still depending, that shall be likewise communicated to you, as soon as they are perfected.

'It is fit I should tell you, the eyes of all Europe are upon this

[1] On the death of James II in exile (September 1701), Louis XIV had recognized his son, James Edward (the 'Old Pretender') as rightful King of England.

Parliament; all matters are at a stand, till your resolutions are known, and therefore no time ought to be lost.

'You have yet an opportunity, by God's blessing, to secure to you and your posterity, the quiet enjoyment of your religion and liberties, if you are not wanting to yourselves, but will exert the ancient vigour of the English nation: But I tell you plainly, my opinion is, if you do not lay hold on this occasion, you have no reason to hope for another. In order to do your part, it will be necessary to have a great strength at sea, and to provide for the security of our ships in harbour; and also, that there be such a force at land, as is expected, in proportion to the forces of our allies.

'Gentlemen of the House of Commons, I do recommend these matters to you, with that concern and earnestness, which their importance requires. At the same time I cannot but press you to take care of the public credit, which cannot be preserved but by keeping sacred that maxim, that they shall never be losers, who trust to a Parliamentary security.

'It is always with regret, when I do ask aids [*subsidies*] of my people; but you will observe that I desire nothing which relates to any personal expense of mine; I am only pressing you to do all you can for your own safety and honour, at so critical and dangerous a time; and am willing that what is given, shall be wholly appropriated to the purposes for which it is intended.[1]

'And since I am speaking on this head, I think it proper to put you in mind, that during the late war [*1688–97*], I ordered the accounts to be laid yearly before the Parliament, and also gave my assent to several bills for taking the public accounts, that my subjects might have satisfaction how the money given for the war was applied; and I am willing that matter may be put in any farther way of examination, that it may appear whether there were any misapplications and mismanagements, or whether the debt that remains upon us, has really arisen from the shortness of the supplies, or the deficiency of the funds.

'I have already told you how necessary dispatch will be for carrying on that great public business, whereon our safety, and all that is valuable to us depends. I hope what time can be spared, will be

---

[1] Since his accession in 1688, William III had earned an unenviable reputation with his Parliaments on account of the sums of money he insisted on spending on the armed forces. Parliament was extremely jealous of the control of the national purse strings, and charges of misappropriating funds were frequently levelled at the King's ministers; hence the careful wording of these new requests.

employed about those other very desirable things, which I have so often recommended to you from the Throne; I mean the forming some good bills for employing the poor, for encouraging trade, and the further suppressing of vice.

'My Lords and Gentlemen, I hope you are come together determined to avoid all manner of disputes and differences, and resolved to act with a general and hearty concurrence, for promoting the common cause; which alone can make this a happy session.

'I should think it as great a blessing as could befall England, if I could observe you as much inclined to lay aside those unhappy, fatal animosities, which divide and weaken you, as I am disposed to make all my subjects safe and easy, as to any, even the highest offences, committed against me.

'Let me conjure you to disappoint the only hopes of our enemies, by your unanimity. I have shown, and will always shew how desirous I am to be the common father of all my people: Do you in like manner lay aside all parties and divisions, let there be no other distinction heard of among us for the future, but of those who are for the Protestant religion, and the present Establishment, and of those who mean a Popish prince, and a French government.

'I will only add this, if you do in good earnest desire to see England hold the balance of Europe, and to be indeed at the head of the Protestant interest, it will appear by your right improving the present opportunity.'

This speech had such an effect on both Houses of Parliament, that they unanimously agreed to everything his Majesty proposed to them; and being truly sensible of their great danger, and of the declining state of the King, they immediately set themselves to work, prepared several valuable bills for the Royal Assent, which he signed with great pleasure, and by the fatal eight [19th] of March 1701-2,[1] had put every thing in a right channel for carrying on a vigorous war.

Queen Anne being seated on the British throne, continued the deceased King's Ministry to a man (a few of her Household only excepted).[2] She continued the same Parliament, confirmed the alliances the King had made, and pursued the same schemes and measures, which he had formed. She made her Royal Consort Prince George of

---

[1] At this period there was still some confusion as to whether the calendar year began on 1 January or on 25 March—hence the double date.

[2] The Ministry centred around Godolphin, the Lord Treasurer, and Lord Nottingham (who was replaced in 1704 by Harley, later Earl of Oxford).

Denmark, Lord High Admiral, and Generalissimo of all her forces by sea and land. She also appointed the Earl of Marlborough Captain-General of all her land forces, and sent him to Holland in quality of her Ambassador Extraordinary, to notify the King's death, and to consult on measures for carrying on an offensive war in the Netherlands.

I am now entering upon the transactions of a second war, the cause whereof was this; that the French King contrary to the faith of treaties had placed his grandson on the Spanish throne. This being done, he soon found means to bring over to his interest, the two ungrateful brothers, the Electors of Bavaria and Cologn [*Cologne*].[1] The first had been made Governor of the Spanish Netherlands, by the means of King William and the Allies: yet on this occasion he received French troops into all his garrisons, and made all those of the Dutch that were in them prisoners; for which good piece of service the French King promised to give him all his assistance, to raise him to the Imperial throne.

The Elector of Cologne had also been promoted to that Electorate by the interest of the Allies, and had been made Bishop of Liège in opposition to the French King, who used all his endeavours in favour of the Archbishop of Furstenburg: Yet he also received French troops into all his garrisons, except Cologne, where the Canons of the city refused to receive either him or them. The French King kept the Dutch troops prisoners, until the States had acknowledged Philip King of Spain: but as soon as their troops returned, they broke through that acknowledgment, and declared war against the two Crowns [*15 May 1702*].

1 The following practice has been followed throughout the volume with regard to spelling: where a place or person is mentioned for the first time the original eighteenth-century form is preserved, the modern spelling being placed after it in parenthesis. All subsequent references to the same name are printed in the modern form.

II

The Campaign of 1702

The first thing the Confederates undertook in the Netherlands was the siege of Keyserswaert, [*Kaiserworth*], a fortress belonging to the Electorate of Cologne, but garrisoned by the French. It lies close on the German side of the Rhine, three leagues above Cleves.[1] The siege was formed in the month of April [*18th*] by the troops of Prussia, Hanover, Hesse, and some Dutch, commanded by the Prince Nassau Sarbruck [*Saarbrücken*]; whereupon the French King sent the Duke of Burgundy and Marshal Bouffliers [*Boufflers*], with an army of something more than 60,000 to raise the siege. They encamped on the hitherside of the Rhine, but dared not venture to pass the river; however they found means to prolong the siege, by sending fresh men in boats every night to the besieged, and bringing back their wounded.

When the French had marched up into these parts, the Earl of Athlone [*or Field-Marshal Ginkel*] took the field with about 24,000, and encamped three leagues beyond Nimeguen [*Nijmegen*], near Cranenburg, in order to cover this part of the country. In this small army was our British infantry, the horse being still in quarters.

The Duke of Burgundy and Marshal Boufflers finding that they could not prevent Kaiserworth from falling into the hands of the Allies, had formed a scheme to cut off Athlone. The two armies were but five leagues distant from each other, but then we had a large thick wood in our front, which they could not possibly march through; wherefore they divided their army, and upon beating Tattoo,[2] decamped on a sudden; the Duke of Burgundy marching with the right wing of the army round by the way of Cleves, and Boufflers with the left round by Gennep [*Genappes*]. They continued marching all that night, and the next day, with design that both wings should cut between us and Nijmegen. Had they succeeded in this, not a man of our small army could have escaped; all must either have been killed or taken. At the same time Nijmegen must also have fallen into their

---

[1] See general map of the Netherlands area, pp. xxvi–vii.

[2] For this, and other military terms, see Glossary of Military Terms, p. 262 below.

hands, which would have opened them a way into the very heart of the Province of Holland, and been a fatal blow to the Allies at this time.

They carried on their march so privately, that our general had not the least notice of it, till noon next day; and he instantly gave orders to strike our camp and march. This surprised us not a little, more especially as many of us had sent our horses to Nijmegen for forage, and for want of them were obliged to leave our tents and baggage behind us: but expresses were sent after them, with orders to throw away their forage, and bring off our tents and baggage, which they luckily effected, and were at Nijmegen before us. We continued marching all night, but were obliged to take a considerable round, in order to leave the great road for the artillery and baggage. By daylight, we were within less than a league of Nijmegen, at which time the enemy's horse began to appear on both sides of us. This made us mend our pace, and they pushed forward to try if they could get between us and the town. Some of their dragoons came so near, as to make a push at the Dutch foot, which put them in some disorder: But the next regiments to them facing about, fired upon them, and made them scour back. At length we arrived safe within the outworks of Nijmegen. My Lord Athlone with the horse kept in the rear of the foot, and behaved with great conduct, and bravery; but was much censured for not having better intelligence; for half an hour more would have cut us all to pieces.[1]

The Governor was an older general than Athlone, and was disgusted that the other had been made a Veldt [Field]-Marshal over his head; and on this occasion there was some reason to suspect he had been tampering with the enemy; for though he saw them close at our heels, within half cannon-shot of the town, yet he had not a cannon mounted on all the ramparts; nor could the burghers obtain the keys of the stores, but were obliged to break them open, to draw the cannon up to the ramparts, and to bring the powder and ball on their backs. When this was done, they fired like fury on the enemy, and made them retire immediately; otherwise as their foot was just come up, it was believed they would have attacked us in those noble advanced works, which had been made there during the short interval of the last peace, by the famous engineer Cohorn. He, as it were, foresaw what had now happened; and it was to these very works that we owed our

---

[1] It would seem that the French lost some 200 casualties to Athlone's 700. The Allies also lost about 300 wagons. (See G. Bodart, *Militär-historisches Kriegs-Lexikon 1618–1905*, p. 126.)

preservation. Whether the Governor was faulty or not, I shall not pretend to say: but it is most certain that the States[1] sent for him in a short time, and he was never heard of after.

The enemy encamped about a league from us, where they stayed two nights only, and then marched back to Cleves. Here they continued destroying the fine improvements of that place, until Kaiserworth surrendered, which it did in a few days.[2] Whereupon they marched, and took up the strong camp of Genappes, having the Wood of Cranenburg on their right, the river Meuse on their left, and a deep swampy river in their front. Here they proposed to continue while they could meet with forage; more especially as this post covered the garrisons they had on the Meuse.

Upon the surrender of Kaiserworth, the Prince of Nassau marched with about 14,000 Prussians, etc., up the Rhine, to clear that river of all the French garrisons as high as Cologne; and the remaining part of these troops came and joined us at Nijmegen.

About the end of June the Earl of Marlborough came and took upon him the command of the Confederate army in the Netherlands. [1 July]. Upon a review he found them to be complete 70,000, well appointed in all respects. The second day after he reviewed them, he marched directly up to the enemy, and encamped at Duckenburg, within two leagues of them, having his right close to the Meuse.

Now my Lord Marlborough, who never had the command of such an army before, knew very well that the eyes of all the Confederates were upon him; more especially those of the States General. They in compliment to the Queen of England, had given him the command of their army; and even the safety of their country depended in a great measure on his conduct. However, that wise state, even in the late King's time (in whom they placed all the confidence imaginable), always sent into the field with him, two of the most experienced of their Council of State, who were to be consulted upon all occasions. They therefore sent at this time with the Lord Marlborough, the Baron de Heyd, and the Heer Guildermaison; which his Lordship could not take amiss, since he knew it had been their constant practice.

My Lord saw that, at his first setting out, it was not very consistent with his honour to lie idle: and finding the enemy resolved on keeping their strong camp, where there was no coming at them; he formed a

---

[1] The States-General constituted the ruling body in the United Provinces.

[2] The siege of Kaiserworth lasted from 18 April to 15 June 1702 N.S. See pp. 242-3.

scheme which obliged them to quit their camp, and dance after him. In order to do this he caused three bridges to be laid over the Meuse, under pretence of supplying his camp with forage from the other side: but the very evening the bridges were finished, he decamped on a sudden, passed the river, and continued marching all that night, and till noon the next day, at which time he came up with the Castle of Gravensbruck. It was a small frontier garrison belonging to the enemy, in which were about 300 men. It held out about three hours, and then surrendered at discretion. From hence we continued our march to Hubertslill [or *Lille St Hubert*], about eight leagues from the place where we passed the Meuse; and by this means we were between the enemy and home.

This sudden march was no small surprise to the Duke of Burgundy and Boufflers. They knew if they fought us, it must be at great disadvantage, and yet could not tell how to get home without it. Early next morning they decamped, but were obliged to keep the same side of the river, till they came within two leagues of Venlo. Here they must either pass it, or run the hazard of a long round about march, which would give Lord Marlborough an opportunity of becoming master of their lines, or of gaining some other considerable advantage over them. At this place therefore they passed the river, and encamped within less than three leagues of us. They were yet in great perplexity how they should pass by us, for we were just between them and home, and they had no way homeward, but by marching over a heath within half a league of our camp.[1]

To cover their design, they made a grand forage the morning after they had passed the river; this looked as if they designed to continue some time in that camp. They had also sent an express to Count Tallard, (who commanded a body of 12,000 men, that were left to cover their lines) to draw toward our right, in order to facilitate their passing by us. The Lord Marlborough immediately judged what they designed by their grand forage; whereupon that very evening he ordered the army to strike their tents, and send them with all their baggage to Gravensbruck. He ordered the army also to lie on their arms all night, to be in readiness to fall on the enemy next morning as they passed the heath; and he had likewise made a disposition for attacking Tallard, in case he should attempt any thing on our right. As his Lordship judged the thing so it happened; for the enemy upon

[1] These operations are usually referred to as 'the Heaths of Peer' (31 July–23 August 1702 N.S.). See Churchill, *Marlborough* (1947), Book One, pp. 582–91.

beating Tattoo decamped, and marched all night with the utmost expedition. By the time it was day, their front had entered the heath, and my Lord Marlborough had his men under arms, and just ready to march, when the Field-Deputies came to him, and prayed him to desist. This greatly surprised him, as they had agreed to his scheme the night before: but being a man of great temper and prudence, and being determined not to do anything this first campaign without their approbation, at their earnest entreaty he desisted.[1] Whereupon the tents and baggage were sent for, and the army pitched their camp again. However, he desired they would ride out with him to see the enemy pass the heath, which they and most of the general officers did, and saw them hurrying over it in the greatest confusion and disorder imaginable; upon this they all acknowledged, that they had lost a fair opportunity of giving the enemy a fatal blow. By this means did young Burgundy and Boufflers escape: but being joined by Tallard, they were more in number than we, and then they faced about, and encamped within two leagues of us; however, they took care to keep within the enclosed grounds, and next day we altered the aspect of our camp in order to front them.

Here we were obliged to wait till our bread-waggons, which were at the [River] Grave, waiting for an escort, should come up. For this purpose General Obdam [Opdam] was sent off with a detachment of 16,000 men. Our Regiment belonged to one brigade of this detachment, which was commanded by the Lord Cutts, and our Colonel, Brigadier Hamilton. When the enemy observed us marching towards the Grave, they made a movement that way, expecting to meet with an opportunity of falling upon us: this was what my Lord Marlborough expected, and thereupon he ordered the army to move gently after the detachment. The enemy perceiving this, stopped short within the enclosures, and suffered Opdam to pass with the convoy. My Lord Marlborough finding that neither the enemy nor the Field-Deputies were inclined to come to an engagement, used all proper methods to draw them into one insensibly. With this view he ordered the army, as they were on the long march, to face about, and march over the great Heath of Dunderslaugh toward Peer, leaving Opdam with the

---

[1] This galling decision illustrates Marlborough's ability to balance military against political considerations in the interest of the long-term view. Rather than cause a serious disagreement with the United Provinces which might have affected the overall conduct of the struggle, he was prepared to abandon the chance of a near-certain success in the field.

convoy to follow at some distance. This he did to draw the enemy out of their enclosures into the heath, in order to fall upon Opdam: the bait took, and out they came at the very place he expected, and were preparing to fall upon him. My Lord, who had his eye that way, halted on a sudden, and stretched the army back toward Opdam. The enemy did not expect we could have been ranged in opposition to them so suddenly, and now to retire to the enclosures must expose their rear to great danger; they therefore put on the best face they could, and drew up in order of battle. It was on the 12th of August, O.S. [22 August] about five in the afternoon, when both armies were drawn up on a large heath, within less than half an English mile of each other; and it was thought impossible for us to part without blows.

The cannon on both sides fired with great fury, and killed a number of men. Here I narrowly escaped a cannon-ball, which I plainly saw coming directly to me, but by stepping nimbly aside, had the good fortune to avoid it. The Field-Deputies finding themselves insensibly led into this scrape, came to his Lordship, just as he was giving orders to begin the battle, and begged him to forbear till morning. My Lord (though it was somewhat late) desired that this second opportunity might not be lost, and told them the enemy would not stay till morning; however, in the end they prevailed on him to desist; so we lay on our arms all night, expecting to begin the battle as soon as it was day. But behold, when day came, there was not an enemy to be seen, except a few squadrons on the other side of the enclosures, bringing up their rear; and these made not the least halt, until they came within their lines. Soon after Tallard marched away to the Rhine with the troops under his command, the Germans having at this time laid siege to Landau [from 18 June].

The Field-Deputies had opposed our coming to a battle, first because their instructions were to avoid it, till such time as the Maese [Meuse] was cleared of the French garrisons up to Maestricht [Maastricht]; and also because they knew not how the Lord Marlborough might behave in a general engagement. These things his Lordship had also considered, and therefore bore the disappointment with great temper, though he saw plainly he had lost great opportunities of attacking the enemy to advantage. The French having now marched off, he was at liberty to clear the Meuse of their garrisons, and ordered General Opdam to march with his detachment and lay siege to Venlo, while he marched with the grand Army, and encamped near Maastricht to cover the besiegers.

On the 16th [27th][1] of August Opdam came before Venlo, in order to attack Fort St Michael, which covered the two on this side, while Prince Nassau (who had cleared the Rhine of the French) came and encamped the next day on the other [east] side of the river to carry on the attack of the town, which lay altogether on that side. On the 20th [31st] the trenches were opened on both sides; and as there happened a very remarkable affair on our side, in which our Regiment in particular was chiefly concerned, I shall be more exact in relating it.

Fort St Michael was a regular fortification of five bastions, etc. We had carried on our approaches against it, until we came to the foot of the glacis; at which time orders were given for attacking the covert [covered]-way, and driving the enemy from thence, in order to make a lodgment on the top of the glacis, and so join the three attacks by a particular line. It happened that our Regiment mounted the trenches of the British attack this morning. About noon the grenadiers and 300 men of the other three regiments of our brigade, joined us soon after; the Lord Cutts, Brigadier Hamilton, and several young noblemen came to see the attack made.

The Lord Cutts sent for all the officers, and told them, that the design of the attack was only to drive the enemy from the covert-way, that they might not disturb the workmen in making their lodgment; however, if they found them give way with precipitation, we were to jump into the covert-way, and pursue them, let the consequence be what it would. We all thought these were very rash orders, contrary both to the rules of war, and the design of the thing.

About four in the afternoon the signal was given, and according to our orders, we rushed up to the covert-way; the enemy gave us one scattering fire only, and away they ran. We jumped into the covert-way, and ran after them. They made to a ravelin, which covered the curtain of the fort, in which were a captain and sixty men. We seeing them get into the ravelin, pursued them, got in with them, and soon put most of them to the sword. They that escaped us, fled over a small wooden bridge, that led over the moat to the fort; and here like madmen without fear or wit, we pursued them over that tottering bridge, exposed to the fire of the great and small shot of the body of the fort. However, we got over the fausse-braye, where we had nothing for it, but to take the fort or die. They that fled before us, climbed up by the long grass, that grew out of the fort, so we climbed after them. Here we were hard put to it, to pull out the palisades,

[1] Most sources say 29th N.S.

which pointed down upon us from the parapet; and was it not for the great surprise and consternation of those within, we could never have surmounted this very point. But as soon as they saw us at this work, they quitted the rampart, and retired down to the parade [-*ground*] in the body of the fort, where they laid down their arms, and cried for quarter, which was readily granted them.

Thus were the unaccountable orders of Lord Cutts as unaccountably executed, to the great surprise of the whole army, and even of ourselves, when we came to reflect on what we had done. However, had not several unforeseen accidents occurred, not a man of us could have escaped. In particular, when we had penetrated as far as the wooden bridge, had the officer drawn the loose plank after him, as he ought (for they were laid loose for that very purpose), we must all have fallen into the moat, which was ten feet deep in water; and again, when we had passed the bridge, which was 120 feet in length, and had got on the fausse-braye, had there been six or eight feet of stone or brick under the sod work (which is always practised in our modern fortifications) or had the Governor kept the grass, by the help of which we climbed, close mown, as he ought to have done, what must have been our fate? But everything fell out fortunately, and Lord Cutts's orders were crowned with success. In the end his Lordship had the glory of the whole action, though he never stirred out of the trenches till all was over. The garrison consisted of 1,500 men, which was more than the party that attacked them. They had about 100 killed and wounded; and what was strange, we had but 27 killed, and about as many wounded.

This affair was the occasion of another almost as surprising. Two days after, an express came to Prince Nassau, which gave an account that Landau was taken [*the town fell on 8 September*]; whereupon he ordered the army on both sides of the river, to draw down as near the town as they could, in order to fire three rounds for the taking of Landau. The cannon also of all the batteries, the mortars and 'Cohorns' loaded with shot, were ordered to fire with the troops, into the town. When the garrison and inhabitants saw us drawing down on all sides, they judged it was with a design of making such an attack on the town, as that we had made on the fort. This struck such a terror into them, that the Magistrates, in the greatest consternation imaginable, begged the Governor[1] to capitulate, and not suffer them all to be put to the sword. By this time the first round of all our batteries began to

1 The Governor was Major-General Labadie, Comte de Varo.

23

fire, and the small shot of the army followed, which so affrighted them, that men, women, and children, came flocking on the ramparts with white cloths in their hands, crying, 'Mercy! Mercy! Quarter, Quarter;' and the Governor, in as great a consternation as the rest, sent out an officer to the Prince to desire a capitulation, which was immediately granted. As we had other sieges to carry on this season, the Prince allowed them honourable terms [*25 September*].

The enemy marched out two days after, and the day following Opdam passed the Meuse, and joined the Prince on his march up the river to Ruremond [*Ruremonde*]; to which place we laid siege, and it surrendered in fourteen days [*in fact nine: 29 September–7 October*]. Within this time my Lord Marlborough for dispatch, had sent detachments from the grand army, which took Stevenswaert [*4 October*], and Maseik [*Maaseyck*], and this cleared the Meuse up to Maastricht.

After this the whole army joined on Petersberg, a league above Maastricht, from whence we marched next day to Liège. Burgundy was now returned to Court, and Boufflers, who commanded in his absence, had drawn the French army to this place, in order to prevent it from falling into the hands of the Allies this year. But at the approach of our army, he retired within his lines, leaving eleven battalions in the citadel, and two in the Fort of the Charter-house [*or Chartreuse*]. The Meuse runs through the town, and this fort lies on the left side of the river.

The city of Liège being a defenceless place, the Magistrates opened their gates, and received a garrison of our troops. It was the first of October, O.S. [*the 12th*][1] when we sat down before the citadel, and by the eleventh [*22nd*] a breach was made fit to be stormed. Whereupon my Lord Marlborough sent to the Governor, to let him know, he should have honourable terms, if he surrendered immediately. The Governor answered, it would be time enough a month hence, to treat of a surrender.[2] Next day therefore, being the 12th [*23rd*] of October (the very day the Duke of Ormonde attacked the Spanish galleons at Vigo), every thing was prepared for a general assault. The attack was made about twelve o'clock, and in less than an hour we carried it sword in hand, with a very inconsiderable loss on our side.

[1] Some sources say 11 October N.S.

[2] By the conventions of the day, a besieged garrison was expected to hold out for forty-eight days. Then, if no relief was in prospect and the besiegers were in a position to attempt a storm, the defending commander was entitled to surrender his position on the best terms he could obtain.

Our men gave no quarter for some time, so that the greater part of the garrison was cut to pieces. They in the Charter house being eye-witnesses of the fate of the Citadel, surrendered next day [*in fact on the 26th N.S.*]. They had liberty to march out with their hands in their pockets,[1] and every man was to go where he pleased, by which means the officers carried but few of them home.

Thus ended the Lord Marlborough's first campaign, which established his character among the Allies, and gave great satisfaction, in particular to the States-General; for not only the Field-Deputies, but even the Earl of Athlone (who at first disputed the command with him), and all their general officers gave an extraordinary character of him.

In a few days after the reduction of Liège, all the British troops were ordered back to Holland, and the rest of the army disposed into proper quarters. The Lord Marlborough and the Field-Deputies went down the Meuse in their yacht; a Lieutenant and 40 men, together with a party of Horse, being ordered to escort them. The Lieutenant stopped short at Venlo, thinking they were past danger, and the horse lost their way in the night. In this situation they were when a French party from Guelders came up with them about two leagues below Venlo, drew the boat to land, and made them all prisoners. The Field-Deputies produced a pass from the Duke of Burgundy, and they not knowing the Lord Marlborough, and being more intent on booty than making prisoners, when they had received a handsome present, let them pass; and the next day they arrived at the Hague.

---

[1] The terms of every capitulation varied considerably according to a number of considerations—the duration of resistance, the losses sustained by the besiegers, the reputation of the garrison, etc. The terms granted to the Chartreuse garrison were reasonably good, but the fact that the troops could disperse at individual discretion virtually meant their disbandment, and clearly they were first deprived of their arms.

III

The Campaign of 1703

Her Majesty being highly pleased with the conduct of the Earl of Marlborough, this winter created him Duke of Marlborough. Early this spring his Grace came over, and having consulted with the States-General, concerning the operations of the campaign, he sent orders to the Prussian, Hanoverian, and Hessian troops to assemble near Bonn; and thither he went soon after to see the siege of that place carried on with dispatch. He ordered the British and Dutch troops to assemble near Maastricht, under the Veldt-Marshal D'Auverquerque [*Overkirk*], Athlone being dead. The Duke formed the siege of Bonn, which surrendered in less than three weeks [*27 April–15 May*]. By this the Rhine was cleared of the French from Holland up to Philipsburg. From Bonn the Duke marched to Limburg,[1] which surrendered in a few days. While his Grace was employed in taking these places, the Marshals Villeroy [*Villeroi*] and Boufflers, at the head of the French army, marched up to the Veldt-Marshal, which obliged him to retire under the cannon of Maastricht, where he entrenched himself. Notwithstanding this Villeroi advanced in order to attack us, and began to cannonade us with great fury; but the cannon of the town, of our camp, and of the Fort of Petersberg, soon made him weary of that work, and obliged him to retire; and upon hearing of the approach of the Duke, he made what haste he could to get within his lines.

As soon as the Duke had joined us, we marched directly up to their lines, and encamped at Hanef [*or Hanoye*], within a league of them. From hence he sent a detachment to take in Huy, which lies on the Meuse half way between Liège and Namur. This was the last town that remained to the ungrateful Elector of Cologne, who was now become a pensioner of France, being turned out of his Electorate, as

1 Parker's chronology becomes a trifle confused here. In point of fact, after capturing Bonn, Marlborough moved on to take Huy (which capitulated on 26 August after an investment of twelve days). The siege of Limburg (10–27 September) was the final operation of the year, following upon the Dutch refusal to countenance Marlborough's plan to storm the French lines stretching north from the vicinity of Namur.

well as the Principality and Bishopric of Liège, by the same powers that gave them to him.

Villeroi's Lines were prodigiously strong,[1] they extended from Namur to the Scheldt below Antwerp, which surrounded the whole Spanish Netherlands; and the Duke finding he would not stir from behind them, made several marches and countermarches, to try if he could meet with an opportunity of forcing them; but Villeroi kept such a watchful eye on all his motions, that he could make nothing of them. At length an affair happened, which drew both armies toward Antwerp. Upon our taking the field, the States had ordered General Opdam with 12,000 of their troops to guard the lines which run from Breda to Fort Lillo on the Scheldt. The French had also an equal number to guard their lines in that quarter.

Now when Villeroi found that the Duke could not force his lines, he slipped off Boufflers with 30,000 men to join the French troops near Antwerp, in order to fall upon Opdam. The Duke having an account of Boufflers' march, immediately judged what his design was, and thereupon marched the army that way; but before we could come up, Boufflers had attacked Opdam at Eckeren [*30 June*], and after several repulses, at length broke into that part where Opdam commanded, and cut between him and the rest of his troops. Upon this he concluded all was lost, and thereupon fled to Breda, from whence he gave the States-General a melancholy account of the affair. But notwithstanding this disadvantage, the Lieutenants-General Slanenberg [*Slangenberg*] and Tilly maintained their ground with great obstinacy, and still repulsed the enemy with great slaughter, until at length they were obliged to quit the attack, either party having suffered very considerably. As soon as the enemy drew off, Slangenberg and Tilly sent an express to the States, with an account of the action,[2] in which they supposed Opdam to be among the slain; but he had assured them to the contrary a little before. However, he never appeared in the army afterward.

The day after the battle our army arrived and Villeroi being joined by Boufflers, drew out of his lines, and declared he would give us battle. The Duke was very ready to take him at his word, and the next day advanced within half a league of him, being determined to attack him the morning following; but Villeroi thought better of it, and

[1] Compare Mérode-Westerloo's opinion, p. 147 below.

[2] For the experiences of a commander in the French army at the battle of Eckeren, see Mérode-Westerloo, pp. 148–52 below.

stole back within his lines, before it was day. It was now about the middle of October, so both armies broke up and went into quarters. Our Regiment had Breda, from whence, in the beginning of December, we marched to Bergen-op-Zoom, to reinforce that garrison during the frost, and in the beginning of February returned to Breda. Soon after 300 men out of each British regiment of foot marched to Maastricht, where we did duty, while the Dutch infantry was throwing up a strong entrenchment on the height of Petersberg, which was of great use to them the two succeeding campaigns.

IV

The Campaign of 1704:
The March to the Danube

Before I enter on the detail of our German campaign, I must premise, that the Elector of Bavaria aspired to the Imperial dignity, that he was supported by the power of France, and that the French King early in the preceding year, had sent Marshal Villars with 30,000 men through the Black Forest to his assistance. The Elector had 40,000 of his own subject troops, and both these joined together, carried all before them that campaign. But as the Elector's temper and the Marshal's haughty spirit did not agree, Villars at his own request was recalled, and Marshal Marsin sent in his stead; and the Elector being joined by him, did not doubt but he should be able to drive the Emperor out of his capital this campaign.

Now the Duke of Marlborough, upon considering the state of the Empire, saw plainly, that unless something extraordinary was undertaken this year for its defence, the Elector of Bavaria would inevitably place himself on the Imperial throne; and in that case he and France would give laws to Europe. Upon this he formed a bold and daring scheme, for marching a good body of troops from the Netherlands to the Danube. He first communicated it to the Queen, and a few of the Privy-Council; then to such of the States-General as he could confide in; for the success of the undertaking depended in a great measure on the secrecy of it. In order to cover his design, he gave out that he would make this campaign on the Moselle; and had ordered great magazines of all manner of necessaries to be laid up at Coblentz [*Coblenz*], at which place the Moselle falls into the Rhine. This answered his purpose, for the court of France made no doubt, but his designs lay that way; in consequence of which, they made great preparations to receive him on that side.

The Duke arrived at the Hague early this spring; and soon after gave orders, for the troops in these parts that were to act under him, to assemble at Ruremonde. Accordingly our garrison of Breda marched on the 28th of April, O.S. and on the 4th of May [*15th*] passed the Meuse at Ruremonde. From hence we marched to Juliers [*Jülich*], where our detachment from Maastricht joined us. Here the Duke reviewed all the troops that had arrived. Those of Great Britain, in particular, were nineteen squadrons of horse and dragoons, and fourteen battalions of foot, which amounted to 14,384 fighting men.[1] From Juliers we marched through the Electorate of Cologne, and so on to Coblenz, where we halted two days, and were joined by the Prussian and Hanoverian troops, that were in British pay.

Marshal Villeroi by this time had arrived at Trèves with the greater part of his army from the Netherlands, to oppose the Duke in this quarter. This made the Dutch easy, for they were apprehensive, that on the Duke's marching from them, the French would over-run their whole country.

And now when we expected to march up the Moselle, to our surprise we passed that river over a stone bridge, and the Rhine over two bridges of boats, and proceeded on our march through the country of Hesse Cassel, where we were joined by the Hereditary Prince (now King of Sweden) with the troops of that country; which made our army 40,000 fighting men complete.

[1] The following British regiments took part in Marlborough's march.

Cavalry and Dragoons:	Title in 1704:
1st King's Dragoon Guards	Lumley's
3rd Dragoon Guards	Wood's
5th Dragoon Guards	Cadogan's
6th Dragoon Guards (Carabineers)	Wyndham's
7th Dragoon Guards	Schomberg's
2nd Dragoons	Ross's

Infantry	
1st Bn, 1st Guards	
1st and 2nd Bns, 1st Foot	Orkney's
3rd Foot	Churchill's
8th Foot	Webb's
10th Foot	North and Grey's
15th Foot	Howe's
16th Foot	Derby's
18th Foot	Hamilton's
21st Foot	Rowe's
23rd Foot	Ingoldsby's
24th Foot	Marlborough's
26th Foot	Ferguson's
37th Foot	Meredith's

Artillery: part of the 1702 Flanders Train.

When we had passed the Rhine, the Duke, for the convenience of forage, advanced a day's march, and took his rout with the horse, different from that of the foot, which was left under the command of General Churchill.[1] We frequently marched three, sometimes four days, successively, and halted a day. We generally began our march about three in the morning, proceeded about four leagues, or four and half each day, and reached our ground about nine. As we marched through the countries of our Allies, commissaries were appointed to furnish us with all manner of necessaries for man and horse; these were brought to the ground before we arrived, and the soldiers had nothing to do, but to pitch their tents, boil their kettles, and lie down to rest. Surely never was such a march carried on with more order and regularity, and with less fatigue both to man and horse. From the country of Hesse, we marched through that of Nassau, into the Electorate of Mentz [Mainz], then through that of Hesse-Darmstadt, and through the Palatinate till we came to Hydelberg [Heidelberg], where we halted three days; and now, and not before, it was publicly known that the Duke's design was against the Elector of Bavaria. It was so much a secret, that General Churchill (the Duke's brother) knew nothing of the matter till this time; and Villeroi's constant attendance on our marches, shewed that the court of France was as much in the dark as we were.

On the 16th [27th] of June, we joined the Imperial army at Gingen [Giengen?], and next day a grand Council of War was held at Hepack [Gross Heppach];[2] in which were present the Prince of Baden, Prince Eugène, the Duke of Marlborough, the Duke of Wirtemberg [Württemberg], the Prince of Hesse, the Prince of Anhalt Dessau, with several generals of note. Here it was agreed that the Prince of Baden, and the Duke of Marlborough should act in conjunction, and command alternately; and that Prince Eugène should command on the Rhine against Villeroi and Tallard, who were now joined near Strasburg [Strasbourg]. It was observed that on the first interview between Prince Eugène and the Duke of Marlborough they contracted an extraordinary friendship for each other; and it held to the last.

The day after this grand consultation, our two generals made a

[1] The Duke's brother, General Charles Churchill.

[2] Parker's chronology again becomes a trifle confused here: the meeting of the Allied leaders at Gross Heppach took place between 11 and 15 June 1704 N.S.; the final junction with the Imperial forces took place at Launsheim on 25 June.

review of their army, and found it about 85,000. On the 20th we advanced towards the enemy, and encamped within sight of them; they having taken up the strong Camp of Dillingen on this side of the Danube. Their army was computed to be about 70,000, of these the Elector had detached 16,000, the evening before, under the Count de Arco [*d'Arco*], to post themselves on the hill of Schelemberg [*Schellenberg*], in order to secure the pass of Donawert [*Donauwörth*].

Our generals, finding the Elector and Marsin so strongly posted that there was no coming at them,[1] decamped next morning, and directed their march toward Donauworth. We encamped this night at Hermendingen [*Amerdingen*], and the day following, being the 22nd of June, O.S. [*2 July*] and the Duke's day of command,[2] he marched by three in the morning at the head of thirty squadrons, three Imperial regiments of grenadiers, and a detachment of 7,000 foot; the whole army marching close after them; and as we marched off from the left, the British troops led the march of the army. The Duke was detained some hours at the River Wrentz [*Wernitz*], in repairing the bridge, and laying others for the army to pass; by which means it was four o'clock, before he reached Donauworth. From thence he saw the Count d'Arco's men hard at work in throwing up an entrenchment on the top of the hill at Schellenberg. As soon as the British troops were all come up, he formed a disposition for attacking them. The hill was in itself very steep and rough, and difficult to ascend. Beside which they had thrown up an entrenchment on the summit of it.

About six in the afternoon the English Guards began the attack, the whole line going on at the same time. The thirty squadrons kept in the rear of the foot, as close as the nature of the ground would permit. The enemy maintained their post with great resolution for an hour and ten minutes; by which time the whole army being come up, and supporting the attack, at length they gave way, and a terrible slaughter ensued, no quarter being given for a long time. Count d'Arco, with the greater part of them made down the back of the hill to the Danube, where they had a bridge of boats; but this breaking under them, great

---

[1] Marlborough's march from the Netherlands had been facilitated by leaving his army's heavier guns behind. As a result he was in no position to batter a breach in strong enemy fortifications.

[2] Officially, Marlborough and Baden shared the command, assuming control on alternate days. In fact, however, the Duke's authority was paramount during this period, although to save the Margrave's face he was permitted to issue the password, etc., on his supposed day of control.

numbers were drowned. The Count with a few others that were well mounted, saved themselves by swimming the river.[1]

The loss of the enemy was computed to be about 7,000 killed, 2,000 drowned, and 3,000 taken, with everything they had. On our side also the loss was very great; for we had about 6,000 killed and wounded. When the Elector saw us pass his camp at Dillingen, he passed the Danube and made what haste he could to succour d'Arco; but he arrived only time enough to be a witness to his fate. Upon which he turned to the right, marched to Augsburg, and entrenched himself under the cannon of that city, where he had laid up great

---

[1] A participant in this dire struggle was Colonel de la Colonie, a French officer serving in d'Arco's force. Part of his description of the action is as follows:

'The enemy broke into the charge, and rushed at full speed, shouting at the top of their voices, to throw themselves into our entrenchments.

'The rapidity of their movements, together with their loud yells, were truly alarming, and as soon as I heard them I ordered our drums to beat the "charge" so as to drown them with their noise, lest they should have a bad effect upon our people. . . .

'The English infantry led this attack with the greatest intrepidity, right up to our parapet, but there they were opposed with a courage at least equal to their own. Rage, fury and desperation were manifested by both sides. . . . The little parapet which separated the two forces became the scene of the bloodiest struggle that could be conceived. . . .

'. . . During this first attack . . . we were all fighting hand to hand, hurling them back as they clutched at the parapet; men were slaying or tearing at the muzzles of guns and at the bayonets which pierced their entrails. . . .

'At last the enemy, after losing more than eight thousand men [*a gross exaggeration*] in this first onslaught, were obliged to relax their hold, and they fell back for shelter to the dip of the slope, where we could not harm them. A sudden calm now reigned amongst us. . . .

'Never was joy greater than our own at the very moment when we were in the greatest danger.

'About 7.30 . . . I noticed all at once an extraordinary movement on the part of our infantry, who were rising up and ceasing fire withal. I glanced around on all sides to see what had caused this behaviour, and then became aware of several lines of infantry in greyish-white uniforms on our left flank. From lack of movement on their part, their dress and bearing, I verily believed that reinforcements had arrived for us, and anybody else would have believed the same. No information whatever had reached us of the enemy's success, or even that any such thing was the least likely, so in the error I laboured under I shouted to my men that they were Frenchmen and friends.

'Having, however, made a closer inspection, I discovered bunches of straw and leaves attached to their standards, badges the enemy are in the custom of wearing on the occasion of battle, and at that very moment was struck by a ball in the right lower jaw, which wounded and stupified me to such an extent that I thought it was smashed.'

(Extracts taken from J. M. de La Colonie, *The Chronicles of an Old Campaigner*, pp. 185–91.)

stores of everything. As he turned off, he sent orders to the Governor of Donauwörth, to set fire to the magazines, and follow him to Augsburg; but the inhabitants found means to give our generals notice of it; and they immediately ordered bridges to be laid both above and below the town, to prevent his retreat. When the Governor perceived this, he did not stay to execute his orders; upon which the inhabitants opened their gates, and received a garrison of our troops.

Our generals having gained this important pass [or *bridgehead*] on the Danube, passed the army to the other side, and marched to the Leck [*Lech*], which is the boundary between Suabia [*Swabia*] and Bavaria; and having passed this river also, we entered the Elector's dominions, and came up to a small fortified town called Rain, which held out only four days. During this time orders were given to all the regiments to send out parties to plunder and maraud the country, but not to burn any place. This was done with a design of bringing the Elector off from the French interest; and it had its effect so far, as that a treaty was set on foot, which put a stop to our marauding. From Rain we marched to Friedburg, not a league from Augsburg, and as we were on a rising ground, we had from hence a fair view both of the Elector's camp and city; but yet we saw plainly that it was impossible to come either at one or the other.

This was the utmost extent of our march into Germany, which, according to our route, was computed to be more than 600 English miles. We lay here about a month, during which time the treaty [or *negotiation*] was carried on with great hope of success; but it was all grimace in the Elector, and designed only to prevent the ruin of his country. For upon the defeat at Schellenberg, he instantly dispatched an express to Villeroi, to send him a strong reinforcement, and insisted, that if he did not, he must be obliged to quit his master's interest, and join with the Allies. Upon this Villeroi sent off the Marshal Tallard with sixty squadrons and forty battalions, all choice men; and marching with all the expedition he could, through the Black Forest, was now arrived at Ulm, from whence he let the Elector know, that in two days he hoped to join him at Lavingen.[1] Upon this he broke off the treaty abruptly, and let our generals know, that he would serve as a dragoon under the King of France, rather than as general of the Emperor's forces. This incensed our generals to that degree, that a great number of parties were sent out far and near,

[1] See below pp. 158–65, for Mérode-Westerloo's fuller account of Tallard's movements during this period.

34

who burned and destroyed all before them; insomuch, that it was said there were 372 towns, villages and farmhouses, laid in ashes; and it was a shocking sight to see the fine country of Bavaria all in a flame. The Elector was an eye-witness of the calamity he had brought upon his country; and as revenge is sweet, he resolved as soon as Tallard had joined him, to make a retaliation on the country of Württemberg. Such are the effects of war, the innocent suffer for the guilty: but let those ambitious men, that occasion such things, take care how they will account for it another day. Certain it is that the Duke of Marlborough would not suffer any of the troops, that were immediately under him, to go out on that burning command.

The day after this conflagration, the Elector drew off from Augsburg, and joined Tallard at Lavingen; and the same day our generals marched back the way they came. On our second day's encampment, just as we were pitching our tents, Prince Eugène came riding along our line, attended by two servants only, and rode directly to the Duke's quarters. He had attended Tallard's march from the Rhine, with 20,000 men, whom he left at the strong camp of Munster, under the command of the Duke of Württemberg. When the Duke and he came to consult, it was soon agreed, that unless something more material was done, before the Duke left the Empire, his great undertaking would avail nothing, and the Elector would carry all before him the next campaign. If things should take this turn, the Duke well knew what must be his fate on his return to England, where he had many powerful enemies. They knew also that the Prince of Baden was a cautious old general, that he was not for fighting without great probability of success; and that it was very necessary notwithstanding to give a bold and a decisive blow at that time; whereupon they contrived it so, as to send the Prince to lay siege to Ingolstadt [11–21 August]; by which they were left at liberty to pursue their own schemes.

These were the results of these two great men, on whose courage and conduct the fate of Europe depended at this critical juncture. The Prince of Baden readily agreed to their scheme, and early next morning marched off for Ingolstadt with 20,000 Imperialists.[1] Upon this Prince Eugène rode directly back to his troops; at the same time the Duke marched with the main body of the army, and in two days joined him at Munster. On the day following [12 August] they both rode out with the picket-guard of horse, to view the ground about

[1] Most accounts place the number at approximately 15,000.

35

Hochstedt [*Hochstadt*], in order to mark out a camp thereon. But as they came within sight of it, they perceived the enemies' quarter-masters marking out a camp on the plain, and the van of their army entering into it; upon which they stopped some time to observe their manner of encampment, and then returned with a resolution of giving them battle next day. As soon as they came to camp, they gave orders for striking our tents, packing up our baggage, and sending all away to the Schellenberg; and that every man should prepare for battle.

V

The Campaign of 1704:
The Battle of Blenheim

We lay on our arms all night, and next day, being the 2nd of August, O.S. [*13th*], we marched by break of day in eight columns up to the enemy. The Duke received the Holy Sacrament this morning at the hands of his Chaplain, Doctor Hare, and upon mounting his horse, he said, 'This day I conquer or die.' A noble instance of the Christian and the hero! Our army consisted of 181 squadrons and 67 battalions.

We had upwards of three leagues to march to the enemy; when we came in sight of them their whole camp was standing [*i.e. the tents were still standing*]; but as soon as they perceived us, they fired three cannon to call in their foragers; so little did they expect a visit from us this morning. They soon struck their camp, and sent their tents, baggage, and everything of value to the town of Hochstadt, which was about half an English mile in their rear; and then drew up in order of battle, being 163 squadrons and 83 battalions. They therefore had 16 battalions more than we, and we had 18 squadrons more than they. They had 120 cannon and mortars, and we 64; so near an equality were both armies.[1]

Prince Eugène with the Imperialists stretched away to our right, and drew up opposite the Elector, and the greater part of the forces under Marsin; and the Duke of Marlborough drew up the forces he brought with him, opposite Tallard and the right of Marsin. About eight o'clock we began to form our lines;[2] at which time the enemy

[1] Churchill, whose figures are generally accepted, gives: 60,000 French and Bavarians (84 battalions and 147 squadrons) with 90 cannon; 56,000 Allies (66 battalions with 160 squadrons) with 66 cannon. (See Churchill, Book One, p. 851.)

[2] At this period, before the institution of corps or even divisional organization, armies habitually drew themselves up for battle in two main lines of units, often with a smaller reserve in rear. Each line comprised a right wing, a left, and a centre, and general officers were told off to command these sectors in strict accordance with their seniority. Each line again generally included a proportion of horse, foot and guns, but the detailed alignment of the troops varied considerably according to the commander-in-chief's whim.

set fire to such villages as might be a shelter to us, and the cannon on both sides fired with great fury. The first shot the enemy fired was at our Regiment, and it fell short; the second killed one man, which was the first blood drawn that day. When we began to form our lines, the Elector, Tallard, and Marsin went up into the steeple of Blenheim, from whence they had a fair view of our army. The Elector told Tallard that Marlborough was drawing up the troops he brought with him in order to attack him, and desired he would draw up his troops close to the morass, and not suffer a man to pass, but what came on the point of his bayonets. Marsin was of the same opinion: but Tallard, a proud, conceited Frenchmen, puffed up with the success of his former campaign (which shall be taken notice of in another place)[1] thought the Elector took upon him to dictate to him; and told him that was not the way to obtain a complete victory, which now offered; and that the utmost that could be made of it in their way, was only a drawn battle: whereas he was for drawing up the army at some distance from the morass; and then the more that came over to them, the more they should kill. The Elector told him, he had often been engaged with these troops, and knew them well; and he insisted on it, that if he once suffered them to come over, he would find it a hard matter to drive them back. But all that he or Marsin could say, could not prevail on him to alter his opinion; so dreading the consequences of his obstinacy, they left him, much dissatisfied. He told them at parting, he saw plainly that that day's victory must be entirely owing to him.[2]

The situation and disposition of the enemy was as follows: They had the Danube on their right, close to which was the village of Blenheim: they had on their left a large thick wood, with the village of Lutzingen close by it, from whence runs a rivulet [R. *Nebel*], which empties itself into the Danube a little below Blenheim. This rivulet they had in their front, which made the ground in most places about it swampy and marshy. The Elector and Marsin drew up their part of the army close to the morass, and determined not to suffer a man to pass, but what should come on the points of their bayonets. But Tallard made quite another sort of a disposition of his troops;

[1] See below, p. 47 Robert Parker evidently added this section as something of an afterthought. If the proper sequence had been adhered to, the passage referred to might well have been placed about p. 29.

[2] For a stimulating account by one of Tallard's army, see below, p. 166 *et seq.*

he posted in the village of Blenheim 28 battalions[1] and 12 squadrons of dragoons. There were two mills on the rivulet a little above Blenheim, in which he posted two battalions; he had therefore but 10 battalions in the field with him; and being joined by 20 squadrons of Marsin's, he had 70 squadrons, on whom was his great dependence. These and his 10 battalions he drew up on the height of the plain, almost half an English mile from the morass. The village of Auberclaw [Oberglau] lay partly on the morass towards our side, and was near their centre; in it Marsin had posted 8 battalions. Now these, with the troops in Blenheim and in the mills, were to march out as soon as they saw the Duke pass the morass, and fall on his rear, by which means Tallard was sure of having him in a trap between two fires. Now as the main part of this battle was fought between the Duke and this mighty Marshal of France, I shall be very particular in describing it.

The Duke of Marlborough, a man of uncommon penetration and presence of mind, soon perceived Tallard's design; and thereupon ordered General Churchill, with 19 battalions to attack the troops in Blenheim, and Lieutenant-General Wood with 8 squadrons to support him.[2] He also ordered the Prince of Holstein-Beck with six battalions to attack the village of Oberglau, and two battalions to attack the mills. The Duke having thus secured his rear, a little before one[3] ordered the signal to be made for attacking the villages and mills; at which time Brigadier Rue [Rowe] at the head of the British Guards, and two British brigades, attacked those in Blenheim, but were repulsed, the Brigadier and a great many men being killed. At this

[1] Churchill estimates twenty-seven battalions; it would also be more accurate to say that these troops were placed 'near' Blenheim village. At the outset only nine battalions were actually manning the defences. However, owing to the errors of judgement displayed by the sector commander, the Marquis de Clérembault, a further seven, and later another eleven battalions were drawn into the perimeter.

Similarly, the twelve squadrons of dismounted dragoons Parker refers to were, in fact, posted slightly to the south of Blenheim to cover the gap dividing the village from the Danube.

[2] In fact, General Lord Cutts ('the Salamander') was in command of the Allied left, which attacked Blenheim village, with, it is generally accepted, twenty battalions and fifteen squadrons. General Charles Churchill (Marlborough's brother) commanded the centre.

[3] This delay in opening the battle was due partly to the late arrival of Prince Eugène and the right wing (delayed by difficult country), and partly to the time it took to draw up the lines of battle.

39

time the rest of the foot coming up, they renewed the charge; and those that had been repulsed, having soon rallied, returned to the charge, and drove the enemy from the skirts of the village, into the very heart of it. Here they had thrown up an entrenchment, within which they were pent up in so narrow a compass, that they had not room to draw up in any manner of order, or even to make use of their arms. Thereupon we drew up in great order about 80 paces from them, from whence we made several vain attempts to break in upon them, in which many brave men were lost to no purpose; and after all, we were obliged to remain where we first drew up. The enemy also made several attempts to come out upon us: but as they were necessarily thrown into confusion in getting over their trenches, so before they could form into any order for attacking us, we mowed them down with our platoons[1] in such numbers, that they were always obliged to retire with great loss; and it was not possible for them to rush out upon us in a disorderly manner, without running upon the very points of our bayonets. This great body of troops therefore was of no further use to Tallard, being obliged to keep on the defensive, in expectation that he might come to relieve them.

Prince Holstein-Beck was repulsed on this attack of Oberglau: yet, though he could not force the enemy from thence, he answered the Duke's intention however, in not suffering them to fall on his rear. They in the mills made but little resistance; so setting them on fire[2] they made off to Tallard, and joined the battalions he had with him.

It may be presumed that the Lord Marlborough was not idle all this while. The very moment that the villages were attacked, he ordered Colonel Palms [*Palmes*] with three British squadrons of horse[3] to enter the morass. These having passed it without any opposition, drew up at some distance from it. Upon which the Duke gave orders, that all the troops should pass with the greatest expedition, while his Grace followed close after Palmes. Tallard, as a man infatuated, stood looking on, without firing a shot great or small; these formed their lines as fast as they passed. At length Tallard seeing Palmes advanced with his squadrons some distance from our lines,

[1] See below, p. 88, and also Appendix I, p. 236, for fuller descriptions and analyses of the advantages conferred by the platoon firing system.

[2] Mérode-Westerloo clearly infers that the French set fire to the mills before the onset of the main battle. (See below, p. 168.)

[3] In fact, Palmes commanded five squadrons; similarly, Tallard ordered out eight—not five—squadrons of the *élite* Gendarmerie to meet them.

ordered out five squadrons (some said seven) to march down and cut
Palmes's squadrons to pieces, and then retire. When the commanding
officer of these squadrons had got clear of their lines, he ordered the
squadron on his right, and that on his left to edge outward, and then
march down till they came on a line with Palmes; at which time they
were to wheel inward, and fall upon his flanks, while he charged him
in front. Palmes perceiving this, ordered Major Oldfield, who commanded the squadron on his right, and Major Creed, who commanded
that on his left, to wheel outward, and charge those squadrons, that
were coming down on them; and he, not in the least doubting but
they would beat them, ordered them when they had done that, to
wheel in upon the flanks of the other squadrons that were coming
upon him, while he charged them in front; and everything succeeded
accordingly. This was a great surprise to Tallard, who had placed such
confidence in his troops, that he verily thought there were not any on
earth able to stand before them. And now in no small hurry, he
ordered his lines to advance, and charge the Duke, who by this time
had all his troops over, and his lines formed.

Here was a fine plain without hedge or ditch, for the cavalry on
both sides to shew their bravery; for there were but few foot to interpose, these being mostly engaged at the villages. Tallard seeing his
five squadrons so shamefully beaten by three, was confounded to that
degree, that he did not recover himself the whole day, for after that,
all his orders were given in hurry and confusion.[1]

When the Duke saw Tallard's lines advance, he ordered his troops
also to advance and meet them. The front line of the enemy was
composed mostly of the Gendarmery [*Gendarmerie*], on whose
bravery Tallard had the greatest dependence. These therefore were
pitched upon to begin the battle; and they indeed made so bold and
resolute a charge, that they broke through our first line: but our
second meeting them, obliged them to retire. This check allayed that
fire, which the French have always been so remarkable for in their
first onsets: and it was observable, that they did not make such another
push that day; for when once they are repulsed, their fire immediately
abates. And now our squadrons charged in their turn, and thus for

---

[1] The importance of this incident in undermining Tallard's morale was borne out by no
less a personage than the French commander himself. Writing in December to explain
his defeat, he asserted: 'First, because the Gendarmerie were not able to break the five
English squadrons.' See Pelet and de Vault, *Mémoires militaires relatifs à la succession
d'Espagne sous Louis XIV*, vol. IV, p. 575.

some hours they charged each other with various success, all sword
in hand. At length the French courage began to abate, and our
squadrons gained ground upon them, until they forced them back to
the height on which they were first drawn up. Here their foot, which
had not fired a shot, interposed, whereupon the Duke ordered his
squadrons to halt. At the same time our foot came up, and Colonel Blood
with nine field-pieces loaded with partridge-shot, fired on their foot,
which obliged them to quit the horse, and stand on their own defence.

The cavalry had this breathing-time, in which both sides were very
busy in putting their squadrons and lines in order. And now Tallard
finding that the troops in Blenheim did not answer his expectation,
sent to them to quit the village, and come to his assistance; but alas!
they were not able to assist themselves. He then sent to Marshal
Marsin for help; but he sent him word, he had too much work on his
own hands. The Duke now finding the enemy very backward in
renewing the battle, and, as it seemed, rather in a tottering condition,
sent orders to all his troops to advance gently, until they came pretty
near them, and then to ride on a full trot up to them. This they did so
effectually, that it decided the fate of the day. The French fire was
quite extinguished, they made not the least resistance, but gave way
and broke at once. Our squadrons drove through the very centre of
them, which put them to an entire rout. About 30 of their squadrons
made toward a bridge of boats they had over the Danube: but the
bridge (as it frequently happens in such cases) broke under the crowd
that rushed upon it, and down they went. At the same time our
squadrons pursued close at their heels, cutting down all before them;
for in all such close pursuits, 'tis very rare that any quarter is given. In
short, they were almost all of them killed or drowned;[1] and the few
that reached the far side of the river, were killed by the boors of the
villages they had burnt. Tallard fled that way, but finding the bridge
broken, he turned up the river toward Höchstadt, and was taken. The
rest of the troops fled toward Lavingen, but were not pursued, because the Elector and Marsin still made good their ground.[2] The Duke

---

[1] Estimates of the number of French cavalry who met their deaths in this way vary
between 2,000 and 3,000.

[2] Parker pays scant attention to the part played by Eugène's wing on the Allied right.
For much of the day he faced unfavourable odds of two to one, but was nevertheless
prepared to detach Fugger's cuirassier brigade to the assistance of Churchill's centre at
the crisis of the deployment over the Nebel. Such selfless co-operation reveals the relationship between Marlborough and his Imperial colleague.

observing this, ordered Lieutenant-General Hompesch to draw together what troops he could, and fall on their flank: but by this time they found that Tallard was routed, and seeing our squadrons drawing toward them, they instantly, and with great dexterity and expedition, formed their troops into three columns, and marched off with the greatest despatch and order imaginable. Prince Eugène by this time had got a good part of his troops over the morass, and was just ready to fall on their rear: but perceiving the squadrons under Hompesch coming down that way, he took them to be some of Tallard's squadrons drawing down to join the Elector; whereupon he halted, lest they should fall on his flank. The Duke also seeing Prince Eugène's troops so near the rear of the Elector's, took them to be a body of Bavarians, making good the Elector's retreat; and thereupon ordered Hompesch to halt. Here they both remained until they were informed of their mistakes by their Aides de Camp; and it was by this means that the Elector and Marsin had time to get over the Pass of Nordlingen which was just before them. Our troops also were much fatigued, and night drew on, all which favoured their retreat. Or perhaps it may rather be said, that Providence interposed, which seeing the slaughter of the day, thought it sufficient: otherwise few, if any of them, could have escaped. As to the battalions which Tallard had with him in the field,[1] they were cut in pieces to a man, such only excepted, as threw themselves down among the dead. I rode through them next morning as they lay dead, in rank and file. As soon as the troops in Blenheim saw the fate of their army in the field, they threw down their arms,[2] and surrendered at discretion; but the troops in Oberglau made off with Marsin.

You have here the most exact account of this memorable battle, that I could possibly learn; for next morning I made it my business to ride over the field of battle, and had very particular information of

[1] Parker is referring to the nine or ten battalions that Tallard had originally placed to strengthen his centre; the remainder of the French infantry, of course, were by this time bottled up uselessly in Blenheim village.

[2] Here Parker misrepresents the facts. The Blenheim garrison, in fact, continued to resist until late into the evening, and occasioned Marlborough no little anxiety, as his own troops were obviously very tired. As it happened, however, there was no firm handling of the French troops in the village. Clérembault had ridden off to his death in the Danube, and there was no obvious replacement. In the end the English bluffed the bewildered—but still fresh—troops into surrendering about 9 p.m. The Regiment of Navarre burnt its colours in despair.

the several transactions I have mentioned, from the parties immediately engaged in them.

The victory of this day was allowed by all, to be chiefly owing (under Divine Providence) to the valour and conduct of the Duke of Marlborough, and the bravery of the troops, which he led from the Meuse to the Danube.[1]

The loss of the enemy was computed to be at least 40,000 killed, drowned and taken. The prisoners of note were, the Marshal Tallard, and 27 officers of the first rank, with 1,500 of inferior rank. The booty also was very great, 103 cannon and 14 mortars, 129 colours, 110 standards, 17 pair of kettle-drums, 3,600 tents, 15 pontoons, 34 coaches, 24 barrels of silver, and 30 laden mules, with all the plate and baggage of the officers.

The true account of this battle was concealed from old Lewis for some time, but when he came to know the truth of it, he was much cast down; it being the first blow of any fatal consequence, his arms had received, during his long reign. And he said in a passion, he had often heard of armies been beaten, but never of one taken before.

The loss on our side also was great, we had near 6,000 killed, and above 8,000 wounded.[2] The troops under Prince Eugène were the greatest sufferers, and in all probability he would not have been able to force the Elector and Marsin from their ground, had not the Duke managed Tallard as he did; and indeed, had that conceited man been advised by the other two, it were hard to say how the day would have ended. The loss of our Regiment was, three captains, and four subalterns, killed: our Major and five officers wounded, with near 100 private men killed and wounded.[3]

The day after the battle, all our wounded were sent to Nordlingen, where our grand hospital was fixed; the prisoners were disposed of and sent off, except Tallard and three more, and in the afternoon, the

[1] See below, p. 174, for Mérode-Westerloo's pertinent opinions.

[2] The casualty figures most generally accepted are as follows: French and Bavarians: 20,000 killed; 14,000 prisoners; 6,000 deserters. Allies about 12,000 killed and wounded. No set of figures, however, can be implicitly trusted.

[3] According to the *Blenheim Roll* (reprinted in Dalton, *English Army Lists*, vol. V, Pt Two, p. 54) the 18th Foot lost the following officer casualties:

	Killed		*Wounded*
Capts	Henry Browne	Maj.	Richard Kane
	Arthur Rolleston	Capts	Frederick de la Penotière
	Vaudin (died of wounds)		Moses Leathes

army marched to Lavingen. Here we halted for our tents and baggage, and to refresh our men. The Sunday following was appointed for a day of Thanksgiving; and after Divine Service, the army drew out to fire for the victory. On this occasion, Tallard, and the officers with him, were desired to ride out to see the army fire, which they did with much persuasion. As they rode along the lines, our Generals paid Tallard the compliment of riding next the army, and ordered all the officers to salute him. When the firing was over, the Duke asked Tallard, how he liked the army? He answered, with a shrug, 'Very well, but they have had the honour of beating the best troops in the world.' The Duke replied readily, 'What will the world think of the troops that beat them?'

I cannot omit taking notice of the compliments that were paid the Duke of Marlborough on this occasion. The first was a letter from the Emperor, written in Latin with his own hand; in which he gives him the appellation of 'most illustrious Cousin, and dear Prince',[1] and then proceeds,

'For it is our will, that this public monument which I have conferred on you, should manifest to all the world, how much myself and the whole Empire (as I here freely acknowledge) owe both to the most serene Queen of Great-Britain, for having sent her powerful assistance, under your conduct as far as Swabia, and even to Bavaria, when my own and the Empire's affairs were not a little disordered by the perfidious revolt of the Bavarian to the French; and also to your

Killed		Wounded
Ensign Wm Moyle		Nathaniel Hussey
	Lieuts	William Weddall
		Samuel Roberts
		Jno. Harvey
	Ensigns	James Pinsent
		Stephen Gilman

Parker agrees with the total of officer casualties (13), but differs on the detail. Sterne gives Vaudin as 'Vaughan' and differs on the names of some of the wounded. (Cannon, p. 26). Kane gives no details.

The *Blenheim Roll* also reveals that the Regiment was commanded at the battle by Lieutenant-Colonel Robert Sterne, and that a total of 33 officers, 32 sergeants, 36 corporals and 479 privates and drummers qualified for the bounty, which ranged from £72 for the Colonel to 20s. for the rank and file. Parker received £14. Wounded officers received double bounty.

[1] In recognition of his services, Marlborough was created Prince of Mindelheim—a small principality of the Holy Roman Empire.

Grace, that all things have been so prudently and successfully carried on. For not only fame, but also the generals of my army, the companions and sharers of your labours and your victories, attribute the same chiefly to your councils and conduct, and to the bravery and fortitude of the English and other forces, that fought under your conduct, etc.'

The States-General, in their compliments to the Duke, use the following expression.

'After the first blow you gave them at Schellenberg, we had reason to expect something greater would follow; but never dared to carry our hopes so far, as to think of so glorious and complete a victory as you have gained over the enemy. The action of that day has placed your merit in its true lustre. A day whose glory might have been envied by the greatest captains of past ages, and whose memory will endure throughout all ages to come, etc.'

VI

The Campaign of 1704:
The Conclusion of the Campaign

The day after our Thanksgiving, we marched toward Ulm, where we stayed two days; and then leaving some troops with Lieutenant-General Thungen, for the taking of that city, we marched in eight columns through the country of Württemberg. Here the inhabitants, who were all Protestants, came out in all places, returning us thanks on their knees, and blessing us for preserving them from the fury of the Elector of Bavaria. On the 16th of August, O.S. [27th], all our columns joined near Philipsburg, where we passed the Rhine; and encamped on the plains of Spirebach [Speyerbach]. This place was remarkable for a victory [15 November 1703] which Marshal Tallard obtained here the last campaign over the Prince of Hesse.

The Marshal at that time had laid siege to Landau [24 October–28 November 1703], and the Prince of Hesse and Count Nassau Homberg, who commanded two separate bodies on the Rhine, were ordered to join on this plain, and endeavour to oblige Tallard to raise the siege; but as a dispute arose between them about the command, they encamped separately, a morass being between them. Tallard being informed of this, decamped privately about the dusk of the evening, leaving a sufficient number of troops to guard his trenches, and by break of day he was up with the Prince. He was not expecting this visit, was soon routed, and retired after the best manner he could, under the cannon of Spire (Speyer). Count Homberg not being able (or perhaps not willing) to assist the Prince, retired under the cannon of a fort on that side of the Rhine opposite Philipsburg; and Tallard returned to Landau and took it. This little success puffed him up to that degree, that he verily thought there were not any troops able to stand before him and his Gendarmerie; but he found himself much mistaken at Blenheim.

Our army lay encamped on these plains, until the Prince of Baden joined us with his troops from Ingolstadt; that place having surrendered [21 August], as soon as they heard of the defeat of the Elector.

But the old gentleman could never forgive our two generals, for robbing him of his part in the glory of the battle.

Much about the same time we were joined by the troops which Prince Eugène had left to guard the lines of Stollhofen. Our army was then computed to be 135,000; and now the siege of the unfortunate town of Landau was undertaken. Thrice was it besieged and thrice taken in three succeeding campaigns. The siege was to be carried on by the Prince of Baden under the King of the Romans [*actually the Emperor*]. All the troops that were not in the late battle, were to be employed in it, and our two generals were to cover the siege. On the last of August [*11 September*] our army advanced to Landau. Villeroi had drawn together all the French troops that were in that country, to try if he could prevent us from sitting down before it; but as we advanced he retired behind the lines of Haguenau. Prince Eugène and the Duke of Marlborough advanced to Cronweissenburg, about three leagues from Landau, and in ten days after the King of the Romans arrived.

While the siege was carrying on, the Duke's thoughts were employed in forming a new scheme for promoting the common cause. He considered that the Netherlands were crowded with a number of the best-fortified towns in Europe, and that they were surrounded with lines almost impregnable; from hence he concluded it next to an impossibility to penetrate into France that way. His scheme therefore was to carry on the war along the Moselle, and having proposed it to Prince Eugène, he immediately approved of it. Whereupon they went to the siege, where, in a council of war, the King of the Romans, the Prince of Baden and all the general-officers fell into it at once. It was then concluded that early in the spring, the Prince of Baden with 40,000 Germans should join the Duke of Marlborough with an equal number of troops on the Moselle. This affair being settled, the Duke undertook immediately to clear the Moselle of all the French garrisons from Coblenz up to Trèves; and thereupon ordered the Prince of Hesse to march with the Prussian, Hanoverian and Hessian troops towards Trèves. His Grace also went with them, and in a short time they took that city [*29 October*] and Traerbach [*Trarbach, 20 December*], and punctually executed what he had undertaken. This being done, he left the Prince with his troops, to take care of that part of the country, and returned to Cronweissenburg. It was now toward the end of October, and Landau still held out:[1] but as it was not in the power of

[1] Landau eventually fell on 28 November N.S.

France to raise the siege, the Duke thought it full time to send off the British and Dutch troops for Holland. Whereupon boats were prepared to carry the foot down the Rhine; while the horse were to march back the same way they came up. Our Regiment was quartered at Ruremonde.

This winter my very good friend and benefactor General Hamilton, being grown old and infirm, resigned his Regiment to Lieutenant-General Ingoldsby.[1]

Immediately after this, the Duke set out to visit several of the courts of Germany, in order to press them to prosecute the war with vigour; and it may well be supposed that the man who had just preserved the Empire, was highly caressed wherever he came.

And now on his return home he was graciously received by her Majesty, highly caressed by all that wished well to their country; and upon his going into the House of Lords, they ordered the Lord-Keeper to make him the following Speech.

'My Lord Duke of Marlborough,

'The happy success that has attended her Majesty's arms, under your Grace's conduct in Germany the last campaign, is so truly great, so truly glorious in all its circumstances, that few instances in former ages can equal, much less excel the lustre of it.

'Your Grace has not overthrown young and unskilful generals, raw and undisciplined troops; but your Grace has conquered the French and Bavarian armies, that were fully instructed in the arts of war: select veteran troops, flushed with former successes and victories, commanded by generals of great experience and bravery. The glorious

---

[1] The successive Colonels of the Royal Regiment of Ireland between 1684 and 1713 were the following:

From 1 March 1684 (raising of the regiment)—Arthur, Earl of Granard
From 1 March 1686—Arthur, Lord Forbes
From 1 March 1689—Sir Jno. Edgeworth
From 1 May 1689—Edward, Earl of Meath
From 19 December 1692—Frederick Hamilton
From 1 October 1695—Frederick Hamilton (recommissioned on retitling of the Regiment to 'The Royal Regiment of Foot of Ireland'. See p. 7 above)
From 1 April 1705—Richard Ingoldsby
From 18 February 1712—Robert Sterne

Information drawn from Dalton, vol. VI. *N.B.*—The Regiment was frequently commanded in the field by brevet-lieutenant-colonels; the Regimental Colonel was often a general officer with higher responsibilities.

victories your Grace has obtained at Schellenberg and Hochstadt[1] are very great, very illustrious in themselves; but they are greater still in their consequences to her Majesty and her Allies. The Emperor is thereby relieved, the Empire itself freed from a dangerous war in the very bowels of it, the exorbitant power of France checked, and I hope a happy step made toward reducing that Monarch within his due bounds, and securing the liberties of Europe. The honour of these glorious victories, great as they are (under the immediate blessing of God) is chiefly owing to your Grace's conduct and valour. This is the unanimous voice of England, and of her Majesty's Allies.

'My Lord, this most honourable House is highly sensible of the great and signal service your Grace has done her Majesty this campaign, and of the immortal honour you have done the English Nation, and have commanded me to give you their thanks for the same. And I do accordingly give your Grace the thanks of this Honourable House, for the great honour you have done the English Nation.'

The Committee of the House of Commons waited on his Grace the same day, with the thanks of that House.[2]

---

[1] To this day German and French historians refer to Blenheim as the battle of Höchstadt. This has occasionally led to some confusion with the battle of that name fought on 20 September 1703, when the Elector of Bavaria and Marshal Villars routed the Imperial general, Count Styrum. The modern spelling of the town's name is Blindheim.

[2] More tangible rewards took the form of the royal gift of the Manor of Woodstock and a large cash grant for the building there of Blenheim Palace, the country seat of the Dukes of Marlborough.

VII

The Campaign of 1705

Early this spring the Duke came over to the Hague [*April*], and having settled matters with the States, he ordered the troops that had acted under him the preceding campaign, to assemble at Maastricht, whither he soon came, and on the 12th of May, O.S. [*23rd*], marched toward the Moselle, leaving the Veldt-Marshal Overkirk, with the Dutch troops, encamped within the entrenchment of Petersberg. By easy marches we arrived on the 24th,[1] on the banks of that river about two leagues above Trèves, where we were joined by the Prince of Hesse and the troops under his command.

Here it was that the Prince of Baden had promised to join the Duke; but he let him know, that for several reasons he could not possibly do it as early as he had engaged; however, in a short time he expected to have everything in readiness, and then he might be sure he would not fail him. Upon the strength of this, the Duke passed the Moselle, and marched on through the Defile of Taverne, which is a narrow pass between two mountains, near two leagues in length. He continued his march the same day three leagues beyond it, and we encamped at Elst, with the Moselle on our right. The Marshal Villars was at this time encamped at Sirque [*Sierck*], two leagues in our front, with an army upwards of 70,000. The Duke waited here above a month, and no appearance of the Prince of Baden. At length he sent the Duke word he was so ill of the gout, that he could not possibly join him. This was generally thought to be done out of pique to the Duke, on account of the battle of Höchstadt; but however that was,[2] the Duke was greatly chagrined at the disappointment, as he had conceived great hopes of penetrating into France that way, which must have obliged the French Court to alter their measures. For had that Prince joined him according to their agreement, the French must

[1] Most authorities state that Marlborough reached Trèves on 26 May N.S. Parker has probably slipped from his usual Old Style dating here. Similarly the opening of the campaign is often given as 18 May.

[2] Other sources claim that Baden pleaded the effects of a slight wound sustained at the Schellenberg to excuse his inaction—the 'Margrave's Toe'. See also Mérode-Westerloo, p. 192 below.

have drawn from the Netherlands a good part of those troops, with which the Elector and Villeroi were at this time carrying all before them. Here their successes were so great, that it obliged the States to write a pressing letter to the Duke, to return to them with all possible expedition; and on the receipt of it, he put all things in order to retire. Here he was obliged to use great caution, lest Villars should attempt to fall on his rear, as he was passing through the Defile of Taverne. This had formerly been the fate of Marshal Crequis [*Créquy*], who being under a necessity of passing this defile with the French army, Charles the old Duke of Lorrain [*Lorraine*], at the head of the German forces, fell on his rear, and pursuing the advantage, gave him an entire overthrow [*Battle of Consarbrück, 15 August 1675 N.S.*]. To prevent a misfortune of this kind, the Duke decamped on our beating Tattoo [*17 June*], and by marching all night, we entered the defile by daybreak; and though Villars had near double our number, and was looked upon to be the most pushing general in the French service, yet he never stirred from his camp. So on we marched without the least disturbance, and repassed the Moselle.

At this time the Duke received an express from the Veldt-Marshal, with an account that the enemy had taken Huy [*10 June*], and were in full march to Liège. This made him hasten his march; insomuch, that we were but half the time in returning, that we took in going up. When we had advanced as far as Aix-la-Chapelle, another express arrived, with an account that the enemy was actually in possession of the city of Liège, and was battering the citadel. Upon which the Duke hastened away with all the horse and dragoons, each of them taking a grenadier behind him; and next morning joined the Veldt-Marshal at Petersberg.[1] General Churchill made what haste he could to bring up the foot: but as soon as the enemy heard of the Duke's approach, they drew off from Liège [*25 June*], and retired within their lines. As soon as the foot were come up, the Duke marched after the enemy, and encamped within a league of their lines; from whence he sent a detachment which retook Huy [*11 July*]. His Grace at this time became acquainted with a gentleman of that country,[2] through whose

[1] According to Sergeant John Millner (pp. 153-4), the joint Allied army totalled 104 battalions and 168 squadrons, with 108 cannon and 20 mortars and howitzers. Churchill puts the figures at 92 battalions and 160 squadrons (as against Villeroi's army of 100 battalions and 147 squadrons).

[2] It is tempting to speculate whether this gentleman was the Count of Mérode-Westerloo; but although he certainly possessed extensive properties in the area of the lines (see

estate the enemy's lines ran; and as he wanted to get clear of such troublesome neighbours, he acquainted the Duke with the situation of two barriers, about three leagues from our right, where the enemy kept but slight guards, and he supplied him with two trusty peasants to guide him thither. Upon this the Duke formed the following scheme.[1]

On the 16th of July, O.S. [*in fact N.S.*], about noon, he ordered the army to strike their camp, and pack up the baggage. This being done, the Veldt-Marshal marched away to the left with all the left wing [*early on the 17th*]; at the same time a detachment of 10,000 foot was made from the right wing, which drew up on the right of all. These were commanded by Count Noyels [*Noyelles*], and Lieutenant-General Ingoldsby, and they, and we on the right wing, lay down on our arms.

The enemy soon had an account of all this, and concluded by the march of our left wing, that we really designed to attack them on that side, while the Duke should at the same time attack them where he stood. Whereupon Villeroi edged with their right wing away to the right, to observe the motions of the Veldt-Marshal: and the Elector drew all the troops that were on their left, close to him, to oppose the Duke. Thus matters stood, till night came on, at which time our right wing stood to their arms, and the horse mounted; and then the detachment, with a good number of pioneers, marched away to the right. The Duke at the head of the right wing of horse, kept close to them, and our right wing of foot, close to the horse; at the same time the Veldt-Marshal, facing about with the left wing, made what haste he could after us. Thus we marched all night. About day-break [*18 July*] the detachment came up to the barriers, where they found but a lieutenant and forty men in each of them; who being much surprised,

---

below, pp. 147 and 194), there is no certain evidence that he was Marlborough's informant. Nevertheless he certainly defected from the Franco-Spanish cause at this very period, and from his own account we learn that he 'wined and dined' many English officers at his house in Aix (p. 192 below), although he denies having met Marlborough in person at this time. Such a revelation—if it took place—might well explain the Duke's reluctance to employ Mérode-Westerloo in any position of high trust. The Captain-General would have had no wish to run the risk of the Count undergoing another change of heart and allegiance—and betraying Allied secrets to his former masters in the process.

[1] This operation is usually called the 'Passage of the Lines of Brabant', 17/18 July 1705. It forms one of Marlborough's masterpieces of manoeuvre.

gave us only one fire, and made off. The detachment soon broke open the barriers, and entered, and the pioneers fell to work in levelling the lines; so that in a short time the Duke with the horse, and the detachment were within them, and soon drew up in great order: and our right wing of foot doubling their pace, passed as fast as they came up and drew up behind the horse.

The Elector and Villeroi were strangely confounded, when their spies came to them a little before day, and told them our army was in full march toward the barriers. Upon this the Elector ordered the Marquis de Alegar [*d'Alègre*] and Count Horn to ride off with the greater part of the left wing of horse, and try to prevent us from coming within the lines, or to force those back that had got within them; while he with the rest followed, leaving orders for the foot to make what haste they could after him. D'Alègre and Horn did not come within sight of the barriers, till it was fair daylight; when, to their surprise, they saw our right wing of horse, and a body of foot behind them, drawn up in great order, and also the remaining part of our foot crowding over the lines, as fast as they could. However, the Marquis and the Count, according to their orders, drew up, and with great resolution charged our horse. In this charge they were both desperately wounded, and made prisoners, and their squadrons drove back in great disorder. By this time the Elector was come up, with the rest of their left wing of horse, who rallying those that were broken, drew them up in conjunction with these he brought with him; and seeing his left wing of foot near at hand, he made another bold push at our horse, but was treated as in the former charge. And now the Duke ordered his squadrons to advance briskly after them; but they were stopped by the fire of some of their foot, that had lined a hollow way. In the meantime our foot coming up, soon drove them from thence. The Elector was now endeavouring to rally his horse, but before they could be brought into any kind of order, our squadrons advanced up to them in a round trot, and put them to an entire rout. They left their foot to shift for themselves, and of these a great number were cut to pieces.[1]

I must not omit taking notice of the gallant behaviour and good discipline of ten Bavarian battalions, who finding themselves aban-

[1] This engagement is usually called the battle of Elixheim (or, occasionally, Wanghé). At one point in the sharp cavalry action Marlborough was in danger of being cut down by a Bavarian officer—but the soldier missed his stroke, fell off his horse, and was killed by Marlborough's trumpeter.

doned by their horse, kept together; and observing that as we had marched all night, our foot was not able to come up with them, they formed themselves into a hollow square. In this form they marched, and notwithstanding that our right wing of horse and dragoons had surrounded them on all sides, yet they dared not venture within reach of their fire; for having divided their grenadiers into two bodies, which kept moving backward and forward to support the parts that were most in danger, the square kept marching on, driving the squadrons before them, out of their way, and so retreated safe to Louvain, which was three leagues from the field of battle. This shews what the foot are capable of doing against the horse, while with resolution they preserve their order, and avoid hurry.[1]

Villeroi made all the haste he could with the right wing to support the Elector; but seeing him defeated, he turned off to the left, and made the best of his way to Louvain, where he found the Elector with his shattered troops cursing his fate. Here they took up the strong camp of Parck, having the Dyle in their front, which is a deep still river, and runs through Louvain.

In this action (which may properly be called half a battle, being fought by half only of each army), the Bavarians were the greatest sufferers; the Elector having had with him 24 squadrons and 22 battalions of his own subject troops, who behaved to admiration: and had the French horse that were joined with them, and were treble their number, behaved with equal bravery, the victory had not come as easy as it did. It was computed that they had about 2,000 killed, and a great number taken, besides two entire regiments taken at Tirlemont, with eighteen pieces of cannon, and a great many colours, standards and kettle-drums. This victory and our gaining these important lines, cost us but a very few men not worth notice.[2] Our army halted near Tirlemont, and we did not march after the enemy till twelve o'clock the next day, for which the Duke was censured by those that did not wish him well. They insisted, that had he pursued with the horse, while the enemy were in so great consternation, and left orders for the foot to follow as fast as they could, it would have obliged Villeroi to take another rout; and then the Elector could not have rallied his shattered troops at Louvain. On the other hand it was

[1] The Bavarian battalions were commanded by Count Pierre Caraman on this noteworthy occasion. During the battle's course the French had brought up secret weapons—namely a number of cannon with triple barrels—but they did them little good.

[2] Allied casualties were about 200 men.

alleged in favour of the Duke, that the army in general, and especially the foot, were greatly fatigued, and that our left wing under the Veldt-Marshal had not passed the lines;[1] and therefore that it had been very imprudent in him to pursue the Elector with his fatigued squadrons alone, lest Villeroi, who had the greater part of their army with him, might have fallen on him with his fresh and unfatigued troops, and overturned all he had done.

However that might have happened, it gave a handle to his Grace's enemies in the House of Lords to move that the Duke of Marlborough's conduct, in relation to this affair, might be examined into: as also with respect to his marching the army up the Moselle, which they urged evidently shewed his design of protracting the war. But this motion was rejected with indignation. It shewed however the spirit of his Grace's enemies, and what he might have expected, had he not succeeded the preceding campaign, in his march up to Germany.

About noon next day we marched after the enemy, and found them encamped on the other side of the Dyle, with their right close to Louvain, where it was impossible to come at them. We encamped within cannon-shot of them, where we lay about ten days. In this time the Duke laid a scheme for passing the river two leagues above the town; and in order to it, General Churchill marched on our beating Tattoo [*29 July*], with a body of 20,000 men to the place where he designed to pass, and soon after his Grace followed with the rest of the army. We had laid our bridges, and passed fifteen battalions, with all our grenadiers, when the Duke came up about sunrise, and perceived the enemy drawing up on the hills, above our men that had passed. He then viewed the ground on both sides of the river, and found it so very swampy, that the horse could not pass it without great difficulty; and thereupon he sent orders to those that had passed, to retire, and bring off the bridges. The enemy perceiving this, drew down their cannon, and began to cannonade us. From hence we marched about two leagues back from the river, where we lay four days; and then the Duke marched the army to the head of the Dyle, to try if he could pass there. Slangenberg (who had been made General of the Dutch infantry in the room of Opdam) was by this time grown so intolerably insolent, that there was no bearing him; and because he

---

[1] In fact, the Dutch flatly refused to undertake the pursuit without a period of rest. In their defence, it should be pointed out that Overkirk's troops had been required to march twenty-seven miles in thirty-one hours. See Churchill, Book One, pp. 956–7.

was not consulted on all occasions he took all opportunities of thwarting the Duke. We were now drawing near the enemy, and his Grace had sent orders that the English train of artillery should make all possible haste up to him; but as they were just upon entering a narrow defile, Slangenberg came up to the head of them, and stopped them for some hours, until his baggage had passed on before them, a thing never known before even for the King's baggage. And this delay it was which prevented the Duke from attacking the enemy.[1] Being disappointed by this means, he turned all his thoughts on demolishing their lines, and taking in St Lue [*Léau*], and Xanvelt, which he finished by the middle of October, and then sent the army into quarters.

The Duke made a proper representation of Slangenberg's behaviour to the States-General, who knowing the pride of the man, readily laid hold of this opportunity, and sent him a dismiss. Lieutenant-General Salish [*Salisch*] was appointed to succeed him as General of the Dutch Infantry. The rise of Mr Salisch is very remarkable. He was born in Switzerland of a family of note, and upon some disgust had listed himself with a Dutch officer, who brought him a recruit to Breda, to the very regiment he was now colonel of. In this regiment he advanced himself by his personal bravery, without any interest or friends, but such as his merit had gained him: till from a private sentinel, he became colonel of the regiment, Governor of Breda, and General of the Dutch infantry; but it was yet more remarkable, that the officer who enlisted him, still continued a lieutenant when our Regiment was quartered at Breda, and it was more than he deserved, for he was an old Geneva sot: however, the General, out of pure compassion to him, kept him constantly confined, where great care was taken of him, as long as he lived.

---

[1] This abortive operation, named by Churchill 'the unfought Waterloo' (for the action—had it taken place—would have been very close to the battlefield of 1815), reached its unfortunate climax on 18 August. Slangenberg's obstructive attitude unfortunately received support from the Dutch Deputies, and accordingly another chance of near-certain victory was let slip.

VIII

The Campaign of 1706: The Battle of Ramillies

The French King being greatly incensed at the Duke of Savoy, was resolved to crush him this campaign; in order to which he sent a powerful army into Italy, to take from him his capital, and drive him out of his dominions.

Upon our taking the field [*18 May*], the Duke of Marlborough ordered six hand-mills for grinding corn to be delivered to every British regiment, as well horse as foot. This occasioned a report, that he designed to march us to Italy, to the relief of the Duke of Savoy, which had been a fine jaunt indeed: but whatever his Grace's design was, it is still a mystery, for anything I have been able to learn;[1] for we never had occasion of hand-mills in Flanders.

In the beginning of May our army took the field, and assembled at Burklone near the demolished lines. Here the Duke had an account, that the Elector and Villeroi were assembling the French army on the plains of Mont St Andrea; whereupon he advanced to Hanoy. At this place he had intelligence, that the enemy had the same day taken up the strong camp of Ramillies, which was within three leagues of us. Thereupon he sent an express to the Duke of Württemberg, who commanded the Danish horse, to let him know that he designed to engage the enemy next day, and therefore that he would join him as soon as possible.

Our army at this time consisted of 117 squadrons (including the Danish horse, which were fourteen of them), and 80 battalions;[2] and

---

[1] Marlborough had indeed at one time contemplated marching to join Prince Eugène in Italy. For his plans—and the reasons for abandoning them—see Churchill, Book Two, pp. 79–84. In the end, however, Eugène won a great victory at Turin (7 September) which effectively cleared North Italy of the French and thus complemented Marlborough's string of successes in the Low Countries. For a brief account of this battle, see Mérode-Westerloo, p. 196 below.

[2] Churchill, following Sergeant Millner (p. 170), estimates the Allied army's strength at 74 battalions, 123 squadrons, with 100 guns and 20 howitzers (Book Two, p. 95).

the next day, being Whitsunday the 12th of May, O.S. [*23rd*], by three in the morning, we marched up to the enemy in four columns.

The enemy had 132 squadrons and 90 battalions,[1] beside the advantage of the ground. It was a spot they had made choice of two months before; for in the month of March, the Elector and Villeroi had taken two engineers with them, and rode out, as it were to divert themselves with hunting and hawking. At this time they examined all the ground from Louvain to the Mehaign [*R. Mehaigne*], and finding the ground about Ramillies the fittest place to draw the Duke of Marlborough to a battle, they ordered the engineers to draw a plan of it, and of the order of battle, and sent it to Court for their approbation. The plan was highly approved of,[2] and such a number of troops sent them as they required; and among them were as many of the Household Troops, as could be spared.

The nature of the ground, and disposition of their army was as follows. They had the Mehaigne on their right, with the village of Franqueines [*Franquenay*] on the bank of it; in this village they had placed a good body of foot and dragoons, and had also thrown up such an entrenchment as the time would admit of.[3] From hence to the village of Ramillies (which was a little to the left of their centre) was a fine plain of near half a league in length, where they knew the main stress of the battle must fall. On this plain therefore, they drew up the choicest, and the greatest number of their cavalry, interlined with their best infantry. In the village of Ramillies (before which they had also thrown up a trench), they placed twenty battalions with ten pieces of cannon. From Ramillies runs the River Gheete [*Geet*], which makes the ground on both sides marshy, and not passable, especially for horse. Along this river to the villages of Offuse [*Offuz*] and Autereglise [*Autre Église*], which covered their left flank, was posted a thin line of the worst of their infantry, with squadrons after a scattering manner posted in their rear. This was the dispositions of the enemy, when our army came up to them.

---

[1] Millner (p. 170) puts Villeroi's strength at 76 battalions, 132 squadrons, 66 cannon and 12 mortars. Churchill estimates that the French fielded 63,000 men to the Allies' 62,000 (Book II, pp. 95 and 120 refer).

[2] The King added, however, that his Commander-in-Chief was to 'pay special attention to that part of the line which will endure the first shock of the English troops'. Villeroi's following of this advice substantially contributed to his losing the battle. (See Pelet and Vault, vol. VI, p. 19.)

[3] See La Colonie (pp. 304–16) for a Bavarian view of the battle on the extreme French right.

We drew up in two lines opposite them, having a rising ground on our right, whereon a great part of our British troops were drawn up. From hence the Duke had a fair view of the enemy, and saw evidently, that the stress of the battle must be on the plain, where they were drawn up in a formidable manner: he saw also, that things must go hard with him, unless he could oblige them to break the disposition they had made on the plain. On this occasion his Grace shewed a genius vastly superior to the French generals; for though he knew the ground along the Geet was not passable, yet he ordered our right wing to march down in great order, with pontoons to lay bridges, as if he designed to attack them in their weak part. The Elector and Villeroi perceiving this, immediately ordered off from the plain an entire line, both of horse and foot, to reinforce those on the Geet. When the Duke observed that these had arrived there, he sent orders to our right wing to retire easily up the hill, without altering their aspect. This we did, until our rear line had got on the back of the rising ground, out of sight of the enemy. But the front line halted on the summit of the hill in full view of them, and there stood, ready to march down, and attack them. As soon as our rear line had retired out of sight of the enemy, they immediately faced to the left, and both horse and foot, with a good many squadrons, that slunk out of the front line, marched down to the plain, as fast as they could;[1] by this time the greater part of our horse of the left wing had arrived there also, and we were now superior in numbers to them in that quarter. The Duke soon put them in order for attacking the enemy on the plain; and about one o'clock sent orders to the Veldt-Marshal to begin the battle on the left. At the same time he ordered four brigades of foot to attack the village of Ramillies, and then ordered the troops on the plain, to advance and charge their main body.

In this engagement there was great variety of action; sometimes their squadrons and sometimes ours giving way in different places; and as the fate of the day depended entirely on the behaviour of the troops on the plain, so both sides exerted themselves with the utmost vigour for a long time. The Duke was in all places where his presence was requisite; and in the hurry of the action happened to be unhorsed, and in great danger of his life; but was remounted by Captain Molesworth, one of his Aides de Camp, the only person of his retinue then near

---

[1] Marlborough's cunning use of 'interior lines' and a useful reverse slope thus enabled him to transfer considerable bodies of troops, unseen by the enemy, from his right to the left centre for the critical engagement.

him; who seeing him in manifest danger of falling into the hands of the pursuing enemy, suddenly threw himself from his horse, and helped the Duke to mount him. His Grace, by this means, got off between our lines; the Captain being immediately after surrounded by the enemy; from which danger (as well as that of our fire) he was, at last, providentially delivered. His Grace, about an hour after, had another narrow escape; when in shifting back from Captain Molesworth's horse to his own, Colonel Bringfield (his first Escuyer [*Equerry*]) holding the stirrup, was killed by a cannon-shot from the village of Ramillies.[1] Notwithstanding which, the Duke immediately rode up to the head of his troops; and his presence animated them to that degree, that they pressed home upon the enemy, and made them shrink and give back. At this very instant the Duke of Württemberg came up with the Danish horse, and perceiving an open between the village of Franquenay and their main body, fell in on the right flank of their horse, with such courage and resolution, that he drove them in upon their centre. This put them into great disorder; and our troops taking this advantage, pressed so close upon them, that they could never recover their order. The Elector and Villeroi did all that was possible to keep them from breaking: but our troops stuck so close to them, that they were put to the rout. The Household troops, who had behaved to admiration during the whole action, rallied and made a stand for some time: but as all the rest had fled, they were obliged to follow them, leaving the foot that had been drawn up with them in the field (who were of no manner of use to them), to be cut to pieces.

The Veldt-Marshal had also routed those where he attacked, who fled in a scattering manner towards Charleroi. The troops in Ramillies defended themselves to the last, till they saw their troops drove out of the field; upon which they drew off, and made toward their left wing: but were most of them cut to pieces before they could reach it. Their left wing, which was posted along the Geet, and the front line of our right wing (in which was our Regiment), stood looking on without firing a shot; and as we were posted on an eminence, and

---

[1] For corroboration of this dramatic incident, we can turn to Lord Orkney: 'Milord Marlborough was rid over, but got other squadrons to his aid which he led up. Major Bingfield, holding his stirrup to give him assistance onto his horse, was shot by a cannon ball that passed through Marlborough's legs; in truth there was no scarcity of 'em: indeed I think I never had more shot about my ears—both musketry and cannon.' ('Letters of the First Lord Orkney', E.H.R., 1904, p. 315.)

were disengaged, we had a fair view of the whole battle on the plain.

When the Elector and Villeroi saw all was lost, they, with such troops as they could bring together, made the best of their way for Louvain, and sent to their left wing to join them there, in order to make a stand at the Dyle, as they had done the last year: but the Lord Marlborough (perhaps sensible of his mistake at that time) pursued so close with the horse, that he cut between their left wing and Louvain, which obliged them to disperse and fly the other way, every man shifting for himself. The Elector and Villeroi finding that the Duke was close at their heels, turned off from Louvain, and made towards Vilvorde, hoping to make [reach] the canal which runs from Brussels thither: but the Duke still pursuing them close, they quitted Vilvorde, and never stopped, until they fled to Lisle [Lille], with about 2,000 horse only. The Duke having passed the canal of Vilvorde, halted at Grimnberg, where he waited for the coming up of the foot. These continued marching after him with all the expedition they could, without observing any other order than this, that every regiment kept their men as close together as they possibly could; and none of them halted above an hour at a time, till they joined him.

Thus ended the famous Battle of Ramillies. The enemy had at least 7,000 killed, and a great many more taken prisoners; and as they were dispersed about the country, their loss by desertion was very considerable. Upon the whole, their loss was computed to be upwards of 30,000, beside 60 pieces of cannon, 8 mortars, a great number of colours, standards and kettle-drums, taken. Their tents and baggage escaped us, having been sent off before the battle. The loss on our side was computed to be more than 5,000 killed and wounded.[1]

---

[1] Millner (p. 175) claims that the French lost 6,759 killed, 5,328 wounded, and 5,729 prisoners, besides 4,000 deserters (a total of 21,816). He places the Allied loss at 4,192 (p. 177). In addition to prisoners, Marlborough took 54 cannon (including 'eleven triple-bored'—see p. 55 n. above), 65 colours, 21 standards, six pairs of kettledrums, and 2,000 wagons. Churchill accepts these figures with only slight variations.

IX

The Campaign of 1706:
The Exploitation of the Victory

We halted at Grimnberg until our tents and baggage came up; in which time the magistrates of Brussels, Louvain, Mechlin, Leer, and Alost, brought their keys to the Duke, and craved his protection. From hence we marched to Alost, and the next day to Ghent, the magistrates of which met the Duke a league from their city with their keys [1 June]; as did also in two days after, those of Bruges, Oudenard [Oudenarde], and Courtray [Courtrai]. Our army halted near Ghent for a fortnight, in which time the Duke went to the Hague, to consult with the States on the future operations of the campaign.

The French Court, which had entertained great hopes of the success of this campaign, was greatly shocked at the loss of the battle: but it was yet more alarmed at the consequences that attended it. For it obliged them not only to recall their favourite general, the Duke of Vendosme [Vendôme], from Italy, to command in the Netherlands, but also to draw a great number of their troops from the Rhine.

On the Lord Marlborough's return from the Hague, the Veldt-Marshal, with part of the army, laid siege to Ostend [19 June]; the Duke at the same time marched the other part to Courtrai, where we lay till Ostend was taken [9 July]. It surrendered in three weeks after opening trenches, but had formerly held out as many years.[1] The Marquis of Terracena, Governor of Antwerp, who had six Spanish, and six French regiments in garrison, obliged Mr Du Pontis, who commanded the French, to capitulate for his marching home, which was granted [16 June]. Upon which the Marquis declared for King Charles, and was continued Governor. Dendermond [Dendermonde] stood a blockade of three months before it surrendered [9 September].

The Veldt-Marshal having joined the Duke, they marched the army up to the lines, which had been the French Barrier all the last

---

[1] The reference here is to the celebrated siege of July 1601–September 1604, when the Dutch patriots successfully withstood all Spanish efforts to take the town until the celebrated General Spinola assumed command of the siege.

war. We encamped at Helchin, from whence a part of the army under General Salisch was ordered to lay siege to Menin [*from 22 July*]. Our Regiment was part of this detachment.

Menin was esteemed to be one of Vauban's masterpieces. It was a regular and well-fortified place, with a garrison of 5,000 men, and well supplied with all manner of necessaries. The Governor disputed every inch of ground with us, till we carried our approaches to the foot of the glacis; and then we made an attack on the covert way.[1] Our entire Regiment was engaged in this attack, and here we paid for our looking on at Ramillies; having had two captains, and five subalterns killed, and eight officers wounded, among whom I was one; having received a contusion on the side of my head, which had like to have been fatal to me. As I was then Captain-Lieutenant and Adjutant, I was upon this occasion made Captain of our Grenadiers.[2]

The day after we had lodged ourselves on the covert-way, the Governor beat the Chamade, and honourable terms were granted him [*22 August*]. While we were carrying on the siege, the Duke employed all the boors of the country, in demolishing the lines, which extended from the Liss [*R. Lys*] to the Scheldt. When this was executed, we marched to the left, and passing the Scheldt at Pont-Espier, we encamped at Gramez, from whence we marched to the plains of Cambron. A detachment was sent off from this place to take in Aeth [*Ath*]; which having surrendered in ten days [*1 October*], we then went into quarters; and this put an end to this glorious campaign, to the immortal honour of the Duke of Marlborough. Surely if he committed a mistake the preceding campaign, he made ample amends for it in this; for never was an enemy so fairly pushed out of a country, as the French were out of the whole Spanish Netherlands. Let his Grace's enemies judge, whether this looks like protracting a war.

Soon after we went into [*winter*] quarters, the Elector of Bavaria,

---

[1] Sterne throws more light on this incident, although he disagrees with Parker's casualty figures: 'This [*the attack on the covered way*] proved warm service; for though we drove the enemy at once out of the counterscarp, they sprung two mines upon us, and from their works plied us with a most violent fire which we lay exposed to until our workmen had thrown up an entrenchment to cover us. In this action our regiment had six officers and upwards of 80 soldiers killed and wounded.' (See Cannon, p. 32.)

[2] Parker's formal appointment as Captain of Grenadiers was gazetted on 11 September 1708. It is possible that he served in this rank in an acting capacity from 1706. He had been promoted captain-lieutenant on 1 May 1706. (See Dalton, vol. V, Pt Two, p. 55, and this volume, p. 10.)

by order of the French King, wrote to the Lord Marlborough, concerning a treaty of peace: but it appeared plainly, that the design of it was only to create a jealousy among the Allies; so that treaty soon came to nothing. The Duke, on his return to England, was received by the Queen with all the esteem imaginable; he also received the thanks of both Houses of Parliament [3 *December*], and the whole nation rang with the highest acclamations of his extraordinary merit.

X

The Campaign of 1707

The young King of Sweden [*Charles XII*] was at this time raising large contributions in Saxony, and had threatened even the Emperor himself. The Allies dreaded the consequences of such an expedition; and had pressed her Majesty to send the Duke of Marlborough to him, to endeavour to persuade him to quit the Empire. Whereupon the Queen wrote a letter to his Swedish Majesty, and gave it to the Duke to deliver to him. Early therefore in the spring his Grace came over, and proceeded to Saxony; and knowing well how to tickle the young hero, he at his first audience [*27 April*] delivered the Queen's letter to him, and addressed him in the following manner.

'Sir, I present your Majesty a letter, not written from the Chancery, but from the heart of the Queen my mistress, and written with her own hand. Had not her sex prevented her, she would have crossed the seas to see a Prince, admired by the whole universe. I am in this respect more happy than the Queen; and I wish I could serve some campaigns, under so great a general as your Majesty, that I may learn what I yet want to know in the art of war.'

It was never known that the King was so much taken with anyone as with the Duke of Marlborough, he engaged him to dine with him that day; and having continued with his Majesty four days, he in that time made use of such prevailing arguments, as quite changed the schemes of that ambitious youth. He had intended to interfere in our war with France: but a new scene was presented to him, he was now determined to revenge himself on the Czar, and to dethrone him as he had Augustus of Poland. Soon after the Duke took leave of him, he marched out of Saxony, and prosecuted his designs on Muscovy with such precipitation, that the Czar artfully drew him on to Pultowa [*Pultava*], and there gave him a total overthrow [*28 June 1709*].

The Duke returned from Saxony in the beginning of May, and gave orders for the army to assemble at Bethlehem near Louvain, from whence in a little time we marched to Meldert.

The Duke of Vendôme drew the French army behind their lines near Mons; and though he outnumbered us considerably, yet he had positive orders not to hazard a battle, unless it was in defence of his lines. We lay at Meldert near six weeks, in hope of drawing him from behind them; at length he ventured out, and encamped at Genappes, six leagues from us. The Duke suffered him to lie quiet about eight or ten days; then on our beating Tattoo, we decamped on a sudden, and sent off our heavy baggage to Louvain. We marched all night, and by the time it was day, the Duke with the right wing of horse, had advanced within less than half a league of the enemy: but they had just struck their tents, and were marching off in some confusion. The Duke immediately ordered Count Tilly to advance with the horse and fall on their rear, and by that means keep them engaged, till the foot should come up. But Tilly could do nothing in the enclosures, as he had none but horse: and the foot being fatigued, could not come up, so Vendôme marched off at his leisure. The Duke therefore seeing that the affair was not practicable, ordered the army to encamp. Vendôme perceiving this, concluded that he had entirely given over that design; and as he had got clear of the enclosed grounds, he encamped at Senef [*Seneffe*], only two leagues from us. This was what the Duke expected; wherefore on our beating Tattoo, we decamped again: but as we began to march it rained so heavily that the foot could hardly stand under it, and it was impossible for them to keep their arms dry. The van of our horse had advanced very near Vendôme's camp, by the time it was day. He not expecting this second visit, struck his camp in great hurry, marched off as fast as he could, and never stopped, till he found himself safe within his lines. In all probability he had paid dear for his halt at Seneffe, had it not been for the rain, which continued so violent for three days together, that our foot was in a miserable condition. The Duke then turned off to the right, and encamped near Soignies [*14 August*], which was but two leagues from our former ground. As short as this march was, yet the rain was so severe, and the ground so poached by the horse that marched first, that many of the foot were smothered in the sloughs, and it was four days before the rest of them came up.

We lay here near three weeks weather-bound; for it was towards the end of July [*in fact August*] before our artillery could be raised off the ground. Our first movement was to the plains of Cambron, where we lay about ten days: and crossing the Scheldt at Pont-Espier, we encamped at Helchin. The French had thrown up new lines last winter, from Warneton, on the Lys to Lille, and so on to Tournai on the Scheldt; and the Duke wanted to take a view of these lines, and of the country about them. With this view he ordered the whole army to make a grand forage that way, he ordered also sixty squadrons and twenty battalions to cover the foragers, and to guard him, while he was viewing the ground; and the whole army was to be in readiness to take arms, and march out, in case Vendôme drew out to disturb him or the foragers. But the Frenchman took care to keep within his lines, and the Duke rode as near them, between Lille and Tournai, as their cannon would permit. As the country was very plentiful, our camp was sufficiently provided with forage till the middle of October, when we went into quarters.

XI

The Campaign of 1708:
The French Offensive

The French King, finding himself hard pressed on all sides,[1] began to listen to the disaffected party in Scotland, who had solicited him a long time to send the Pretender to them, with a few troops and a great many arms. Whereupon he caused a squadron of 24 light ships to be fitted up at Dunkirk. The squadron was commanded by the Chevalier Forbin, and on board of it embarked the Pretender, with twelve battalions and a great many arms, etc.

The Queen had timely notice of the French preparations; and in a short time had a fleet of 36 men of war in the Downs, under the command of Sir George Byng. In the beginning of March Forbin sailed out of Dunkirk, steering along the coast of Holland. He had the start of Sir George by eighteen hours; who finding Forbin had slipped him, made all the sail he could along the coast of England, for the Firth of Edinburgh. On this occasion ten battalions were ordered from Flanders (our Regiment was one of them) and Sir George, on his sailing from the Downs, had sent Admiral Baker with ten men of war to convoy us. We embarked on board transports, and sailed [*28 March; from Ostend*] to the mouth of the Tyne; where we lay on board, waiting for the event of what might happen between Sir George and Forbin. The latter having made the length of Scotland, stood over for that coast: but coming near shore, he found he had over-shot the Firth; whereupon he tacked, and stood off shore till he recovered his port. Just as he was standing into the Firth, he discovered

---

[1] Although Parker does not choose to mention it, 1707 in fact proved a year of considerable success for the French and their allies. Besides Vendôme's success in preventing Marlborough from achieving anything notable in the Low Countries, another French army under Marshal Villars successfully stormed the lines of Stollhofen (22 May 1707) and penetrated deep into Germany, while in Spain the Allies sustained a heavy defeat at Almanza (25 April) at the hands of Marshal Berwick. A final blow for the Grand Alliance was the failure of Prince Eugène to capture Toulon (July–August). The scare engendered by the 'Jacobite Raid'—mentioned here by Parker—also caused the British Government considerable anxiety in early 1708.

Sir George. Upon which Forbin, who never had any opinion of the undertaking, and dreaded the consequence of being imbayed [*trapped on a lee shore*] by him, tacked about, and made all the sail he could homeward. Sir George made what sail he could after him, but as they were all clean light ships, they out-sailed him. However, we retook the *Salisbury*, in which were the Lord Griffin, Lord Clermont, a son of Lord Middleton's, Colonel Wachop [*Wanchope*], with several others of note. This famous expedition being over, our ten battalions sailed back to Ostend, where we disembarked the 14th of April [*25th*].

The French Court being disappointed in this attempt, had now formed the following scheme to drive the Duke of Marlborough out of the Netherlands. The Elector of Bavaria, who had been formerly Governor of the Spanish Netherlands, and had lived in a genteel and profuse manner among them, had gained much on the people, and was in particular a high favourite of the ladies. He had always kept up a secret correspondence with the leading men of their great towns, who were rather inclined to the French and Spanish interest, than to that of the Allies; and had prevailed with them to throw open their gates, and receive him, whenever he came before them. He had also assured them, that the French would have such an army in the field this campaign, as would be able to drive the Allies out of the Netherlands, if they did their part and would not suffer themselves to be besieged.

The Duke of Marlborough, whose intelligence at the French Court never failed him, had early notice of all this; and Prince Eugène (having in the three last campaigns driven the French quite out of Italy) was now at leisure to join the Duke. He thereupon sent to him to meet him at the Hague; which he accordingly did, and there they settled matters so [*12 April 1708*], that the Prince was to join him with 30,000 Germans, to oppose the French in their designs on the Netherlands.

In the beginning of May the Duke of Vendôme took the field, and encamped on the plains of Cambron [*near Mons*]. His army consisted of 139 battalions and 204 squadrons. From thence he marched to Soignies, where he waited for the arrival of the Duke of Burgundy, who was to command the army, and have the glory of the campaign. He arrived at Soignies about the middle of June, attended by the Duke of Berry, and the Pretender, who was called the Chevalier de St George.

My Lord Marlborough drew his army together at Terbanck,

between Louvain and Brussels, in order to cover these towns, and to be in the way to join Prince Eugène. Our army consisted of 110 battalions, and 176 squadrons. When the enemy advanced to Soignies, the Duke imagined they had a design on Brussels, and therefore marched to Anderlecht. The enemy, finding they could not come at Brussels, resolved to push for Ghent. On the 25th of June, O.S., on their beating Tattoo, they decamped suddenly, and marched thither, as expeditiously as they could. When they came before it [*in fact 5 July N.S.*], they sent a formal message to the magistrates, that if they did not open their gates, they would burn the town about their ears. Upon which they assembled (as formerly) to consult, whether they should open their gates to the French, or receive General Murray, who was just arrived at Bruges-Port with four regiments from Courtrai. The few that were not in the secret, declared for receiving Murray; but the majority were for the French. Whereupon they admitted them, and shut out Murray, who marched back to Courtrai.[1] Lieutenant-General La Motte entered Ghent with 20,000 French; and next morning he sent off 5,000 of them to Bruges, which also threw open her gates to them [*in fact 5 July N.S.*].[2] The Duke of Burgundy's next design was upon Oudenarde; and had he met with equal success here, it had cut us off from all communication with our garrisons on the other side of the Scarpe and the Lys.

[1] See Mérode-Westerloo, p. 201 below.

[2] Parker confuses the facts here; Ghent town surrendered to the advance guard of the Duke of Burgundy's Grand Army on 5 July N.S., and the citadel fell two days later. Count de la Motte, meanwhile, with a separate force, had marched from Comines to Bruges, which admitted the French at 3 a.m. on the 5th.

XII

The Campaign of 1708:
The Battle of Oudenarde

My Lord Marlborough finding that the enemy had stolen this march of him, and imagining they designed for Ghent, decamped next morning; and marched directly for Oudenarde.[1] When we arrived there, the French were also on their march thither, and had advanced as far as Gaver [*Gavre*], within two leagues of it; but finding that we were beforehand with them, they stopped short, and passed the Scheldt there, with a design of marching that way back toward Lille. The Duke upon this ordered two bridges to be laid over the Scheldt below the town, and left orders for the foot to pass as fast as they came up: while he at the head of the horse passed through the town with such despatch, that our army had got between them and home. Things being thus circumstanced, they were under a necessity either of fighting their way through us, or of retiring back to Ghent.

Upon this a dispute arose between Burgundy and Vendôme. The latter and the old generals dreaded the consequences of a battle, and therefore were for retiring toward Ghent, until La Motte had joined them; though by that means they must be pent up in a corner of the country, and cut off from all their garrisons: but Burgundy and the young gentlemen were for fighting. And indeed it is not easy to say which was the best course to take, especially as Prince Eugène's troops were within two days' march of us.[2] However, Burgundy prevailed, which disgusted Vendôme so, that they were continually jarring all the rest of the campaign. Vendôme finding that it must come to a battle, and that the management of it must lie on him and the old

---

[1] During the night of 10/11 July N.S. Marlborough forced-marched his men over a distance of fifteen miles from Lessines to reach Oudenarde before the French could cover the mere six miles separating them from Gavre.

[2] The approach of Eugène's army had been materially hampered by the covering moves executed by Marshal Berwick and his French army. On 11 July only Prince Eugène and his immediate escort were actually present at Oudenarde.

generals that had opposed it, set himself to work with some reluctance, and drew up the army on an advantageous piece of ground.

His left flank was covered by the Scheldt, the ground about being full of enclosures. They had a rivulet in their front [R. *Norken*], and the village of Hyne [*Eyne*] advanced a little before it, in which he posted a body of foot and some dragoons. A marshy piece of ground, full of trees and brushwood extended from hence, something beyond their centre: here he posted the greater part of his infantry, who cut down a number of trees, and laid them in such a manner as to prevent our coming at them. Near the springs which occasioned this marshy ground is a spacious plain (where our army lay encamped for some time in the year '94); here he drew up the greater part of his cavalry. At the end of this plain is the village Orchies [*Oycke*], near the Lys, which covered their right flank; and here he also posted a good body of foot and dragoons.

It was now the 30th of June, O.S. [*11 July*]; the Lord Marlborough having got all his troops over the Scheldt, immediately ordered the first brigade of foot that passed the bridges to march up and attack the village of Eyne, which they did with such resolution, that the enemy made but little resistance; though they afterwards made some attempts to recover it, but in vain. While this prelude to the battle was acting, the lines were forming with all possible expedition; at which time Prince Eugène came up, but had left his troops more than a day's march behind him.

The lines being formed,[1] our main body of foot attacked the enemy in the marshy ground. At the same time also the village of Oycke was attacked by the foot on our left. The main battle was fought on the plain, where most of the cavalry on both sides were fairly engaged. As the enemy had some foot drawn up with their horse, the Prince of Orange attacked them with fifteen Dutch battalions. At the same time also our horse advanced and charged their horse with such resolution, as made them give way at the very first charge; nor did they make one gallant charge the whole day, but still gave way as our squadrons pushed at them. Our generals observing this, pressed still

---

1 The Allies probably fielded some 80,000 men (85 battalions and 150 squadrons) against Burgundy's 85,000 (90 battalions and 170 squadrons). At the outset, however, the enemy enjoyed a far larger advantage than these total figures indicate. Marlborough took a very real risk in advancing over the Scheldt—inviting defeat in detail. However, the dissensions dividing the councils of Burgundy and Vendôme, and the fine fighting quality of the Allied troops, swung the fortunes of the day in the Duke's favour.

the more upon them, until with very little resistance they were entirely routed; insomuch that they could not be prevailed upon to rally, even so far as to help off their foot. As for the Dukes of Burgundy and Berry, the Chevalier, and some of the other sparks, they were perched on a steeple in the rear of their army [*probably at Royegem*], to behold the battle; and when they saw their horse give way, they immediately came down, and were the first that carried the news of the defeat to Ghent: those in the village maintained their ground till they saw their horse driven out of the field, on which they quitted, and made along the Lys toward Ghent: but their foot that were drawn up with the horse on the plain, met with the usual fate of such, that is, they were cut to pieces. The Prince of Orange having despatched these with the help of the horse, wheeled with his battalions on the right flank of their main body of foot in the marshy ground, and fell upon them; and they being hard pressed both in front and flank, made down to the Scheldt where were such enclosures that our horse could not come at them; and the foot being fatigued, could not follow them far. These made toward Ghent with the crowd; and never thought themselves safe till they had passed through it, and were drawn up along the canal, that runs from thence to Bruges.[1]

The loss of the enemy was computed to be near 5,000 killed, and as many taken, their foot being the greatest sufferers. As for their horse, though a great number of them were the Household troops attending the Princes of the Blood, yet they made but a poor shameful fight of it, and saved themselves by their horses' heels. Our loss was no more,

---

[1] Parker's account of Oudenarde is somewhat sketchy. He does not convey the critical, escalating nature of this encounter-type struggle on the plain, where first Cadogan, and later Marlborough and Eugène, were hard pressed by the French forces. However, by continually feeding into the firing line the new battalions and squadrons as they made their appearance from the Scheldt bridges, the Allied commanders retained the initiative on the right and centre, thanks to the reluctance of large parts of Burgundy's forces to join in the fray. Then, after sending Overkirk and the Prince of Orange through dead ground from Oudenarde to the vicinity of Oycke (*c.* 8 p.m.), Marlborough was able to turn the right flank of the French front line, supplementing Overkirk's onslaught on the left by a complementary attack by Prince Eugène on the right. Vendôme had long since lost control of the battle, plunging into the fighting pike in hand, and very soon practically half the French army were almost surrounded. However, the jaws of the trap never quite closed, for the onset of darkness caused several converging Allied units to fire at one another. Marlborough thereupon ordered a ceasefire (9 p.m.), and many French escaped through a gap in the Allied lines.

by an exact computation, than 824 killed and 2,146 wounded.[1] We took also a great many cannon, standards, colours, kettle-drums, etc.

In this battle, his Highness, the Electoral Prince of Hanover (now George II of England), distinguished himself with singular bravery, and had his horse shot under him, as he charged at the head of his father's troops.[2]

The day after the battle, the Duke sent a detachment to take possession of the lines of Warneton; and the day following Prince Eugène's troops joined us. And now a council of war was held, in which the siege of Lille was resolved on.

But here I must take leave of the army for some time; for our Colonel, Lieutenant-General Ingoldsby, being appointed Commander in chief of the troops in Ireland (on the death of Lord Cutts), on his arrival in that kingdom, found them very defective in their discipline, especially the foot. Whereupon he applied to the Duke of Marlborough to suffer me to go thither, in order to introduce among them the discipline practised in Flanders. Accordingly I left the army at Helchin, embarked at Helvoetsluys [*Hellevoetsluis*], arrived soon after at Solbay [*Solebay*], and from thence proceeded for Dublin. I continued two years disciplining the foot of that kingdom, in which time all the regiments of foot passed through my hands. When I had finished the work, the Government ordered me a gratuity of 200 [*pounds*] and then I returned to Flanders.[3]

---

[1] Millner (pp. 218–19) puts the enemy loss at 16,400 (4,200 killed and wounded, 9,800 prisoners and 2,400 deserters), together with ten guns. The same source computes total Allied loses at 3,040. According to Sterne (Cannon; pp. 33–34), the Royal Irish, 'though the first that engaged, had only one lieutenant and 8 men killed, and 12 men wounded.'

[2] To the end of his life King George II remained proud of his presence at Oudenarde. At the battle of Dettingen (27 June 1743) he proudly donned the aged red coat worn at the battle in his youth, thirty-five years earlier, and wearing it led his troops to victory over the Duc de Noailles. This was the last occasion that a King of England personally led his troops in battle.

[3] See the letter written by Parker from Dublin, p. 8 above.

XIII

The Campaign of 1708:
The Siege of Lille

I left the army then (as has been related), at Helchin [*12 August*] on their march toward Lille.[1] They invested the city on the 2nd of August O.S. [*13th*]. Prince Eugène and the Prince of Orange under him carried on the siege with fifty battalions, and forty squadrons, while the Duke and the Veldt-Marshal covered them with the rest of the army.

The defeat at Oudenarde was a heavy stroke to the French Court: but their concern was much greater, when they found that their beloved city of Lille was invested. The King had expended vast sums of money in pulling down the old buildings, and laying out the streets in a most regular and spacious manner. His famous engineer Vaubon [*Vauban*] had exerted his utmost skill, as well in the beautiful and exact model of the new buildings, as in its noble and extraordinary fortifications; insomuch that his Majesty came thither to see it, and named it Petit Paris.

Upon the defeat of their army, they were apprehensive that the Allies would lay siege to it; and as our generals could not possibly invest it sooner than they did, the French had time to supply it with all manner of provisions, and stores in abundance. The Marshal Boufflers also, who was governor of it, had got in with a good body of troops; so that the garrison consisted of 14,000 regular troops, besides a number of inhabitants that were of service on many occasions. They had likewise sent orders to the Duke of Berwick, to bring all the troops that could be spared from the Rhine, to reinforce the Duke of Burgundy. He arrived accordingly toward the end of August with 14,000 men, and encamped between Douay [*Douai*] and Tournai, to cover that part of the country from our parties and foragers. At the same time the Duke of Burgundy passed through Ghent with the army, and marched up to the Scheldt, leaving La Motte with 10,000

---

[1] Churchill calls Lille 'the second greatest city of France'. Its fate was therefore of symbolical importance as well as military.

men to take care of his new conquest, and having repassed the Scheldt near Tournai, he joined the Duke of Berwick. In short they had drained all their garrisons far and near, and had drawn together an army of 120,000 and upwards, exclusive of the detachment under La Motte. On the other side the Allies were obliged to keep strong garrisons at Oudenarde, Brussels, and other places, to keep open a communication with the other side of the Scheldt, from whence they had all their provisions and stores; so that they had 100,000 men only, both to carry on the siege, and at the same time to cover it against that numerous army. This gave the French Court great hopes, not only that the siege must be raised but also that they might soon be revenged of us for the affront at Oudenarde. Accordingly they sent positive orders to oblige us to raise the siege, or to give us battle; however to act with caution.

The Duke of Marlborough lay with the covering army, at some distance without the line of circumvallation, and was not much more than half the number of the enemy; whereupon the Dukes of Burgundy, Vendôme, and Berwick, advanced up to him in order of battle, and seemed determined to attack him. Prince Eugène observing this, came and joined him with such troops as could be spared from the siege, leaving the Prince of Orange with a sufficient number to guard the trenches. The enemy drew up within cannon-shot of us, at which time both sides began to cannonade each other with great fury [5 September]; our generals expecting every moment when they would advance to begin the battle: but their hearts failed them, and when it grew dark, they drew back about half a league. Our generals found by this, that they were afraid to venture a battle; and that their design was rather to protract the siege by alarming us frequently, and so oblige us to waste our ammunition in cannonading, which might be wanted at the siege. They therefore caused a strong entrenchment to be thrown up along the front of the army, to cover their men from the enemy's cannon; and then Prince Eugène returned with his troops to the siege. Three days after the enemy advanced as before, and began to cannonade us; and Prince Eugène with a few squadrons only, came again to the Duke. They continued cannonading all that day, and at night lay down on their arms, which looked as if they designed to attack us early next morning. Our army also lay on their arms all night, and Prince Eugène sent for the rest of his troops, who were up with him before it was day. In the morning the enemy began to cannonade, and continued it the whole day, to very little purpose. We

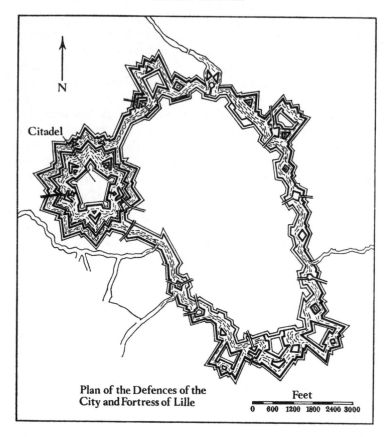

Plan of the Defences of the
City and Fortress of Lille

Feet

0   600   1200 1800 2400 3000

fired but seldom, and when it grew dark, they drew off silently, and made no further attempts in that way.

Next day the French generals held a grand consultation, in which all agreed that it was not safe to attack the Duke of Marlborough in the situation he was in; and thereupon they came to a resolution of cutting off our communication with our garrisons on the other side of the Scheldt; by which means we should be deprived of all provisions and necessaries for carrying on the siege. They sent an express to Court with an account of what they had done, and what they proposed to do; and were answered, Any way, so they could preserve Lille. On the return of the express they marched, and passing the Scheldt a little below Tournai, they stretched their army along that side of the river. They then threw up an entrenchment all the way to Oudenarde, and continued it round the town on to Gavre, which effectually answered their design in that respect. But the Lord Marlborough, who never wanted a ready thought, was apprehensive [*aware*] of all this; and had already sent expresses to England and Holland, to desire they would immediately send great stores of provisions and ammunition to Ostend. It happened very lucky at this juncture, that Lieutenant-General Earl, who had embarked with 7,000 foot designed for Spain, was detained at Spithead by contrary winds. He thereupon was ordered to take in great store of provisions and necessaries, and sail directly for Ostend. Upon this the Duke marched the covering army to Rosselaer, to be at hand to send escorts to bring up the convoys. As soon as Earl arrived, he immediately sent off a convoy of 600 waggons, and the Duke ordered Major-General Webb with 6,000 foot, and about 100 horse to bring it up. The fate of Lille depended in a great measure upon the success of this affair; for at this time all manner of provisions began to grow very scarce, and the ammunition of the besiegers began to fall short.

The Duke of Burgundy had an account of all this, and ordered La Motte to march with a body of 24,000 horse and foot, and 12 pieces of cannon to intercept this convoy. La Motte came up with Webb as he was passing on the back of the wood of Wynendale [*Wynendael, 28 September*]. Upon his appearing Webb drew up his men within an open [*clearing*] in the wood, by which both his flanks were covered. He was drawn up in four lines, and the situation is such, that La Motte could not bring more men in front to attack him, than he had to defend himself.

La Motte drew up his foot in nine lines, and his horse in the rear of them, and began to cannonade: this however did little execution, as Webb had ordered his men to lie flat on the ground, while the cannon were firing. La Motte's foot advanced, and attacked Webb's several times, but were still repulsed with considerable loss. The Duke being informed of La Motte's design, ordered Major-General Cadogan to march with a good body of horse to reinforce Webb; he upon hearing La Motte's cannon, hastened his march, and La Motte on the first sight of his squadrons, immediately drew off with great precipitation, leaving all his cannon, and a great many men killed and wounded behind him.[1] In consequence of this action, that great convoy arrived

[1] Millner (p. 235) puts the French loss at 4,000 killed and wounded besides deserters; the Allies appear to have lost some 140 killed and 800 wounded.

safe; and this in effect was the taking of Lille. Webb very deservedly acquired great honour and reputation by this gallant action; but then he spoiled all by making it the subject of his conversation on all occasions. This he should have left to fame, which seldom fails to give the hero all due praise, and does him infinitely greater honour than all his own vain boasting. And after all, had not Cadogan come up with his squadrons, it would be hard to say what might have been the consequence.

While the covering army lay at Rosselaer, the brave Veldt-Marshal Overkirk died in the eightieth year of his age. He had served his country from his youth, and distinguished himself in many gallant actions; was regretted by all, and had been singularly esteemed by the Duke of Marlborough.

Boufflers at first had been somewhat too lavish of his ammunition, and began now to want powder. He found means to let the Duke of Burgundy know it, who was at a loss to know how to supply him, until the Duke of Luxembourg undertook it. His method was this. He took about 2,000 choice horse, each of which carried behind him a bag of powder, containing about 100 weight. These put green boughs in their hats, and marched with the Duke in great order from Douai. About the dusk of the evening they came up to the outer barrier of our circumvallation line, and pretending to be a party of German horse, that had been out on an expedition, and were returned with some prisoners, the officer opened the barrier, and let them in: from thence they rode on gently to the next officer's guard, where there was no barrier, and he asking some questions which the Duke did not like, they clapped spurs to their horses, and rode in a full gallop through the intervals of our camp towards the town, but the officer ordering his guard to fire, it gave the alarm, and the Quarter-Guards turning out, and the soldiers of the camp running to their arms, all fired upon them. This set many of their powder-bags on fire, and the fire in the crowd, catching from one to the other, many of them were blown up. In the end Luxembourg with about 1,000 of them got safe into the town; but not one half of them carried in their powder with them. The rest were most of them killed or taken, a few only excepted that had not got within the barrier. This affair happened on the very same day with the action of Wynendael.[1]

After the first great convoy, two lesser ones arrived, which just did the business. The Duke of Vendôme finding (when it was too late)

[1] Compare this account with Mérode-Westerloo's, pp. 206–7 below.

that our army was supplied with everything from Ostend, marched a great part of his army that way, and taking the forts of Plassendal and Lessingen, found means, by cutting the dykes, to lay all that part of the country under water. This indeed cut off our communication effectually; but it was done too late. Boufflers in a few days after, on the 12th of October [*in fact 22 October N.S.*], surrendered the town, and retired into the citadel, with about 5,000 men, which were the remains of his garrison.

The Elector of Bavaria, who had been principally concerned in forming the schemes of this campaign, had a notion that the inhabitants of Brussels would rise in his favour against the garrison, and open the gates to him, if he appeared before it, with anything like an army. Accordingly a little before the surrender of the town of Lille, he sat down before it with 12,000 men. The inhabitants (as he expected) were inclined to receive him, but were prevented by the vigilance of Count Paskal [*Pascale*],[1] the Governor, who had a garrison of 5,000 men in it. However he opened trenches before it, carried on his approaches, and made a lodgment on the covert-way, and such a breach as he designed to storm in a day or two; but the Governor making a sally with all his garrison, drove them from their lodgment, demolished their works, and killed a great many men. Notwithstanding this, he persisted in carrying on the siege; but as Prince Eugène was by this time in possession of the town of Lille, the Duke of Marlborough marched with the covering army toward the Scheldt, and sent two detachments before him, one under the Lord Orkney and Count Lotum [*Lottum*]; the other under General Cadogan and Brigadier Evans: the former passed the Scheldt at Gavern below Oudenarde; the other at Kirkhoven above it, without the least opposition, to the great surprise of all Europe, and to the scandal of the French arms. They had declared that they would make our army eat their horses, nay that they would make them all prisoners: yet now upon sight of a part of our army only, they shamefully abandoned those mighty works, which they had boasted of so much, and without firing a gun, they instantly dispersed and fled, leaving behind them upwards of forty pieces of cannon, with a great quantity of powder and ball. The Duke with the main body of the army passed at Kirkhoven, and directed his march to Brussels. Whereupon the unfortunate Elector of Bavaria fled by night to Namur, leaving all his artillery, ammunition, and sick and wounded behind him. In the end

1 One of Mérode-Westerloo's particular *bêtes noires*. See below, pp. 208–10 and 214.

this mighty army of France, which was to have done wonders this campaign, was baffled, dispersed, and obliged to steal home different ways, leaving their beloved city of Lille a prey to the Allies; for Boufflers finding that there was no prospect of relief, surrendered the citadel about the end of November [*in fact 10 December N.S.*].[1]

The Dukes of Burgundy, Berry, Vendôme, and the Chevalier stole home by the way of Nieuport; Berwick by the way of Tournai, and the Elector (as was said) by that of Namur. La Motte only stayed behind them, with a body of troops to preserve Ghent and Bruges: but the Lord Marlborough (late in the year as it was) resolved that he should not winter in Ghent. He sat down before it on the 7th of December, O.S. [*18 December*], and La Motte surrendered it on the 24th [*4 January 1709 N.S.*], having liberty to march home the same way his generals had gone before him, and to take with him the garrisons in Bruges, and other places. This put an end to this long and glorious campaign, to the great mortification of the Court of France, and to the immortal honour of our two heroes, who now resolved to push on the war jointly in these parts.

The Duke on his return to England was received as usual by the Queen, and by both Houses of Parliament; and was indeed very justly the joy of the whole nation. I mention this that it may be remembered hereafter, when in a short time you will find him treated in as vile a manner as if he had been a notorious traitor to his Queen and country.

---

[1] Five British battalions took a leading part in the siege—namely the 16th, 18th (Royal Irish), 21st, 23rd and 24th Foot. Between them they sustained a total of 1,500 casualties by 10 December. (See C. T. Atkinson, p. 205 'Marlborough's Sieges'.) Colonel Sterne states, that the Royal Irish suffered over 200 casualties. (See Cannon, p. 34.)

XIV

The Campaign of 1709:
The Siege of Tournai

As our army had kept the field a long time the last campaign, and as this spring was very wet, it was the beginning of June [*13th N.S.*] before we could take the field. Our first rendezvous was near Lille.[1]

The French Court being greatly dissatisfied at the conduct of Vendôme, had now appointed the Marshal Villars to command in the Netherlands; but he would not accept the command, if the Duke of Burgundy was sent with him; for Vendôme had laid on him the load of all the misfortunes of the last campaign. Villars was looked upon at this time to be the best general in the French service. He was certainly a gallant enterprising man, and had been more than a match for the Prince of Baden and the other generals he had to deal with on the Rhine or elsewhere: but then he was intolerably vain, and full of himself; and when anything happened amiss under any other of their generals, he used to shrug his shoulders, and say, 'Villars cannot be everywhere.'

The French had, with great expense and labour, thrown up new lines, from the Lys, to the Scharp [*Scharpe*]; and Villars drew up his army behind them at Pont-à-Vendin. On the 18th of June, O.S.[2] our generals advanced up to him, and made preparations for attacking him in his lines. Upon which Villars drained all the garrisons near him to give them a warm reception; particularly from Tournai he drew 3,000 of their best troops. This was what our generals wanted, for

---

[1] It should be pointed out that the winter had seen protracted attempts to reach a negotiated peace. These negotiations, however, had all foundered. The Allies—overconfident of ultimate success—pitched their demands too high, even requiring Louis XIV to undertake to remove his grandson from the Spanish throne by force of French arms, if necessary. Such extreme demands only served to harden Louis's determination to continue the struggle, and from early 1709 there were considerable signs of popular support within France for his stand.

[2] This date should probably read '14th of June O.S. [*25th*]', for almost all accounts agree that the siege of Tournai opened on 27 June.

the very evening that these troops had joined him, on beating Tattoo, our army decamped, and marched away to the left. When day appeared they found themselves before Tournai, which was invested immediately, and that in such a manner, that it was impossible for Villars to return the troops he had drawn from thence. This finesse fretted Villars to the quick; and the French Court was not a little concerned at it, when they found that neither Villars, nor any man among them were able to cope with the superior genius of our two generals. However, as they had already tried them all, they had no remedy left, and were obliged to continue him, and join the Marshal Boufflers with him; the chief command being in Villars.

Prince Eugène undertook to carry on the siege [*with 40,000 men*], and the Duke was to cover him. The Marquis De Surville, who commanded the garrison of Tournai [*7,000 strong*], made heavy complaints at the Court of France, that the best of his troops were drawn from him: however, he made a gallant defence for a month, then surrendered the town [*28 July*], and retired into the citadel.

The Citadel of Tournai is famous for its underground works. It is situated on a rising ground, with a gentle ascent to it from the town; and was made and fortified by the famous engineer Major-General Ma'Griny, from whom Vauban learned the rudiments of that art. When he had finished the underground works of this citadel, the fame of it was such, the King came from Paris on purpose to view it, and was so well pleased with the performance, that he made Ma'Griny Governor of it. He accepted the command, and told the King, he only wished he might live to see himself besieged in it. The old gentleman had now his wish, but not with all the advantages he expected; for he had not a complete garrison in it, nor did he command in chief. At which he was so much chagrined, that he did not act with his usual vigour and resolution; and when it was taken, he quitted the service, retired to a country seat, and died with grief soon after.

Our approaches against this citadel were carried on mostly under ground, by sinking pits several fathom deep, and working from thence, until we came to their casemates and mines. These extended a great way from the body of the citadel, and in them our men and the enemy frequently met and fought it out with sword and pistol. We could not prevent them however, from springing several mines, which blew up some of our batteries, guns and all, and a great many men; in particular a captain, lieutenant, and forty men of our Regiment.

When we had battered what was to be seen of it above ground, into a mere heap of rubbish, we yet dared not venture to attack it by storm. On the 22nd of August [*in fact 23rd O.S., or 3 September N.S.*] it surrendered on honourable terms; and it was allowed on all hands, that we could not have made so easy a conquest, had not the Duke, by the feint above mentioned, obliged Villars to draw so many men out of it; for now they had not enough left to man their underground works. Hence it was that the few that remained were never off duty, and they were fatigued to that degree, that their guards had been often taken fast asleep in their casemates.

Our generals having taken Tournai without the least disturbance from Villars, resolved upon the siege of Mons; in order to which, they sent the Prince of Hesse with a strong detachment before them, to dislodge some dragoons that were posted near it. Some few regiments (of which ours was one) were left at Tournai, to level the approaches we had thrown up; and the rest of the army marched after the Prince of Hesse. Villars crossed the Scheldt near Valenciennes, with a design of cutting off the detachment under the Prince: but perceiving that our army was very near him, he stopped short at Malplaquet; and as that place was well situated, either for disturbing the siege, or standing a battle, he set his men to work in cutting down the trees of those woods, within which he had drawn up his army; and in throwing up several strong entrenchments, one behind another, in the intervals of the woods.

XV

The Campaign of 1709:
The Battle of Malplaquet

Our generals finding that Villars had posted himself so near them, did not think it proper to suffer him to remain there, while they were carrying on the siege; whereupon they marched up to him, and would have engaged him that evening, had all the army come up time enough. They therefore deferred it till the next morning; and in the meantime the armies cannonaded each other, till night came on.[1]

Villars seeing plainly that our generals were determined to attack him in the morning, resolved to stand his ground; and thereupon kept his men hard at work all night, to finish the works he had begun. In the morning the army seemed to be drawn up within a fortification in a wood. He had the wood of Lamert [*more usually called Lanières*] on his right, that of Janfart [*or Tiry*] in his centre, and that of Sart [*or Taisnières*] on his left. In the intervals between the woods were double and treble entrenchments; and in short, they were in all respects so strongly posted, that it was thought we should not have attacked them: but as our two generals were flushed with success, on they would go. So on the 31st of August, O.S. [*11 September*], about eight in the morning the battle began; for as both armies had cannonaded each other from the first light of day, some breaches had by this time been made in their works. Prince Eugène commanded on the right, the Prince of Orange and Count Tilly on the left, and the Duke of Marlborough in the centre.[2]

[1] This delay has been much criticized. See, for example, Mérode-Westerloo, p. 215 below.

[2] According to Millner (p. 272), the Allies deployed 152 battalions, 271 squadrons and 88 cannon to Villars's 160 battalions, 300 squadrons and 80 cannon (or 120,000 men). These figures have been challenged, and it would seem more probable that Marlborough and Eugène had 128 battalions, 253 squadrons and 100 guns (or 110,000 men) on the battlefield. The French commanders, on the other hand, probably controlled 80,000 men—96 battalions, 180 squadrons and 60 guns. Thus the Allies enjoyed a considerably greater advantage than Millner would allow. Neither Parker nor Mérode-Westerloo have much to communicate on the subject.

General Schulemberg [*Schulenburg*], at the head of 36 German battalions, attacked the enemy on their left, in the wood of Sart: the Earl of Orkney, with the other British generals, attacked the village of Tanieres [*Taisnières*], and the opens between the woods of Sart and Janfart: the Prince of Hesse attacked the village of Blaregnies, and the opens between the woods of Lamert and Janfart; and the Prince of Orange, with other Dutch generals, attacked the village of Malplaquet, and their right in the wood of Lamert. Thus were the infantry on both sides engaged with a most terrible fire, and prodigious slaughter. As our infantry advanced, the cavalry kept close in the rear of them. The battle held till near four in the afternoon, at which time Schulenburg broke in on their left, and soon after their whole army gave way. Our men immediately entered their works [*in the centre*], when a most terrible slaughter ensued,[1] which fell entirely on their foot; the horse on either side having had little to do, till our foot broke through their entrenchments, and made way for them to advance.

No man could behave with more bravery than Villars did on this occasion, until he received a shot in his knee, which disabled him from acting, and obliged them to carry him off a little before his troops gave way. Boufflers also acted the part of a brave and good officer; for when he saw the foot put to the rout, he drew up all his cavalry in great order, and made a bold stand against our horse, until the foot made off and then he made a gallant retreat in the rear of his flying foot, until he got within the lines, that run from Quesnoy to Valenciennes.

Our generals having had enough of this dear bought victory, did not pursue farther than to the verge of the wood; so that Boufflers retreated at his leisure. This was the most obstinate and bloody battle that had been fought in the memory of any then living; and our generals were greatly condemned for throwing away so many brave men, when there was not any necessity of coming to a battle; for the siege might have been carried on without it. And indeed it was the only rash action that either of these great men had been guilty of in the course of the war. It was said however that the Duke of

---

[1] In fact, owing to Marlborough's typical skill, Marshal Villars had been induced to withdraw practically all his troops from his entrenched central positions to strengthen his wavering left wing. The fortifications were consequently occupied by British battalions with relatively little trouble. The worst casualties were, in fact, borne by the Dutch on the Allied left, whose advance, thrice repeated, was enfiladed by a well-sited French battery.

Marlborough was much against it, and endeavoured to bring over Prince Eugène to his opinion: but be that as it will, it gave a handle to his Grace's enemies at home to exclaim loudly against him.

The loss was very great, and near an equality on both sides, there being upwards of 16,000 killed and wounded on each side:[1] but we took a great many prisoners, with most of their artillery, and a great many Colours. Their tents and baggage escaped us, for they had been sent off the night before the battle.

The part which our Regiment acted in this battle was something remarkable. We happened to be the last of the regiments that had been left at Tournai to level our approaches, and therefore could not come up till the lines were all formed and closed, so that there was no place for us to fall into. We were ordered therefore to draw up by ourselves, on the right of the whole army, opposite to a skirt of the wood of Sart [or *Taisnières*]; and when the army advanced to attack the enemy, we also advanced into that part of the wood, which was in our front. We continued marching slowly on, till we came to an open in the wood. It was a small plain, on the opposite side of which we perceived a battalion of the enemy drawn up, a skirt of the wood being in the rear of them. Upon this Colonel Kane, who was then at the head of the Regiment,[2] having drawn us up, and formed our platoons, advanced gently toward them, with the six platoons of our first fire made ready.[3] When we had advanced within a hundred paces of them, they gave us a fire of one of their ranks: whereupon we halted, and returned them the fire of our six platoons at once; and immediately made ready the six platoons of our second fire, and advanced upon them again. They then gave us the fire of another rank, and we returned them a second fire, which made them shrink; however, they gave us the fire of a third rank after a scattering

[1] Even Millner (p. 279) admits 19,718 Allied casualties, but it would seem that 24,000 (or 20 per cent of those engaged) is the more accurate figure. As for the French, their losses would appear to have been considerably less—probably 12,000–14,000, or 15 per cent. The Royal Regiment, by December, required 119 recruits to make good the year's losses. (See document in P.R.O., War Office Papers IV, vol. 9.)

[2] Richard Kane, at the time a brevet-lieutenant-colonel, was in acting command of the Regiment in the absence of Colonel Sterne. (See Introduction, p. xvii.)

[3] Parker's description of this operation—although presumably based on reported evidence, as he was stationed in Ireland at the time of the battle—is probably the most celebrated and illuminating account of the 'platoon firing system' in operation that has survived from this period.

manner, and then retired into the wood in great disorder: on which we sent our third fire after them, and saw them no more. We advanced cautiously up to the ground which they had quitted, and found several of them killed and wounded; among the latter was one Lieutenant O'Sullivan, who told us the battalion we had engaged was the Royal Regiment of Ireland.[1] Here, therefore, there was a fair trial of skill between the two Royal Regiments of Ireland, one in the British, the other in the French service; for we met each other upon equal terms, and there was none else to interpose. We had but four men killed, and six wounded: and found near forty of them on the spot killed and wounded.[2]

The advantage on our side will be easily accounted for, first from the weight of our ball; for the French arms carry bullets of 24 to the pound; whereas our British firelocks carry balls of 16 only to the pound, which will make a considerable difference in the execution. Again, the manner of our firing was different from theirs; the French at that time fired all by ranks, which can never do equal execution with our platoon-firing, especially when six platoons are fired together. This is undoubtedly the best method that has yet been discovered for fighting a battalion; especially when two battalions only engage each other.

The day after the battle Mons was invested. It held out till the 28th of September, O.S. [*in fact 20 October N.S.*], and soon after both armies went into quarters [*from 28 October*]. The campaign being ended, the French King renewed the negotiations for a peace, and seemed to be very sincere. The Allies, also being ready to hearken to any reasonable proposals, Gertruydenburg was appointed for the place of conference, and it was generally thought it would end in a peace.[3]

On the Duke of Marlborough's return to England, his enemies exclaimed loudly against him on account of the late battle,[4] and the

1 A regiment formed from Irish Catholic exiles—supporting the claims of the Old Pretender to the throne of England.

2 The total number of casualties inflicted is remarkably light, considering that some 500 shots were fired at ranges of 100 yards or less; clearly the British musket was not very accurate. Nevertheless, it should be noted that the enemy battalion fared by far the worse in this exchange of fire.

3 The relatively fortunate outcome of Malplaquet for the French forces did a great deal to strengthen French national morale for the years of struggle that still lay ahead.

4 Many historians date the first waning of the Marlborough influence from this period.

Duke of Argyle in particular, speeched largely against him in the House of Lords; which his Grace had not deserved from that gentleman. However, his speech weighed very little with the House, as appears by the following Address to her Majesty.

'Most Gracious Sovereign,

'We etc., having reasons to believe that the negotiations for peace will speedily be renewed in Holland, and being justly apprehensive of the crafty and insinuating designs of the enemy, to create divisions among your Allies, or by amusing them with deceitful expectations of peace, to retard their preparations for war, do think ourselves bound in duty most humbly to represent to your Majesty, of how great importance we conceive it is to the interest of the common cause, that the Duke of Marlborough should be abroad at this juncture.

'We cannot but take this opportunity to express the great and unparalleled services of the Duke of Marlborough, and with all imaginable duty to applaud your Majesty's great wisdom in having honoured the same person, with the great character of General of your army, and Ambassador Extraordinary to the States-General. Our humble opinion is, etc.'

To which her Majesty answered,

'I am so sensible of the necessity of the Duke of Marlborough's presence in Holland, at this critical juncture, that I have already given the necessary directions for his immediate departure; and I am very glad to find by this Address, that you concur with me in the just sense of the Duke of Marlborough's eminent services.'

The Duke set out the very next day for Harwich, and landed in Holland about the end of February. The negotiations that were then on foot, soon after came to nothing. However, the joint Address of both Houses of Parliament, shews evident their sense of the Duke's extraordinary merit and services: but whether her Majesty was sincere in her answer, will appear by what soon followed.

XVI

The Campaign of 1710

Notwithstanding the Treaty of Gertruydenberg, the Allies did not in the least slacken their preparations for war; so in the beginning of April, our two generals assembled the army near Tournai, and on the ninth [*20th*] in the evening marched up to the enemy's lines, and passed them without opposition at Pont-à-Vendin, and advanced into the plains of Douay [*Douai*]; our army consisting of 155 battalions and 262 squadrons [*and 102 cannon*].

The French affairs at this time were in such a situation that Villars could not bring his army into the field time enough to oppose our passing their lines. He was at this time assembling them behind the Scharpe: but upon our marching up to him, he retired very precipitately behind the Senset [*Sensée*], where there was no coming at him, leaving some of his tents and baggage behind him. Upon this our generals invested Douai [*23 April*], in which was a garrison of 10,000 regular troops, commanded by Lieutenant-General Albergotti, a brave old experienced officer. The works were strong, and a great many of them, and well stored with all manner of necessaries.

Soon after Douai was invested, Villars had brought all his army together. It consisted of 153 battalions, 266 squadrons;[1] and then he drew from behind the Sensée: and encamped on the plains before Arras, from whence he advanced and drew up within cannon-shot of the covering army. He seemed determined to give the Duke battle, and began to cannonade us with great fury, and this brought Prince Eugène from the siege, with as many men as could be spared.[2] The cannonading held till night; at which time he retired out of reach of gun-shot, and there stood looking at us all the next day. Upon this we fell to throwing up a sort of an entrenchment, to cover our men from his cannon: and then the Prince returned to the siege, and Villars retired to the plains before Arras.

---

[1] Millner (pp. 289–90), repeated by Churchill (Book Two, p. 681), puts Villars's initial strength as high as 204 battalions, 308 squadrons, 96 cannon and 16 mortars and howitzers.

[2] Prince Eugène's portion of the Allied army amounted to 45 battalions and 101 squadrons.

Albergotti made a gallant defence, and disputed every inch of ground with us. He also made a great many desperate sallies, which played off a number of men on both sides. However, after a siege of eight weeks, he capitulated, and surrendered both the town and fort of Scharpe, on the 18th of June, O.S. [*in fact the 14th O.S. or 25th N.S.*].

After the surrender of Douai, our generals advanced up to Villars, to try if he would stand a battle: but he thought fit to retire behind the Sensée, where he secured his army, and at the same time prevented us from laying siege to Arras. Upon this we invested Bethune [*15 July*], which surrendered the ninth of August [*in fact 28 August N.S.*]. We afterward laid siege to Aire and St Venant at the same time [*from 12 and 5 September respectively*]. The latter surrendered in a fortnight [*29 September*]: but Aire held out till toward the end of October. While we lay at this siege, provisions happened to fall short; for a party from Ypres had destroyed our boats laden with provisions and stores, as they were coming to us up the Lys. The country about Aire indeed is noted for its great produce of all sorts of grain: but the enemy had removed it out of our reach. However, we met with a considerable supply, by means which I fear will scarcely be believed by any, but those that saw it. But fact it is, that the soldiers found concealment underground, which the mice had laid up for their winter store, and that in such abundance, that it was a great relief to us toward the end of the siege. These hoards were from four to six feet under ground, and in many of them our men found some pecks of corn.[1] The siege being ended [*8 November*], both armies went into winter quarters.

Such had been the progress of her Majesty's arms for several campaigns successively, all these conquests had been made by the Allies, the war was brought to the very borders of Old France, their armies cowed and beaten in all places, their finances sunk to a very low ebb, and the whole kingdom reduced to a miserable condition, and yet to the surprise of all men, old Lewis, then turned of seventy, still persisted in carrying on the war. He alleged that the Allies insisted upon very severe terms, though they required no more than that he should

---

[1] Colonel Sterne describes this incident as follows: 'During the siege of Aire, provisions were very scarce; but one thing gave the soldiers relief and it is indeed almost incredible —and it was the the hoards of corn which the mice had laid up in storehouses in the earth, which our men found, and came home daily loaded with corn which they got out of these hoards.' (Cannon, p. 38 n.)

During this siege the Royal Irish suffered eight officer and 80 other rank casualties.

restore what he had wrested from his neighbours, and that France might be reduced to the bounds within which he found it; that so it may not be in the power of that aspiring nation to disturb the repose of Europe, as it had done for upwards of sixty years past. His proposals of peace were always insidious, and were made with no other intention but that of creating jealousy and dividing the Allies, which at length he effected, to the great reproach of the British nation: or rather of a British Ministry; for it was as much against the sense, as against the honour and interest of the nation.

While Prince George of Denmark lived, he kept the Queen steady: but having lost her bosom friend, she lay open to the insinuations of her new favourites. Among these the first was Mrs Hill (afterwards Lady Masham) who had been recommended to the Queen by the Duchess of Marlborough (not above twelve months before) for her tire-woman. She being a crafty woman, had in this short time insinuated herself so far into her Majesty's affections, that she prevailed on her to change that wise and faithful Ministry, which had raised the glory of the British nation above any that had gone before them. The first she began with was the Earl of Sunderland, Secretary of State. She proceeded next to displace the Earl of Godolphin, and in fine never stopped till she had made a thorough change.

This new female favourite had prevailed on the Queen to make Mr Harley Prime Minister and sole manager of the Treasury. His merit (I presume) was that having been lately Secretary of State, he was dismissed from his office, on account of Greg, one of her clerks, who was executed for holding a secret correspondence with the enemy. He had also this farther merit, that he had employed Valière and Bara, two vile Frenchmen, as his spies, who had been apprehended for carrying intelligence to France.

Mr St John, for his bright parts, and ready wit, had been brought in by the old Ministry, to be Secretary at War. His other extraordinary qualifications were not then known; for he turned out afterwards a very vicious and profligate man, and was entirely devoted to the interest of the Pretender. These qualifications, but in particular the last, recommended him so effectually to the good graces of Mrs Hill, that he was made principal Secretary of State. He was afterwards created Viscount Bullinbroke [Bolingbroke], as was Harley, Earl of Oxford and Mortimer; and between these two, and their patroness Mrs Hill, the whole affairs of the nation were transacted.

This unaccountable and sudden turn in the British Court, surprised all the Allies. Had England at this time stood firm to her engagements, France must have submitted to any terms we should grant her: but when the French King found all these alterations made in the Court of London, and saw clearly that several of his friends were brought into the new Ministry, it revived the old gentleman's heart once more, and put him off from closing with the Allies.

As the old Ministry is now retiring to make way for one of a very different stamp,[1] we cannot in justice take leave of them, without observing to their honour, that it was in their administration (on the death of the Duke of Gloucester) that the succession of the Crown was settled on the Protestant line, in the present Royal Family;[2] the happy effects of which are felt not by Great Britain only, but also by all the Protestant powers of Europe at this day.

It was they that assisted the late King William of glorious memory, in cementing the present Grand Alliance; and, as they were for the most part continued by her Majesty, it was they who assisted her in carrying on the war, hitherto with wonderful and surprising success. It was they also who had the glory of effecting the Union of the two Kingdoms of England and Scotland;[3] a work which had been often attempted; but it was reserved for their superior wisdom to perfect it. In short, throughout their whole administration the affairs of the nation were conducted both wisely and happily; and as they were charged by their successors with embezzling the public money, it gave them an opportunity of vindicating their integrity to the satisfaction of every honest man in the nation.

The conduct of their worthy successors comes next under our consideration. And here it will not be doubted, that the French King soon made it his business to feel the pulse of the new gentlemen; and it is beyond question that he found them much more tractable than their predecessors. The leading men of them came poor into the Ministry; and as much was expected from them, it was necessary to bribe high. Hence it was, that the Sun-Guineas which were coined in France on this occasion, became in a short time as common in

[1] Parker, as a staunch Irish Protestant, was certainly of the Whig persuasion as regards his political loyalties. He is consequently highly critical of the Tory Ministry's showing and makes no secret of his antipathy. Nevertheless he avoids the temptation to make undue political capital out of this, and is generally accurate in his facts even if his opinions are somewhat biased on occasion.

[2] The Hanoverian dynasty.

[3] Effected by the Act of Union, 1707.

England, as our own. This soon brought on a secret treaty in London, between the two Courts, which was carried on for some time before it was discovered by the Allies. As soon as they came to the knowledge of it, their Ministers complained loudly of this unfair method of proceeding, as being directly contrary to the stipulations of the Grand Alliance; to which our Ministry replied impudently (without having the least regard for her Majesty's honour) that it was impertinent in them to inquire into the Queen's affairs. At the same time it was said, her Majesty knew little of what they were doing, except what they were pleased to tell her. On this occasion they caused several pamphlets to be published, wherein they condemned the Allies for not furnishing their quotas, and asserted several other notorious falsehoods; all which they made appear in their answers. But this was designed to pick a quarrel with them, and to blind the eyes of the nation; in which last they succeeded but too well. This was a bold stroke at their first setting out; and now the French Ministers began to speak in a language very different from what they had lately made use of: there was yet one material point, which the partisans of France were very felicitous about; and that was to have the Duke of Marlborough turned out: but as France was something backward in coming up to their terms, they reserved him for another campaign.

My Lord Marlborough was greatly chagrined at all these monstrous proceedings, and daily expected to be dismissed with the rest of his friends; for now this great man, who had been so long the darling favourite of the Queen, could not be admitted to her presence, but when she had a crowd of his enemies at her elbow; so that he could not have an opportunity to expostulate matters with her. He had then thoughts of laying down all his employments of himself; but by the pressing instances of the Allies and all his friends, he was prevailed on to make the following campaign.

XVII

The Campaign of 1711:
The Lines of *Ne Plus Ultra*

In the month of April the Duke of Marlborough met Prince Eugène at the Hague, where they settled for the operations of the campaign. The army was ordered to assemble at Douai, where our two generals reviewed them separately. The Prince's forces were 47 battalions and 111 squadrons; those belonging to the Duke were 94 battalions and 145 squadrons. The whole amounted to 141 battalions and 256 squadrons. Marshal Villars at the same time assembled the French army behind the Sensée, and found them to be 146 battalions, and 227 squadrons.[1]

The French Court had last winter concerted matters with the Elector of Bavaria to send him with a body of troops this spring into his own country, to kindle the war again in the heart of Germany. The Emperor Joseph also died about this time [*17 April*], and both these incidents obliged Prince Eugène to march his troops with all the expedition he could up to the Rhine; as well to secure the election of Charles the late Emperor's brother, as to prevent the Elector from marching into his own country; and he had the good fortune to come up time enough to effect both.

When the Prince marched off, Villars sent a detachment to the Rhine, of 40 squadrons and 36 battalions; so that he still out-numbered the Duke by 42 squadrons, and 16 battalions [*about 16,000 men*].

Before I enter on the particulars of this campaign, I must premise that Marshal Villars was esteemed at this time, the best general in the French service; and in fact he had made it appear upon several occasions that he was a gallant enterprising man. Now as he had a force, superior to the Duke, it was expected by most men that he would do something very extraordinary; but it was not doubted by any, but he would at least defend his lines, which were reckoned almost impregnable. In either case the Duke's enemies at home hoped for an opportunity of

[1] Both the Allies and the French were in a position to field about 120,000 men at the outset.

exclaiming against him; for whether he lay idle the whole campaign, or suffered himself to be affronted by Villars, it would have given some colour for what they had often asserted, that he could do nothing without Prince Eugène.

Notwithstanding the number of the enemy, the Duke had a great desire to come to a battle with them; in order to which, as soon as Prince Eugène marched off, and Villars had sent the detachment to the Rhine, he advanced into the plains of Lens, and encamped about two leagues from their lines: but Villars, as was believed, had orders not to stir from behind his lines, and was very punctual in observing them. These lines extended from Dunkirk to Arras, and were made very strong with several fortified places on them. From Arras the Sensée branches out in several rivulets, which form a great morass from thence on to Bouchain; over this morass two causeys [*causeways*] had been made for the convenience of the country people. The uppermost of these was called Arleux, and as this was the best and largest, Villars had caused a strong fort to be built on the higher end of it; the other about half a league below it, was called Bachablan, and not being of that importance, it had only a redoubt thrown up before it.

When the Duke found he could not draw Villars from behind his almost inaccessible lines, he set that great genius of his to work, and formed as noble a scheme for passing them, as is perhaps to be met with in history; and it is very well worth while to remark all the various steps and stratagems he made use of to effect it. He saw plainly that there was no possibility of passing the lines, but at these causeys, and for that purpose he wanted to have the Fort of Arleux demolished. He knew he could take it when he pleased, and demolish it when it was in his hands; but he knew also that if he demolished it, Villars would certainly rebuild it whenever he turned his back. His Grace's scheme therefore was to manage matters in such a way, as that Villars himself should demolish the fort; and it was with this view, he first resolved on taking it. The matter being thus fixed, he made a strong detachment of horse and foot, in order to attack the Fort of Arleux. This detachment was to be commanded by Lieutenant-General Hompesch, Governor of Douai, and was ordered to encamp on the glacis of that town, until materials were prepared for carrying on the siege.

Hompesch and most of the general officers lay in the town, and those of them who lay in the camp, were not under any apprehension of danger, as they were immediately under the cannon of Douai; insomuch that they neglected to keep the common outguards of their camp. Villars had an account of this, and immediately ordered a good body of horse and dragoons to pass the morass at Arleux, Bachablan, and Bouchain (the farthest of them not being more than two leagues and a half from Douai). They joined about a league from our detachment, and Villars putting himself at the head of them, they marched with all the silence imaginable; till about twelve at night, without being so much as challenged by any one sentry, they fell upon the right flank of our horse, trampling and cutting down all before them; and had they not fallen to plunder too soon (a bewitching thing to soldiers of all nations), they might have driven through our whole detachment; but while they were rifling the horse, the quarter-guards of the foot firing on them, gave the alarm to the foot regiments; and these running out in their shirts, fired among them at random, and in great confusion in the dark, which however soon made them scamper off. They suffered little or nothing, but killed and wounded many of our troopers, and carried off a considerable number of our horses. This was indeed a bold push [11–12 July], and might have been fatal to the whole detachment, had it been rightly conducted. It was without question the only affront which the Duke had ever received from any of the French generals; and even this was not the fault of his Grace, but of his officers. However, Villars, who was naturally vain, boasted greatly of it, and it was magnified prodigiously in the Paris gazettes. But none were better pleased at it, than our own gentlemen at the helm.

My Lord Marlborough bore all this with his usual temper, and went on with his scheme. Four days after, all things being in readiness, he ordered General Hompesch to march and lay siege to Arleux; which he took in eight days;[1] while Villars who was not quite an English mile from it, stood looking on from the other side of the morass. As soon as it was taken, the Duke gave orders to repair the breaches of it instantly, and to add several new works to it. Then leaving a slender garrison [400 men] in it, away he marched the army, upwards of fifteen leagues on a stretch to the right. Villars at the same time

---

[1] Churchill, Book Two (p. 842) places the capture of Arleux as 6 July—and the French surprise of the garrison as taking place three days later. Millner confuses the issue still further by dating Villars's raid as 1 July O.S.—or 12 July N.S.—explaining away the Allied *débâcle*, incidentally, as caused by 'a prodigious great fog' (p. 319). However, he places the capture of Arleux at 25 June O.S. (or 6 July N.S.). C. T. Atkinson (*Marlborough and the Rise of the British Army*, p. 443) agrees with Millner's first date, and gives 12/23 July as the date of the French recapture of Arleux (and the 11th previous for Villars's first onslaught). Parker would appear to have mixed his sequence of events here.

marched his army within his lines up that way; but left a detachment behind him who immediately passed the morass, and laid siege to Arleux. On this the Governor sent an express to the Duke, to let him know that unless he was speedily relieved, he must give up the fort, the works being in such a condition that he could not hold out three days. The Duke was arrived at Cote before the express overtook him, and had given orders that the army should lay in all the forage they could get; which looked as if he designed to settle for some time in that camp.

On the arrival of the express he seemed very much cast down, and immediately ordered General Cadogan to march, with all the grenadiers of the army, and forty squadrons to the relief of Arleux. Accordingly Cadogan marched, but not in such haste as the occasion seemed to require; so that by the time he had advanced as far as Lens, he had an account that Arleux was taken [23 July], and that the enemy were hard at work in demolishing it. This gave Villars another occasion of bouncing, and he signified to the French King, that he had brought the Duke of Marlborough to his *ne plus ultra*.[1] This it seems was the motto of his Grace's coat [-of-arms], and the Marshal was pleased to be witty on it. His enemies at home exclaimed loudly on this occasion, and indeed his friends seemed to allow that he had not acted with his usual prudence and conduct. What added to our concern was that the Duke seemed to take it much to heart; for upon Cadogan's return, he appeared to have lost his wonted calmness of temper, became peevish, saw little company, and said publicly in a sort of a passion, that he would be even with Villars, intimating that he would at all adventures attack him in the post he was in. The lines here were on an open plain, between the head of Sensée and the Canche, where he had neither river nor morass before him, but the lines of themselves were prodigious strong, having a double fausse [*ditch*] before them. Villars hearing how much the Duke was concerned at his taking and demolishing the fort of Arleux, that he had expressed himself in so warm a manner, and was determined to attack him in the post he was in, prepared to give him a warm reception; and not being content with the troops he then had, he not only drew all the troops and cannon that could be spared from Arras and Cambray

1 Villars was borrowing a joke then current in the Allied army. It appears that Marlborough's tailor used the phrase—in fact, one of Marlborough's mottoes—when he saw a new scarlet coat of startling cut recently bought by the Duke. An approximate translation would be 'Nothing further is possible'.

[*Cambrai*], but did not leave a man to guard the lines, from the post he then occupied, all the way on to Bouchain. And now being thus prepared, he sent an express to his Court, to let them know that he did not doubt, but in a few days, he should give them a good account of the Duke of Marlborough and his army.

My Lord Marlborough still continued in a sullen dissatisfied humour, and notwithstanding that Villars was so strongly posted, he seemed determined to attack him. In order to which, the morning after Cadogan returned, he sent off all the heavy baggage, and with it twelve squadrons and six battalions, directing their march toward Douai. Next day he sent off all the lumber of the train with more squadrons and battalions; and the day following he slipped off all the artillery, except a few light field-pieces; in short he sent off all the wheel-carriages of the army, insomuch that he did not reserve a coach or chaise for himself; with these also went off some squadrons and battalions.

And now in this flying condition he marched up to Villars, and encamped at Villar-Brulain, within a small league of his lines. He immediately ordered the horse and dragoons to cut fascines, and carry them into the plain between our camp and their lines, which Villars could easily perceive. Early next morning [*4 August*] the Duke rode out with our general officers to reconnoitre the enemy's lines: all the grenadiers of the army, with eighty squadrons of horse and dragoons having marched out before, in order to cover him in case the enemy should sally out upon him.

I was posted with my company under the command of Brigadier Durel [*Durell*]; and as this affair seemed to have something extraordinary in it, I desired he would give me leave to ride out with the Duke, in order to make my observations. This was readily granted, and thereupon I kept as near his Grace as I possibly could. He rode upwards of a league along their lines, as near as their cannon would permit. From thence I could discern plainly by the help of a prospective [*spyglass*] that the lines were very strong and high, and crowded with men and cannon, and that the ground before them was levelled and cleared of everything that might be any kind of shelter to those that approached them. Notwithstanding all this, the Duke's countenance was now cleared up, and with an air of assurance, and as if he was confident of success, he pointed out to the army general officers, the manner in which the army was to be drawn up, the places that were to be attacked, and how to be sustained. In short he talked more than his friends about him thought was discreet, considering that Villars had spies at his very elbow. And indeed some began to suspect that the ill treatment he had met with at home or the affront he had lately received from Villars, might have turned his brain, and made him desperate.

When I found the Duke had almost done, I returned to my post; at this time I observed General Cadogan steal out of the crowd, attended by one servant only, and he made all the haste he could to camp. I did not think much of this circumstance at that time: but on his return to the Duke's quarters, there were forty hussars waiting for him, with whom he slipped off unobserved, and made the best of his way to Douai. The Brigadier on my return asked me what my opinion was? I told him what I had observed of the lines, and what I heard the Duke say; and yet that I could not help thinking that his Grace had something else in his head. He replied, that the Duke was determined on it, and that he would certainly attack Villars in those very lines. Soon after the Duke returned to camp, he gave orders that the army should prepare for battle, against the next morning.

And now both armies were big with thought, what was to be the fate of the next day. Villars longed for its coming; his army was no less impatient, being assured of having full satisfaction for all the affronts they had received from the Duke. On the other hand, we plainly saw, that things had but a dismal aspect. We knew that our army had been considerably lessened by the many detachments, that had been sent off, insomuch, that the enemy was near double our number: our heavy cannon also had been sent off; but all which we concluded, that the Duke was become desperate, and cared not what became of himself or the army. These were our apprehensions for the remaining part of the day. But on our beating Tattoo, to our great joy, orders came along both lines, to strike our tents, and form our regiments with all despatch imaginable; and in less than an hour, the whole army was on a full march away to the left. This was no small surprise to us; nor could we yet conceive what he meant by it. We continued marching all night, being favoured by the light of a bright full moon, and fine calm weather. A little before day [*about 3 a.m. on the 5th*], the Duke being at the head of the march, an express arrived from General Cadogan, signifying that he and General Hompesch had passed the causeway of Arleux without opposition, between twelve and one that morning, and that they were in possession of the enemy's lines. Upon this the Duke rode off with all the left wing of horse; at the same time

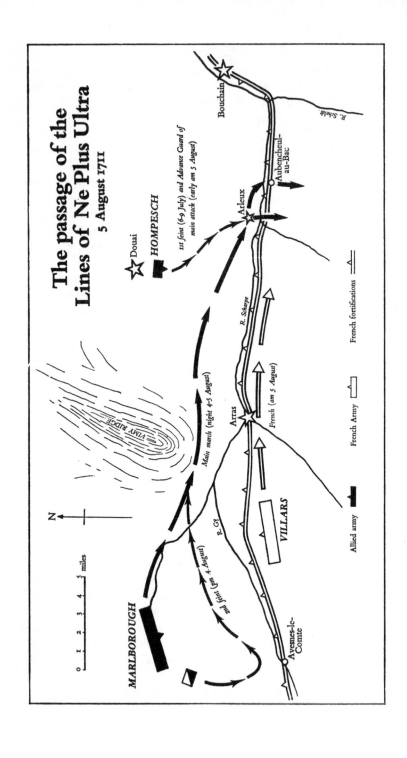

The passage of the Lines of Ne Plus Ultra
5 August 1711

Douai

HOMPESCH

1st feint (6–9 July) and Advance Guard of main attack (early am 5 August)

Bouchain

R. Scheldt

Aubencheul-au-Bac

Arleux

R. Scarpe

VIMY RIDGE

Main march (night 4–5 August)

Arras

French (am 5 August)

VILLARS

R. Gy

N

2nd feint (pm 4 August)

MARLBOROUGH

Avesnes-le-Comte

0 1 2 3 4 5 miles

Allied army

French Army

French fortifications

he sent an account of it to every particular regiment of foot, with orders to continue their march with all the expedition they possibly could. Now it is not possible to express the joy of the army on hearing this very important piece of news; and to do them justice, never did men exert themselves more heartily on such an occasion. But as for Villars, he was quite stunned at it. The moment he heard it, he took with him a hundred choice dragoons only (leaving orders for the army to follow as fast as they could) and rode like a mad man, until he came with Cadogan's out-guards. He was amazed to that degree, that he was not aware of it, until he saw them surrounding him; and then ordering them to throw themselves within the walls of an old castle that was at hand, he with two more rode through an open between our men, and got clear of us, but the dragoons were taken.

Our army continued their march with all the cheerfulness imaginable, not making the least halt, or observing any kind of order; but every regiment of foot brought up as many men as they could, without waiting for any that dropped behind. The enemy also pushed on their march with the utmost expedition, insomuch, that it was a perfect race between the two armies: but we having the start of them by some hours, constantly kept ahead of them. As our foot was marching over the plains before Arras, the front of their horse appeared upon the rising grounds on the other side the Sensée: but their foot was a great way behind. The front of their horse, and the foremost of our foot, marched in fair view of each other, sometimes within half cannon-shot; and had not the Sensée and the morass been between us, we could not have avoided coming to blows with them. Villars finding that the Lord Marlborough had joined Cadogan with his left wing of horse, turned his march to the right toward Cambrai. Our Regiment passed over at Arleux about four in the afternoon: but then half of our men dropped behind, which was the case of all the foot, as our march had been full thirteen leagues [or *39 miles*] in eighteen hours. This is a great march for a foot soldier, with all his luggage, computed to be near fifty pounds weight. It was the third day before the last of our men came up. The Duke had foreseen this, and therefore ordered the right wing of horse, which brought up the rear of our march, to see all the foot up before them. Thus did the Duke of Marlborough carry the Marshal's lines (which were esteemed inaccessible) by dint of art and stratagem only, and without the loss of a man. And indeed, never did a player on the stage act a part to greater perfection, than did his Grace through the whole course of this complicated scheme. As the success of it depended entirely on its being kept secret, it was communicated to a few only, and for the most part to such as were to put it in execution; these were the Field-Deputies, the Prussian General, and the Generals Hompesch and Cadogan.

The whole procedure of the affair was thus; for the scheme was so fine, that it will bear a repetition. First he determined to take the fort of Arleux, and to fortify it when taken. This he knew would influence Villars to demolish it, which was what he wanted to have done. Then to give him an opportunity of destroying it, as well as to draw him, and his whole force far off from that post, he marched his army as has been already related. But here was the master-piece of the whole, when he had brought Villars to answer his purpose, by destroying the fort; he then appeared sullen, seemed to be quite disconcerted, and gave out in a passion, that he would attack him in those very lines, which he had drawn him up to. This Villars readily believed, and therefore did not attend to what the Duke was doing, when he was sending off so many squadrons and battalions toward Douai; where the Governor took care to have them dispersed in the adjacent villages, as they came up. This was managed so nicely, that it did not make any show, nor was any notice taken of it; insomuch that the several parties that were sent thither, knew nothing of each other. Then his marching in a heat up to Villars: his ordering a number of fascines to be cut: his reconnoitring the lines with so much parade: all these were carried on with such an air, and favoured the deceit so effectually, that he not only deceived Villars, but the generals of his own army also; for some of them believed him crazed. No notice was taken of Cadogan's slipping out of the camp. He arrived at Douai about ten at night; where he found Hompesch at the head of forty squadrons of horse and dragoons, and twenty battalions, drawn up on a plain at a little distance from the town. These troops dropped in accidentally as it were, about half an hour before Cadogan arrived. This was transacted between the 12th and 13th of July, O.S. [*in fact 24/25 July O.S. or 4/5 August N.S.*].[1] From hence they marched directly to Arleux, which was only two small leagues from them; and here without any opposition, they passed the causeway, and took possession of those prodigious lines, which Villars in the height of his vanity, called the Duke of Marlborough's *ne plus ultra*.

So far was this great undertaking happily executed. And indeed it

[1] Parker is still some twelve days out in his reckoning.

may be justly said, that Providence favoured us in it; for in my life I never saw finer weather, which continued till all our men came up. It was a further argument of the Duke's forecast, that he had fixed this march in the time of a full moon; for it had been next to an impossibility to have made so hasty a march in the dark. Besides which, as Villars had caused the causeway to be broken up in several places, it had been very difficult for Cadogan and Hompesch to pass it without lights; and this must have discovered the whole affair.

XVIII

The Campaign of 1711:
The Siege of Bouchain

Now the taking these lines was but a part of the scheme, and as one step only to what was principally intended. The Duke, from the beginning, had his eye on Bouchain, this was the main point; for Bouchain is a fortress situate on this morass, which opens a passage into the Kingdom of France. We lay on our arms two days, and in this time we had a good many of our field cannon and pontoons etc. brought to us from Douai. The next day we passed the morass; and here we found that Villars had drawn up his army about half a league in our front, with the right wing close to the works of Cambrai, his left covered by a morass, and along his front were several hollow ways; so that he was very strongly posted.

My Lord Marlborough having received everything he wanted from Douai, drew up his army in order of battle; and then ordering them to face to the left, we marched in this manner at mid-day [*6 August*], over a fine plain, along Villars's front, toward the Scheldt, and so near him, that he now and then saluted us with a cannon-ball, which was all the disturbance he gave us. Now, although his orders might have been not to fight, unless it were in defence of his lines, yet surely in the present conjuncture, when he had so fair an opportunity, he might well have answered it, had he given the Duke battle, in order to drive him back again: especially as he saw, that he was marching to Bouchain, to take post on those very lines, which he had such positive orders to defend. But the truth is, Villars was so baffled and confounded, that he knew not what to do, against an antagonist so vastly superior to him, in all respects.

When we came up to the Scheldt, the Duke drew up the army fronting the right of the enemy. Here we stood looking at each other, while our bridges were laying. These were not finished till near sunset; at which time the Duke ordered the army to pass, leaving Lieutenant-General Ross with the cavalry of the right wing, and all the grenadiers of the same wing, to bring up the rear. By the time it was day, the whole army had passed, the bridges were taken up, and we were on a full march to Bouchain, which was above two leagues from the place, where we passed the Scheldt.[1]

Bouchain is situated at the confluence of the Scheldt and the Sensée, in the midst of the morass, which is not as broad here as above. It is a small town, but strongly fortified; its works extending from one side of the morass to the other.

The day after we came before it [*i.e.* 7 *August*], bridges were laid over the Scheldt, and the morass below the town, over which the Duke ordered General Fagel to pass with forty squadrons and thirty battalions, in order to carry on the siege on that side, which is easiest of approach; and also to keep open a communication with Douai, Marchiennes, and other garrisons on that side. Our Regiment was of this detachment. The Duke took up his quarters at Avoinlesecq on the French side of the town, as well to have an eye on the motions of Villars, as to see the siege carried on on that side.

Villars by this time had recovered out of the panic that had seized him; and being very sensible of what fatal consequence it must be to France, should Bouchain fall into the hands of the Allies, he took courage, and resolved to do his utmost to prevent it; yet he dreaded much the consequence of a battle. On the other hand, as this was the principal point of the Duke's whole scheme, he was resolved to take it, cost what it would.

The day we came before Bouchain, Villars marched his army, between the Scheldt and the Sensée, as near the town as the morass would permit, and encamped within cannon-shot of the Duke, the Scheldt being between them. From thence he sent General Albergotti the same day, with a good body of troops over the morass and Sensée, to entrench himself on the hill of Wavrechin, in order to preserve the line of communication which runs from thence through the morass, between the Scheldt and Sensée to the town of Bouchain; for he judged that from this post he could at any time relieve the town, and prevent us from carrying on the siege on that side. When the Duke observed the French troops on the hill of Wavrechin, he imagined they were posted there, in order to fall on the troops under Fagel; whereupon he ordered them to return the same evening, and lie on their arms that night by the bridges. Next morning [*9 August*],

[1] This tricky series of operations—performed in close proximity to the foe—was accomplished without the loss of a single life. Contemporary experts hailed it as an even greater masterpiece than the passage of the lines of *Ne Plus Ultra* that immediately preceded it.

finding the enemy hard at work on the hill, he ordered General
Cadogan to join Fagel with sixteen squadrons and twenty battalions,
and to pass on to the other side; and as the enemy still continued their
works, the morning following he sent orders to Fagel and Cadogan to
march and dislodge them from thence. When we approached near
them, we observed that they had entrenched themselves up to their
eyes, and that they had a large deep fausse before them, with a number
of cannon mounted thereon. Villars seeing us advance, brought into
the works as many troops as they could contain: notwithstanding
which, our generals made a disposition for attacking them. Our
British grenadiers were ordered to march up to the top of the hill on
the left of their works, in order to begin the attack on that side. Here
we were posted in a large high grown field of wheat, about seventy or
eighty paces from their works, expecting every moment when the
signal should be given to fall on.

I must confess I did not like the aspect of the thing. We plainly
saw that their entrenchment was a perfect bulwark, strong and lofty,
and crowded with men and cannon pointed directly at us; yet did
they not fire a shot great or small, reserving all for us, on our advancing up to them. We wished much that the Duke might take a nearer
view of the thing: and yet we judged that he chose rather to continue
on the other side, in order to observe the motions of the enemy on
that side, while we were attacking them on this. But while I was
musing, the Duke of Marlborough (ever watchful, ever right) rode
up quite unattended and alone, and posted himself a little on the right
of my company of grenadiers, from whence he had a fair view of the
greater part of the enemy's works. It is quite impossible for me to
express the joy, which the sight of this man gave me at this very critical
moment. I was now well satisfied, that he would not push the thing,
unless he saw a strong probability of success; nor was this my notion
alone; it was the sense of the whole army, both officer and soldier,
British and foreigner. And indeed we had all the reason in the world
for it; for he never led us on to any one action, that we did not succeed
in. He stayed only three or four minutes, and then rode back. We were
in pain for him while he stayed, lest the enemy might have discovered
him, and fired at him; in which case they could not well have missed
him. He had not been longer from us, than he stayed, when orders came
to us to retire. It may be presumed we were not long about it, and
as the corn we stood in was high, we slipped off undiscovered, and
were a good way down the hill before they perceived that we were

retiring; and then they let fly all their great and small shot after us: but as we were by this time under the brow of the hill, all their shot went over our heads, insomuch that there was not a single man of all the grenadiers hurt.

The rest of the troops retired immediately, leaving Villars in possession of his post, which elated him not a little. Upon this he drew out all the horse he had in the entrenchment, and pursued our squadrons that brought up the rear. Our troops retired faster than ordinary, in order to get out of the reach of their cannon; which Villars perceiving, imagined they were flying before him, and thereupon drove furiously after them, at the head of his squadrons. The Duke saw the thing, and ordered us to make the more haste, which brought him on with greater eagerness, until he had drawn him on toward the top of a rising ground. When our squadrons had passed the summit of this rising ground, they were out of Villars's sight, and here he ordered them as they came up to face about, and put themselves in order to charge him the moment he appeared on the top of the hill. Villars, not knowing anything of the matter, came driving on; when on a sudden our squadrons charged him with such resolution, that they immediately broke through all those that were up with him, and would certainly have either killed or taken him prisoner, had not a brigadier, that was close at his heels, interposed with singular bravery, and rescued his general. But the gallant brigadier paid dearly for it, he being desperately wounded and taken prisoner, and most of his men cut to pieces: and Villars, with his shattered squadrons, was glad to scamper back in greater haste than he came on.

The brigadier happened about three years before, to have taken General Cadogan prisoner [*19 August 1706*], as he was on a foraging party, and had treated him with great civility. As soon as he was made a prisoner, he sent his name to Cadogan, who came to him instantly, sent him to his own quarters, ordered several of the best physicians and surgeons in the army to attend him, and when he was perfectly recovered, sent him back. This humane and generous treatment is for the most part the practice of all European nations, when once the heat of action is over: but it must be allowed to their honour, that none are so remarkable for it as the English and French; insomuch that with them it prevails, even among the common soldiers.

My Lord Marlborough finding that it must be exceeding difficult to force the entrenchments of Wavrechin, called the principal engineers of the army to him, to know whether Bouchain was to be taken without removing the enemy from thence. To this they all answered in the negative, except Colonel Armstrong. He insisted on it, that it was to be done, and was ready to undertake the most difficult part of it. The Duke, who well knew the capacity of the man in that respect, was very well pleased, and ordered him to proceed upon it immediately. Whereupon ten squadrons, and as many battalions were ordered to march as soon as it grew dark, and post themselves in the valley, between Wavrechin and the rising ground whereon Villars had been ruffled. Here we stood all night with our arms in our hands, to cover Colonel Armstrong, while he, with 5,000 men, were throwing up works on the rising ground behind us; and as soon as day began to appear, we were ordered to retire. The squadrons marched to their ground of encampment; but the battalions retired into a most noble, and indeed surprising redoubt, with a double fausse, which the Colonel had caused to be thrown up that night, and had mounted thereon twenty-four large pieces of cannon with the British standard of our train flying. At the first light of day, he saluted the enemy in the works on Wavrechin, with several rounds of his cannon.

Beside the works already mentioned, he had also thrown up a strong entrenchment, from the redoubt down to the morass, which covered all that quarter from the insults of the enemy; and as all this was executed in one night, it is not easy to say whether the Duke, the enemy, or our own army were most surprised at it. About four in the afternoon our ten battalions were relieved, and on coming to our ground, we pitched our tents, stripped and went to bed, which was the first time our Regiment had done so from the day we marched from Villarbrulain, that is from the 12th to the 25th of July [*23 July to 5 August*]. This I must say was the greatest fatigue I ever underwent at any one time of my life.

This being happily executed, the Colonel proceeded to throw up a strong entrenchment from the redoubt round our camp, and from thence on to the Scheldt below the town, which served for our line of circumvallation. He afterwards carried on this circumvallation line, from the Scheldt below the town, round the Duke's camp to the Scheldt above the town, which secured our camps on both sides of the river. But the greatest difficulty was to come; the enemy posted on Wavrechin, had a communication with the town, and unless this was cut off we should meet with insurmountable difficulties in taking the town. Here the Colonel was hard put to it; for the enemy by keeping the sluices of the town close shut, had raised a very great inundation in the morass on both sides of their line of communication. But Armstrong being a man of invincible resolution, and extraordinary knowledge in these matters, worked through all difficulties with uncommon spirit. By the assistance of a prodigious number of hands, by the means of fascines innumerable, and by his own indefatigable labour, he at length wrought through the inundation; laid bridges over both rivers; attacked their line of communication; drove the enemy from thence, though the cannon both from Wavrechin and from the town continually fired on him with great fury; and in the end carried the line of circumvallation through the morass which entirely cut off all relief from the town.

And now Colonel Armstrong having with great applause finished what he had undertaken, and in much less time than was expected, the Duke ordered the other engineers to go on with the less difficult part of the siege. The approaches of our British attack were carried on between Wavrechin and the town. Here we were cannonaded and bombarded in our trenches from both; notwithstanding which in less than three weeks after opening trenches, the Governor, Major-General De Ravignau beat the Chamade [12 September], not doubting but he should have honourable terms granted him: but he was much chagrined, when the Duke let him know that he would not enter into any capitulation with him; and that he must not expect any other terms, than that he and his garrison should surrender prisoners of war. The Governor at first refused to submit; but as we had made two large breaches fit to be stormed; as we were lodged on their covert-way, and had all things prepared for an attack, he at last submitted [13 September]. But he exclaimed loudly against Villars, who stood looking on with an army much superior to that of the Allies, and yet could suffer him to be drove to these dishonourable terms; and it is certain that the Duke treated him in this way, to humble the impotent pride and vanity of the Marshal; otherwise he had granted him the usual honours of war. Villars soon after had the mortification to see the garrison march out with their hands in their pockets [14 September].[1]

My Lord Marlborough continued the army about Bouchain, till he saw all the works we had raised levelled with the ground, the breaches made up, and everything put into such a condition, as that it

[1] The French casualties sustained at Bouchain (Millner, p. 338) were 2,550 killed and wounded, besides 3,000 taken prisoner of war. The Allies lost at least 4,080 casualties, but Atkinson places the figure as high as 5,172. (See also Appendix II, p. 242–3 below.)

might not be in the power of France to retake it the following winter.

This was the last campaign his Grace ever made, and it may be justly and truly said, that it crowned all the great actions of his life. It appears plainly from the whole of this narrative, that neither Villars, nor all the Marshals of France, nor the French King with all his politicians, were able to cope with him, either in the cabinet or in the field. His successes were so great, that he became the terror of France (who were but the other day the bullies of Europe), the ornament of Britain, and admired by all the world; except a villainous faction at home. It is to be hoped that Britain, in some fortunate age, may produce a genius sufficiently qualified to do justice to the merit of her hero; in the mean time let his actions speak for him. We are next to say, how he was rewarded by his country, for all his great and signal services.

XIX

The Fall of Marlborough

On the change of the Ministry a new Parliament was called; and as the trial of Dr Sacheverel [*Sacheverell*] came on about this time, that, together with his cavalcade round a great part of the kingdom, had so poisoned the minds of the people, with a notion that the Church was in danger, that the Tory party had a great majority in the House of Commons; and the Ministry being supported by them, began now to cavil with the Allies. The Lords on the other hand kept staunch to their former resolutions; they were determined that the war should be carried on in conjunction with the Allies, until the Spanish Monarchy was taken entirely from the House of Bourbon. Upon this twelve new lords were brought into the House at once, which carried the majority on the side of the Ministry; and now our secret treaty at London was changed into a public treaty at Utrecht [*11 April 1713*], notwithstanding the representations of the Allies in general against it: and in particular of the Elector of Hanover, which was so highly resented, that his Minister was forbid the Court.

The Duke of Marlborough still held all his employments, and it was necessary to blacken him, in order to turn him out with a better grace. Whereupon they had the assurance to attack him in Parliament on account of certain perquisites, which had been received not by him only, but by the late King also, and by every commander in chief in the Netherlands. These were a yearly premium paid by the contractors for the bread for the army; and a perquisite of two and a half per cent from the foreign troops in British pay. These had always been allowed to the commander in chief, in aid of the £10,000 which was yearly granted by Parliament, for secret service. And surely if we are to judge by the success that constantly attended all his undertakings, never was money more honestly or wisely applied to the purposes for which it was granted. If we are to give credit to his Grace's letters in relation to that affair, his intelligence cost him a great deal more. Nevertheless these gentlemen represented it to the House as an abuse, and there it was voted, 'That his accepting the bread-money was arbitrary and illegal: and that the two and a half per cent deducted from the foreign troops was public money, and ought to be accounted for.' These resolutions being laid before the Queen, she was pleased to dismiss the Duke of Marlborough from all his employments [*31 December 1711 O.S. or 10 January N.S.*]; and at the same time the Attorney-General was ordered to prosecute him. The Duke of Ormonde was declared Captain-General in his room;[1] and it is remarkable, that he declared he would not accept the command, unless these same perquisites were allowed him. Whereupon these very men who voted the receiving them so great a crime in one duke, without any hesitation confirmed them to the other. Nay, what is yet more strange, these perquisites were granted to the Duke of Ormonde in February, and in April following the Duke of Marlborough was prosecuted for receiving them. Was ever anything equal to this? Or is it possible that posterity can believe it? But the thing was so flagrant, that the Attorney-General was ashamed of the prosecution and dropped it.

When the party failed in a public prosecution, they stooped so low as to let loose their little mercenary scribblers at him.[2] In one of their celebrated papers called the *Examiner*, I remember to have read a passage wherein the author asserts, 'That the Duke of Marlborough was naturally a very great coward: that all the victories and successes that attended him were owing to mere chance, and to those about him; for whenever he came to be engaged in action, he was always in a great hurry, and very much confounded upon every little emergency that happened, and would cry in great confusion to those about him, what shall we do now?' Had I not read these very words, I should never have believed that any man could have the face to publish so notorious a falsehood. But however base and scandalous all this was, it answered the purposes of the faction. It inflamed a Jacobite mob against the Duke to that degree that it was not thought advisable for his Grace to continue in the Kingdom; so he and his Duchess embarked with a small retinue at Dover on board the Ostend packet-boat, where he landed soon after. From thence he made a tour into Germany, to visit his Principality of Mindelheim; which is elegantly set forth by Mr Addison in the following lines.

---

[1] Ormonde also took over the colonelcy of the First Guards; Lord Rivers became Master-General of the Ordnance.

[2] Prominent amongst these was Dean Swift.

Go, mighty Prince, and those great Nations see,
Which thy victorious Arms did once make free;
View that fam'd Column, where thy name ingrav'd
Shall tell their Children, who their Empire sav'd.
Point out that Marble, where thy worth is shown
To every grateful Country, but thy own.
O Censure undeserv'd, unequal Fate!
Who strove to lessen him that made thee great.
Who, pamper'd with Success, and rich in Fame,
Extol'd his Conquests, but condemn'd his Name.
But Virtue is a crime, when plac'd on high,
Tho' all the fault's in the Beholder's Eye.
Yet be untouch'd, as in the heat of Wars,
Flies from no dangers, but domestic Jars.
Smiles at the dart, which angry Envy shakes,
And only fears for her, whom he forsakes.
He grieves to find the course of virtue cross'd,
Blushing to see our Blood no better lost.
Disdains in factious Parties to contend,
And proves in absence most Britannia's Friend.
So the great Scipio of old to shun
That glorious Envy, which his Arms had won,
Far from his dear ungrateful Rome retir'd,
Prepar'd whene'er his Country's Cause requir'd,
To shine in Peace and War, and be again admir'd.

It may be thought perhaps that I am prejudiced against the men
that were then at the helm, and that I am too sanguine in favour of the
Duke of Marlborough, and that my attachment to him may be
occasioned by favours received from him. But for my part, I never
lay under any private or personal obligations to his Grace; on the
contrary he once did me injustice by putting a captain over my head.
This however I knew he could not well avoid doing sometimes, for
men in power are not to be disobliged. My zeal for the man is founded
on his merit and his service, and I do him no more than bare justice.
I had been an eyewitness of most of his great actions. I knew that he
never slipped an opportunity of fighting the enemy whenever he
could come at them; that to the last moment he pushed on the war,
with a sincere desire of reducing France within her proper bounds,
and of securing the succession in the illustrious House of Hanover;

and it must affect every man of virtue or spirit, to see him oppressed by a set of men, who at the same time were selling their country, and his great actions to the declared enemies of the nation.

This winter died our Colonel, Lieutenant-General Ingoldsby, and was succeeded by Robert Stearn [*Sterne*], Esq., our Lieutenant-Colonel. He had served in the Regiment from its first establishment; and being a brave and gallant man, he rose gradually by long service and good fortune, until from an ensign, he now became our Colonel.

XX

The Campaign of 1712:
The Desertion of the Allies

I come now to the last and most inglorious campaign of this war, which is a blot and a dishonour to the British nation.

The Duke of Ormonde was a man of expense, ambitious, good-natured and easily imposed on; these qualifications pointed him out to the Ministry, as a proper tool to execute their purposes; but whether he was at first let into the secret of what they really designed, is yet a mystery. In the beginning of May he arrived at Tournai: the Queen having just before written a favourable letter to the States-General, and another to the Earl of Strafford (then engaged at the conferences at Utrecht), wherein she declared her resolution, that her troops should act against France with the same vigour, as if there was no negotiation on foot. This letter bore date the 18th of April, a little before the Duke left London; from whence it should seem probable, that he then imagined he was to act against France as the Duke of Marlborough had done. Notwithstanding which Prince Eugène had a private hint from London, that if the Duke of Ormonde had not already orders not to act against France, he soon would. Upon which he waited on his Grace, and put it home to him; his Grace replied positively, that he would fight. The Prince returned perfectly satisfied, and soon after the two armies, which were then encamped separately on the plains between Douai and Marchiennes, joined and were complete 295 squadrons, and 145 battalions, amounting to something more than 122,000 fighting men.

On the 12th of May O.S. [*23rd*] they decamped, and marched in four columns up to the Scheldt; and having passed that river a little below Bouchain (the Ministry's pigeon-house, as they were pleased to call it in derision to the Duke of Marlborough, on his taking it) they continued their march, and encamped on the other side of the Sell [*Selle*], between Noailles and Montrecourt. The morning after we came to this ground our generals agreed to ride out and take a view of the situation of the enemy. They were encamped within sight of us, their left being close to the works of Cambrai, their right extending toward the head of the Scheldt, with that river in their front, and their number not exceeding 90,000.

All the grenadiers of the army, with eighty squadrons of horse and dragoons were appointed to cover our generals, and for that purpose they marched early in the morning towards Villars's encampment. He, at first sight of us, imagined that our whole army was on the march, and was exceedingly surprised, having had assurances from Court, that the Duke of Ormonde would not act against him: but when he perceived us still advancing, he said in a passion, that France was undone and betrayed by England. And immediately ordered his artillery and heavy baggage to march with all the expedition they possibly could, until they had passed the Somme; and he was just upon decamping, in order to march after them, when he observed our troops to halt: but as he did not see the army on the march after them, he concluded it to be only a reconnoitring party, as it really was. This gave Monsieur great spirits, and he ordered his artillery and baggage to return.

Our British grenadiers on this occasion marched a little way into Picardy, where the houses were all left desolate, the peasants having fled beyond the Somme with all their best effects. On our return to camp in the evening, we found the face of affairs quite changed; for about twelve at night Sir Thomas Hanmer arrived at the Duke's quarters, with a letter from Lord Bolingbroke wherein he said it was the Queen's orders, that his Grace should not advance nearer to France (for they supposed him then at Douai), nor engage in action till further orders. The Duke seemed very much startled at it, and having communicated it early in the morning to Prince Eugène, desired to be excused from riding out with him as he had promised.

Now how it came to pass that the Queen changed her mind, so soon after the letter she wrote to the States-General is not easy to say. It is not altogether certain whether Bolingbroke may not have written the fatal letter without the Queen's order; but that affair, for anything I have been able to learn, remains a secret to this day. Sir Thomas was a leading man in the House of Commons, and very intimate with the Duke, and for these reasons was pitched upon to deliver the letter. The expedition he made shewed evidently his zeal for the party: for had the Duke engaged the French before his arrival, their hopeful scheme, which was now almost completed, had been dashed to pieces at once. Whether the Duke of Ormonde was really concerned at receiving these orders, I shall not take upon me to say: but however that was, most certain it is, that he was extremely punctual in observing, not them only, but also all others of the same tendency, which came to him afterward; and in short went heartily into all the measures of the party.

This occasioned great disputes in the army, the Duke's friends alleging in his favour, that if he disobeyed the Queen's order, it must cost him his head. But to this it was answered, by those that wished well to their country, and to the common cause, that the Duke should have considered that he was not under an absolute, but a limited government; that consequently he, as general and commander in chief, was accountable not to the Queen only, but to the nation also; and further, that not only the general, but the Secretary [-at-War] and everyone that advised or assisted the Queen in these destructive measures, were accountable to their country for it. Besides the orders in question were signed by the Secretary, and not by the Queen, which single circumstance in a case of this nature, may very well justify his disobedience. And in short had orders of such fatal tendency been signed by her Majesty, he should have known that he was answerable to the nation how he put them in execution.

Had the Duke considered the matter in this light (which is very consistent with the constitution of the English government), what a glorious campaign might he have made? Had he advanced as Prince Eugène requested, but two days' march further, the French King must have met him with a carte blanche [or unconditional surrender], rather than expose his country to be wasted by the enraged soldiery of all nations, who longed for nothing so much as to be revenged on France, for the many and great devastations she had committed on all her neighbours. France at this time was so much reduced, that nothing could have hindered us from marching to the gates of Paris, and exacting any conditions we pleased; and then pray, who would dare think of calling the Duke of Ormonde to account for disobeying the Secretary's order? Would he not rather have shone in our British annals, and his name have been transmitted with honour to posterity? Soon after the arrival of King George the First, a pamphlet was published in justification of the Duke's conduct; the substance of it was, to set forth how punctual he was in obeying the Queen's orders; but not a tittle of the common cause, the independency of Europe, or the good of his country. The key to this whole proceeding, this mystery of iniquity is this; the party at this time reckoned they had carried their point, and were well assured that the person in whose favour the whole scheme was formed, would rather reward than call them to account for deserting our Allies, and prostituting the honour and interest of the nation. But to return.

The Duke soon took care to acquaint Villars with the orders he had received, and to assure him they should be punctually observed. It is easy to judge how Prince Eugène was affected with all this. However, to make the best of the matter, he proposed to take Quesnoy and Landrecy [*Landrécies*], in order to draw a line from the latter to Bouchain, and he desired the Duke to join him in besieging these places. The Duke answered, that that was disobedience to the Queen's orders, which he could not answer; he told him however, that while he continued in that camp he would take care that Villars should not disturb him; but added, that he did not know how soon he should have orders to march, and that then he must take care of himself. The Prince upon this marched with the German and Dutch troops, and laid siege to Quesnoy [*8 June*], having first posted a body of about 14,000 men under the Earl of Albemarle at Denain two leagues below Bouchain, in order to keep open a communication with Douai, Marchiennes, and other garrisons on that side of the Scheldt, from whence he had all his stores and provisions. As this was a post of great consequence, the Earl set all hands to work to fortify it, and at the request of the Prince and the Field-Deputies, the Duke lent them as many pontoon-boats as laid two bridges over the Scheldt, at Denain: all those that belonged to his Highness being employed at the siege, except a few that were sufficient to make a third bridge only.

The day that the Prince marched to Quesnoy, the Duke decamped and retired with all the troops that were in British pay, to the other side of the Selle, in order to have that river in their front; the Duke taking up his quarters at Château Cambrésis. Here we lay until the Prince had taken Quesnoy, which was somewhat more than three weeks [*4 July*].

The soldiers had nothing now to do, but their quarter-guard duty, and from a rising ground in the front of our camp, had a fair view of that rich part of France, which they reckoned they had dearly earned the plunder of. They were greatly exasperated at the disappointment, and were continually murmuring at those who brought them within sight of the 'Promised Land', as they called it, and yet would not suffer them to take the milk and honey it abounded with. Here they often lamented the loss of the Old Corporal, which was a favourite name they had given the Duke of Marlborough; and to make the matter worse, through the carelessness of the contractors, their bread was so intolerably bad, that it was with great difficulty the officers could restrain them from mutinying. This prepared them for mischief, and they were resolved to pay a visit to France, before they left the quarters they were then in. As forage grew scarce in our camp, and none was to be had near us, but in Picardy, we had liberty by the favour of Villars, to forage in that country. It nettled our soldiers that their general should condescend to ask leave: however they were determined to lay hold of this opportunity of tasting some of the sweets of France.

Upon all foragings a strong detachment was sent out the night before, under the command of a general officer, to keep the foragers within bounds, to cover them from the enemy, and to prevent irregularities and abuses.[1] When the detachment marched off, a number of soldiers of all nations stole out of camp with their arms, they chose officers and swore obedience to them, their principal care being to keep at a distance from the covering detachment. Among these one party of British soldiers to the number of 600, came to a village called Molain, where the inhabitants were in arms, and had barricaded all the avenues to the town. Upon this an engagement ensued, in which some of the soldiers fell; this enraged the rest to that degree, that they rushed up to the barrier, and drove the inhabitants into the church; but as they again fired on them from thence, in their fury they set fire to the church, burnt it to the ground, and upwards of four hundred persons perished in the flames; then plundering the town, they set it on fire; and as it grew dark, stole privately into camp. Two days after a complaint was made to the general, and the affair was inquired into, but no discovery could be made. This was a taste of what France might have expected, and I mention it for that purpose only; for the action in itself is utterly inexcusable.

Our plenipotentiaries at Utrecht had by this time brought the treaty to a conclusion;[2] and to our shame clapped up a separate peace

[1] Including the possibility of desertions *en masse* by disaffected elements. The safeguards taken on such occasions were usually very comprehensive. A detailed order—'Memoir for a foraging foray between Sarren and Hautsamen'—issued at the camp of Roussellar, 30 June 1706, is preserved in the British Museum (the Trelawney Papers, Add. MSS 23,642 f. 23). It shows that 1,000 infantry and 160 cavalry were employed to seal off the area, deployed in a comprehensive series of posts, patrols and main guards.

[2] Parker is no doubt referring here to the secret negotiations between London and Versailles which resulted in Ormonde being ordered to suspend active hostilities on 10 May 1712. The Peace of Utrecht, properly so called, was not signed until 11 April 1713.

[*or, rather, armistice*], exclusive of our Allies, the effects of which we feel at this day. By it Dunkirk was put into the hands of the Queen. And now the Duke of Ormonde had orders to march off, and quit the Allies, bringing with him all the troops that were in British pay [*16 July*]. But when he sent these orders to the generals of the auxiliary troops,[1] none observed them, except the Major-Generals Barnard and Wallis: the former commanded four squadrons of dragoons, and one battalion of foot belonging to the Duke of Holstein Gottorp: the latter one regiment of dragoons of Liège. The rest declared they had orders from their principals not to quit the Allies; and that if he marched off, they must join Prince Eugène. The Duke was nettled at the thing, and told them they were to expect no further pay from the Queen.

Prince Eugène having taken Quesnoy and being assured by most of the generals of the British auxiliaries, that they had orders to join him, resolved to proceed on his scheme, and accordingly laid siege to Landrécies [*7 July*]. This was the rashest action which that great man had ever been guilty of. The Prince of Anhalt Dessau carried on the siege, while his Highness commanded the covering army. [*Meanwhile*] we decamped from Château Cambrésis the 16th of June, O.S. [*27th*],[2] and the same day Prince Eugène was joined by most of the British auxiliaries. Our first day's march was to Avoinlesecq near Bouchain, where the Duke ordered a cessation of arms, between Great Britain and France, to be declared at the head of every regiment; upon which occasion it was expected they would have made a general huzza: but instead of that, nothing was heard, but a continued hiss throughout the whole army. This, together with the separation of the auxiliary troops, gave the Duke great offence; and this very afternoon he sent to Denain, and required that his pontoon boats should be taken up, and delivered to him on his march the next day. The Prince and the Field-Deputies requested earnestly that he would spare them a week or ten days only, and he well knew they were absolutely necessary to them, yet he would not comply.

It must be observed, that Villars had caused a cessation of arms to be declared in his camp this same day, where no doubt there were great rejoicings for it; on which occasion he sent a Lieutenant-General

---

[1] In other words, the foreign troops in English pay.

[2] Parker's dating must be in error here; '16th of *July* O.S.' would seem to make better sense.

to compliment the Duke: but his instructions were to press his Grace above all things, to carry off his pontoon boats that were at Denain. Now whether the Duke had determined on this, before the arrival of this gentleman, I cannot pretend to say: but certain it is, that in a very little time after, he sent a peremptory order to have his pontoon boats taken up. It was said also, and indeed generally believed, that the French General brought with him two engineers, who went in disguise with those that were sent to Denain, and made such observations on the works there, as were of great use to Villars when he attacked that post. This indeed might have been done without the Duke's privity [*knowledge*]: but however that was, his conduct was censured very deservedly; insomuch that it gave the Allies cause to suspect at least, that the affairs of the pontoons, and the attack at Denain, might probably have been concerted between him and Villars. Next day being the 17th, we marched from Avoinlesecq, and passing the Scheldt, and the Scharpe, we encamped at Anchin, where our pontoons joined us from Denain.[1]

[1] C. T. Atkinson has described these unhappy events as 'perhaps the most painful episode in the annals of the British Army'. (*Marlborough and the Rise of the British Army*, p. 473.)

XXI

The Campaign of 1712:
The Battle of Denain

As Dunkirk was now put into the hands of the Queen [*on 19 July*],
Villars was reinforced with the troops of that garrison, and of those
that were round about it; by which means his army was much more
numerous than that of the Allies,[1] the Prince notwithstanding was so
obstinate, that he would continue the siege of Landrécies; whereupon
Villars formed a scheme for attacking the post of Denain.

On the 18th [*in fact the 24th N.S.*], early in the morning, as we were
preparing to march from Anchin, we heard great firing toward Denain, from whence we concluded that Villars had attacked that post.[2]
It cannot be conceived how enraged our soldiers were, exclaiming
heavily, and cursing those that had sold their good friends and allies
to the enemy. The day following the Duke received a fulsome letter
from Villars, giving an account of the action, and of the success of it.
In it he ran out in large encomiums on the Duke's consummate conduct and courage, and loyalty to his royal mistress. Then he concludes
that the courage of the Allies was gone off with the brave English
troops, under his Grace's command. This letter, though it was no
more than a fulsome banter, which ought rather to have been burned
than made public, was yet handed about the army, and many copies
taken of it. The only effect it had, was to confirm the Allies in their
opinion, that they had not been fairly dealt with in relation to the
pontoons; for certain it is that the want of these was the loss of
Denain.

The Prince [*Eugène*] had heard of Villars's design, and marched up

---

[1] Millner estimates that Villars commanded 150 battalions and 300 squadrons; Prince
Eugène, on the other hand, is considered to have been left with 148 battalions and 292
squadrons following the withdrawal of Ormonde's 12,000 British troops (p. 359). If
these figures are correct, the numerical disparity may be less than Parker asserts, but
Villars undoubtedly succeeded in massing a considerably superior force before Denain
itself.

[2] See La Colonie's account of this battle as seen from the French side.

to Lord Albemarle time enough to sustain him:[1] but as there was but one bridge left, Albemarle on the approach of Villars, had ordered all the baggage to pass the river on it, and by crowding on it too hastily, it broke. So the Prince was obliged to look on, while his men were cut in pieces, without being able to give them the least assistance; for it was impossible for him to get over the river, as it was exceeding deep, and its banks steep and oozy. In the end every man of that great body was either killed or taken.[2] This was a fatal blow to the Allies, and turned the scale altogether to the French side; and was the first effect of our cessation of arms. The Prince being now cut off from his magazines and stores, was obliged to rise from before Landrécies [2 August], and march by the way of Quesnoy round to Tournai, leaving Villars to carry all before him. And he was not wanting to improve all the advantages he had gained; for as Prince Eugène was not able to look him in the face, he in a very short time retook Marchiennes [30 July], Douai [8 September], Bouchain [19 October], Quesnoy [4 October], with some other towns of less note.[3] This leads me by way of digression, to express my sentiments concerning the conduct of the three great captains of the age; I mean the Duke of Marlborough, Prince Eugène and Marshal Villars.

At first, as to the Duke of Marlborough (for I cannot forbear giving him the precedence) it was allowed by all men, nay even by France itself, that he was more than a match for all the generals of that nation. This he made appear beyond contradiction, in the ten campaigns he made against them; during all which time it cannot be said

[1] It is generally considered that Villars outgeneralled Eugène on this occasion, and that Albemarle's forces met their fate in isolation—the main Allied army being still three hours' march away at the crisis. (See Churchill, Book Two, p. 960.)

[2] Millner (p. 360) gives two sets of Allied casualty figures. The first claims that Albemarle, five other generals, 94 more junior officers and 1,500 other ranks became prisoners. The second puts the prisoner total at 2,200—besides 12 brass cannon—together with 'one thousand killed on the spot, one thousand five hundred drowned'. Albemarle's total force seems to have been about 8,000 men (17 battalions and 12 cannon). The French appear to have lost about 400 casualties from their total of 25,000 men (42 battalions) engaged.

Denain was France's only battle success in the Low Countries during the war. Its effect on French morale was understandably great, and it returned the initiative to the French for the last months of the war and doubtless helped secure them favourable terms.

[3] In all, these disasters (including Denain) are estimated to have cost the Allies the equivalent of 57 battalions—or 34,000 men—practically one-third of Eugène's army.

that he ever slipped an opportunity of fighting, when there was any probability of coming at his enemy: and upon all occasions he concerted matters with so much judgement and forecast, that he never fought a battle, which he did not gain, nor laid siege to a town which he did not take. It is needless to make a repetition of his great actions, more than this, that the last campaign he made [*that of 1711*], notwithstanding the provocations of his enemies, by their scurrilous pamphlets and malicious invectives, in ridiculing his great actions, in hopes thereby to ruffle his temper and raise his passion, so as to put him upon doing some rash action, which might in some measure justify what they alleged against him. And indeed no man but the Duke of Marlborough himself could have borne with the invidious treatment he received. Yet with what temper did he bear all their reproaches, and with what calmness and serenity of mind, and air of grimace, did he carry on that noble scheme he had formed to get within Villars's lines, that were thought inaccessible, in which he shewed the greatest courage and most undaunted resolution? He was peculiarly happy in an invincible calmness of temper and serenity of mind; and had a surprising readiness of thought, even in the heat of battle. But the master-piece of all was his last campaign. The noble scheme he formed for passing Villars's lines: the infinite arts and stratagems he used to deceive him: his passing the lines without the loss of a man; his insulting Villars afterwards, and daring him, by marching with an inferior force at mid-day along the front of his army, and within cannon-shot of him: his passing the Scheldt unmolested in the face of his army, and taking the fortress of Bouchain, the key and inlet into the kingdom of France, while Villars stood looking on, advantageously posted, and with a superior force, yet not daring to interfere: all this is stupendous, and inimitably great.

In short, he confounded and baffled Villars to that degree, that he knew not how to act against him; which shews how far he surpassed the top Marshals of France in the art of war. And indeed had not I been an eyewitness of those things, I should hardly have believed them; and how this great man was rewarded for the great honour and service he did his country, has been already related.

As to Prince Eugène the glorious actions he had performed in Hungary against the Turk, and in Italy and elsewhere against France, evidently shew him to have been a very great man. For my part, I reckon him equal to the Duke of Marlborough, in every respect but this, that he had not altogether that command of temper, which was his Grace's peculiar excellency: and it was this heat and warmth of his temper, which led him once (and once only, as far as I can recollect) into a fatal mistake; this was his persisting in his resolution to lay siege to Landrécies, though the Duke of Ormonde had carried off the British troops. It must be allowed he had met with great provocation; for Ormonde had assured him that he would act in conjunction with him against France, as vigorously as ever the Duke of Marlborough had done. Upon this he formed his scheme, when to his surprise, all on a sudden, Ormonde deserts him. This touched him to the quick, and in the heat of his passion, he determined to let the world see he could execute his scheme without him; so down he sat before Landrécies, not being at that time calm enough to foresee the train of fatal consequences that probably must have attended that ill-concerted undertaking. In this single instance the warmth of his temper misled him; and if you except this only, I judge him in every other respect equal to the British chief.[1]

It is my judgement (all partiality being laid aside) that I pay Marshal Villars all due honour, if I assign him the third place. The first affair of any consequence that he was concerned in, was in the year 1702; when he was ordered to march with a body of French troops through the Black Forest, to join the Elector of Bavaria. The Prince of Baden had posted himself in his way within the lines of Friedlingen, and Villars made a vigorous assault on the lines, but was repulsed, and obliged to desist for the present: however, early in the spring following, he found means, by a stratagem, to deceive the Prince of Baden, and joined the Elector, where they carried all before them.[2] And could Villars, who was exceedingly haughty, have submitted to the Elector's authority, or had the Elector taken his advice, they might have done much more: but they were each of them equally high, and therefore Villars, at his own request, was recalled. The year following [*1704*] he was employed against the Cevennes,[3] whom he subdued in

---

[1] Parker makes no specific mention of Eugène's greatest claims to fame—namely the battles of Zenta (1697) and Turin (1706) and the battle and siege of Belgrade (1717) against the Turks. Nor does he mention the Prince's least fortunate incident—Toulon (1707).

[2] Including winning the first battle of Hochstadt (20 September 1703), where Count Styrum was heavily defeated. This success caused the crisis on the Danube which took up all of Marlborough's attention the following year.

[3] Against disaffected elements of the French populace, known as the 'Camisards' or 'white-shirts,' many of them Huguenots. Villars suppressed these unfortunates with a heavy hand.

a manner, by fair means. The year following he commanded the French army on the Moselle, against the Duke of Marlborough, and when the Duke marched back to the Netherlands, he was sent to command on the Rhine, where, by his exquisite schemes and stratagems, he acquired great reputation [*especially in 1707*]. At length, when the French Court had tried almost all their generals round, they pitched upon Marshal Villars to command in the Netherlands. How shamefully he was baffled there, you have already read; and therefore, that he was not, in any shape, equal to the Duke of Marlborough, seems indisputable. Nor can I, by any means, put him on a level with Prince Eugène, notwithstanding the advantage he had over him at Denain; where it was Ormonde that gave the victory to the French, by withdrawing his pontoons, basely at least, if not corruptly also.

I know it is said in favour of Villars, that he did more after the affair at Denain than they had done in the two preceding campaigns; and it is true enough. But it should be remembered that he then fought without an antagonist, that the Allies had not a man in the field to oppose him, and that the garrisons were not sufficiently provided for a siege, as the Allies did not suspect that England would desert them. Whereas Marlborough and Eugène had always a superior army of veterans to contend with; and the French garrisons were always abundantly supplied in every respect,[1] which makes a very material difference in the case. But to return.

[1] Although this is rather a generalized statement, it is nevertheless basically correct. One of the most important—though unsung—heroes of the French war effort in the Netherlands region was the Intendant of Lille, who was a genius of an administrator.

XXII

The End of the War

From Anchin we proceeded by easy marches to Ghent, and here we were received with open arms.[1] Part of our troops were quartered here, and the rest were ordered to Bruges. At this time the Treaty of Utrecht was drawing near a conclusion; and now our plenipotentiaries found, that since the fatal blow at Denain, the French Ministers talked quite a different language from what they had done. They now receded from several things that had been agreed on in the private treaty at London; and had France been really conqueror in the war, they could not well have insisted on higher terms. All the blood and treasure of ten successful campaigns were sacrificed at once; and the haughty Monarch of France, though reduced to the last extremity, now takes upon him to prescribe to Great Britain, and to our shame he carried his point: for the Ministry, or I should rather say Harley, St John and Lady Masham, had already gone such lengths, that it was too late to look back, and in the end we were obliged to submit to such terms as the French plenipo's [*plenipotentiaries*] were pleased to grant us. In particular, it had been agreed on in London, that England should be mediator between France and the Allies; yet now they would not suffer us to have any thing to do in that affair; so each party was obliged to make the best terms he could for himself. Thus ended this inglorious campaign, to the dishonour of England, or rather of her Majesty, who suffered herself to be imposed on, and wholly governed by a few ill-designing favourites.

This occasioned that satirical saying of the Duke of Buckingham's, when the articles of the Peace were laid before the Privy Council: 'Good God' (says his Grace, lifting up his hands) 'How has this poor nation been governed in my time! during the Reign of King Charles the Second, we were governed by a parcel of French whores: in King James the Second's time, by a parcel of Popish priests: in King William's time, by a parcel of Dutch footmen: and now we are

[1] Most towns, however, shut their gates in the faces of the British forces, who were themselves disgusted with the treachery (as they saw it) of their leaders and the Tory Ministry in England.

governed by a dirty chambermaid, a Welsh attorney, and a profligate wretch, that has neither honour nor honesty.'

The war being over, a reduction of the army was soon expected. Upon this occasion several colonels complained that injustice had been done to their regiments, in respect to their ranks [or *seniority*] in the army; and her Majesty was pleased to order a board of general officers to inquire into the affair, and allow every regiment to have rank from the time it was raised. Our Regiment had suffered in this respect from the time that it was given against us. Rosebeck and we expected to have justice done us on this occasion. I was pitched upon with the approbation of our officers, to go over to London, and lay the pretensions of our Regiment before the Board. And as the Duke of Ormonde had known it from its first establishment, and was sensible of the injustice that had been done us, he ordered the Colonel to bring me to him, that he might write a letter by me, on that subject, to Sir William Wyndham, then Secretary at War. The Duke remembered me perfectly well, though he had not seen me from the time that I carried a wooden gun in his company of boys,[1] and was pleased to ask, why he had not seen me before. I had the honour of dining with his Grace, and after dinner, he delivered me his letter to the Secretary. Had I made my court to him, it is probable I might have raised my self by it: But according to my notion of things, he had taken the wrong cause in hand; for which reason I was never at his *Levée* before or after, for I could not act the hypocrite.

Upon my arrival at London I delivered the Duke's letter to Sir William, who assured me he would do us all the service in his power. Soon after I laid the pretensions of our Regiment before the Board of General Officers; and was answered, that the case of our Regiment, in particular, was different from that of any other, as having been already decided in the time of the late King. For which reason they would not take upon them to make any alteration therein, until they had laid before her Majesty the inconveniences that must attend it; for they alleged that if the alteration I contended for, was made in the army, the Scotch Guards would dispute their rank with the English Guards. Upon this the Queen issued a second Order [-*in-Council*], wherein she declared it was her pleasure, that the Board should take cognizance of the ranks of such regiments only, as had been raised during her own reign: but that all others should continue in the same rank they had

[1] See 'The Career of Robert Parker', p. 5 above.

in the late King's time. This second Order hindered me effectually from proceeding any further in that affair.[1]

The Duke having settled the quarters of the British troops in Ghent and Bruges, left Major-General Sabine to command in the former, and Brigadier Sutton in the latter; where they were to remain till the Barrier in the Netherlands was settled.[2] Then he returned to England, to give an account of his most extraordinary campaign, for which he was highly applauded by her Majesty; and, which is much more strange, he received the thanks of both Houses of Parliament, in as great form as ever the Duke of Marlborough had done. Such was the influence which the [Tory] Party at this time had over the nation.

The soldiers, almost to a man, were highly dissatisfied, from the time that the Duke of Ormonde had declared he was not to act against France, and continually disliked every thing he did. To make the matter worse, they had another real cause of complaint, which was, the extreme badness of their bread. This prepared them to mutiny; and some sly villains finding the generality of them in this disposition, artfully insinuated, that they had a considerable arrear of pay due to them; that the war being over, the greater part of them would soon be disbanded, and that consequently they must expect to lose all that arrear, unless they did themselves justice while they had their arms in their hands. This took with the giddy unthinking part of the soldiery, and a villainous and bloody design was formed. They went so far as to appoint a time and place for rising, when they were to take possession of the garrison, and to seize and murder such officers as should oppose them: then they were to set fire to the town, in several places at once, and while the inhabitants were employed in extinguishing it, they were to plunder the town, and then every one to shift for himself. This was the design of several of the principal mutineers, as they confessed at their execution: but the generality of them thought of nothing further, than demanding what they really thought was due to them, with their arms in their hands.

The officers had an early account of their design, for there were several worthy men in every regiment that heartily abhorred the thing. They were suffered however to go on, till the night before it was to be put in execution. At which time the officers were ordered to

---

[1] The 18th Royal Regiment of Foot of Ireland had hoped to be raised to the place of sixth in the order of battle.

[2] 'The Barrier' was the name given to the string of fortresses that the Dutch insisted they required to safeguard them against any future French aggression.

have them all under arms, to place men they could depend on in proper places, and to watch them closely. Notwithstanding all their care, they slipped off, to the number of about 3,000. These assembled at the place appointed for their rendezvous, where they barricaded themselves on all hands. From hence they sent a menacing letter to the general, wherein they complained of the hardships they suffered by the badness of their bread, and insisted peremptorily that their arrears might be immediately paid off.

They stood it resolutely for some time, though they saw four field-pieces planted against them; for they expected every moment when the soldiers would have seized their officers: but when they saw themselves hemmed in on all sides, especially when Brigadier Sutton arrived from Bruges with the Inniskilling Dragoons, their hearts failed them, and they proposed to capitulate. The general would not hear of any capitulation, but required them to lay down their arms, and submit to his mercy. The ringleaders declared for fighting it out, unless a general pardon was granted without any exception: but they that had been led into the scrape, seized on those that had seduced them, and threw down their arms. A court-martial was immediately held, and ten of the chiefs were found guilty, and executed on the spot. After the execution, the rest of the mutineers were ordered to go for their arms, and fall into the ranks of their respective regiments.

I must not omit the case of one Halfhide, a lieutenant in our Regiment. He had been a pettyfogging attorney in London, and was so used to the squabbles of the town, that he loved contention in every shape.[1] The general ordered him to be tried the next day before the same court-martial, where it was proved that he had been at several of their private meetings, that he encouraged them greatly to the mutiny, and gave his advice how they should proceed. Whereupon he was found guilty, and condemned to be shot. The general however, deferred the execution, until he laid the matter before the Duke. But the Lieutenant having some relations of note to intercede for him, the Duke mitigated the sentence, and ordered him to be cashiered with infamy. Thus ended this dangerous mutiny.

This winter all the British troops were ordered home, except Webb's Regiment and ours, who were to keep possession of the castle

---

[1] The proverbial 'barrack-room lawyer'. According to Dalton (vol. VI, p. 335), this same Halfhide was able to continue his military career, and was still serving with the 18th Foot as captain-lieutenant in 1740.

of Ghent, until the Barrier was thoroughly settled between the Emperor and the States-General; the Barrier with France having been settled some time before.[1]

[Here ends Captain Robert Parker's description of the War of the Spanish Succession. For a summary of his later adventures, see p. 9–10 above.]

[1] See Chronological Table, p. 242–3.

Comte de Mérode-Westerloo

Newly translated and edited extracts from:
Mémoires du Feld-Maréchal Comte de Mérode-Westerloo,
Chevalier de la Toison d'Or, Capitaine des Trabans
de l'Empereur Charles VI, etc., etc.

The extracts are drawn from Volume I, chapters 11, 12 and 13; and
from Volume II, chapters 14 to 18 inclusive, of his great-grandson,
the Comte de Mérode-Westerloo's edition (2 vols, Brussels, 1840).
The original chapter headings have been omitted, being replaced by
short titles.

Editor's Note

All dates are given in New Style. Where necessary, adjustments in dating have been added to the main text in square brackets.

The Career of Feld-Maréchal Comte de Mérode-Westerloo

Eugène-Jean-Philippe was born at Brussels on 22 June 1674, the only son of Maximillian, baron of Mérode, Petersheim and Stein, and his wife, Isabella, heiress of Westerloo. His father died within twelve months of his birth, and two years later his mother married Joachim-Ernest, Duke of Holstein-Retwisch. It was under this stepfather's influence, therefore, that the young Count grew up.

As a child Mérode-Westerloo's health was very feeble, but he somehow survived to enter, at the age of eighteen, into his considerable paternal inheritance. The greater part of the family possessions were situated in the Spanish Netherlands, but there were also large estates in Germany, and but for the depredations of a series of armies fighting their way to and fro across the 'Cockpit of Europe', and the failure of his various masters to pay him adequately for his not inconsiderable services over a period of almost forty years, the Count would have been of truly vast wealth and importance.

Following the normal pattern of existence for a youth of his station, Mérode-Westerloo travelled extensively from the age of eight, visiting Denmark, Holland, Germany, France and Spain. This provided an education of a sort, but in later years the Count deplored the gaps in his upbringing. 'Unhappily my education was badly neglected', he wrote. 'Not only did I remain far too long in charge of women, but I had the misfortune never to have near me a man of real merit and knowledge.'[1] His stepfather, though amiable enough, had little time to spare for his youthful charge. His mother was both proud and domineering, and to the end of her life their relationship was a strained one. Consequently the Count was often left in the care of his Flemish valet and an old soldier called Captain Segard.

On several occasions, however, his stepfather took the youth with him on his journeys, and on one such in 1688 the Count accompanied him to the siege of Oran. Their role there was purely that of spectators, but King Charles II of Spain saw fit to create the Duke a Spanish grandee in recognition of his services and on the young Count's request bestowed on him the coveted Order of the Golden Fleece.

[1] Mérode-Westerloo, vol. I, pp. 68–69.

Mérode-Westerloo greatly enjoyed this visit to Spain, and to the end of his days professed the greatest respect for the sickly, scorned, inbred and miserable last scion of the Spanish Habsburgs.

As a nobleman with vast estates in what was then known as the Spanish Netherlands, the Count was a vassal of the Spanish crown. The outbreak of the Nine Years War in 1688 found Spain allied with England, the United Provinces and the Holy Roman Empire against the overweening ambitions of Louis XIV, and accordingly Mérode-Westerloo saw his first real service in the army of King William III between the years 1692 and 1695. Throughout this period he served as a Gentleman-Volunteer, for his mother, having no wish to see her headstrong progeny waste his talents on a military career, succeeded in frustrating his early attempts to gain a commission. As a result he was present as a simple cavalry trooper at the gory battle of Steinkirk (3 August 1692), 'where, for the first time, I truly underwent fire',[1] and later took part in the battle of Neerwinden (where he saved the life of his stepfather)—besides being present at both sieges of Namur (1692 and 1695). His rash bravery earned him William III's commendation on several occasions, although the self-assertion, arrogance and touchy pride of the youthful warrior must have made him something of a trial. The Count certainly seems to have lost few opportunities of telling the King how he should conduct his army, but William with masterly restraint 'smiled under his large hat and said not a word'.[2] Indeed, on a later occasion the King said of Mérode-Westerloo, '*Il est de bonne race*', and told him to his face that 'he had not enough troopers of my calibre in his army, and that he in no way disapproved of seeing the insignia of the Golden Fleece atop a bandolier, although it was the first time he had so seen one'.[3]

Following the destruction of his mansion in Brussels during the French bombardment of 1695, and tiring of the ceaseless obstructions placed in his way by his scheming mother, the Count determined to take his sword to the distant Italian scene. There he fought two hard campaigns (1696 and 1697) against the French forces of Marshal Catinat, and at last, through the good offices of the King of Spain, received command over two troops of Milanese cavalry. Besides sundry martial adventures at Turin and elsewhere, the Count cut

[1] Mérode-Westerloo, vol. I, p. 81.

[2] Ibid., p. 82.

[3] Ibid., p. 95.

something of a dash in Savoyard court circles, being presented to
Victor Amadeus, the Duke (and later King) of Savoy, and his two
daughters—'neither of them was beautiful but they made up for it
with all the spirit in the world'.[1] He was also invited to dine with
Prince Eugène—another firebrand of great military talent, and, 'as he
was too impatient to await his sedan-chair porters, he wanted to go
on foot, and I went with him'.[2] Nevertheless Mérode-Westerloo
declined Eugène's suggestion that the Count should serve a campaign
with him—'a great mistake', as he afterwards admitted, 'for he fought
and won the great battle of Zenta that campaign [11 September 1697]
and I might have been there'.[3]

The Peace of Ryswick brought the war to a close, and Mérode-
Westerloo returned to his homeland, where his combative nature
soon incurred the severe displeasure of the Elector of Bavaria, the
King of Spain's Viceroy in the Netherlands. He also became involved
in a series of protracted and complex lawsuits with his spiteful mother.
The death of his stepfather removed one of his most valued friends—
for he had generally supported him against his mother, at least when
at a safe distance from the latter—and the Count soon found himself
faced with a new series of problems as the scheming dame attempted
to marry him off to various ladies of her selection. In this she had no
success whatsoever, for her son had already set his heart on gaining
the hand of a Spanish lady of the house of Monteleone, whom he had
first met in Madrid some twelve years before. After a somewhat protracted courtship, carried on by proxies and third parties, and made
all the more difficult by feuds dividing the Spanish nobility, they
married in late 1701. The Count was evidently an ardent bridegroom,
for he tells us that he covered the distance between Brussels and Bayonne on horseback in just six and a half days to meet his bride, Maria-
Theresa d'Aragon y Pignatelli. After their marriage at Bayonne, the
couple made a leisurely journey through France, visiting *Le Roi Soleil*
at Versailles. 'The King received me in his great cabinet, beside his
bed. He was sitting up in the centre of the room. After I had saluted
him he talked very graciously to me. When I took my leave and the
two doors had been opened, he took two or three steps forwards—
which produced a sensation.'[4] Such a formal court etiquette was

1 Mérode-Westerloo, vol. I, p. 111.

2 Ibid., p. 113.

3 Ibid., p. 130.   4 Ibid., p. 205.

always most dear to the heart of the decidedly snobbish Count of Mérode-Westerloo!

Before these events in the Count's private life, the unfortunate King Charles of Spain had at last died (1700), being succeeded to everyone's surprise—and to the fury of many—by Philip of Anjou, Louis XIV's grandson. One immediate effect of this was a *renversement des alliances*; henceforward the inhabitants of the Spanish Netherlands found themselves in a state of alliance with France against their former allies of the previous war as William III completed the formation of the Second Grand Alliance in the hope of redressing the balance of power. The fact that he was now the official foe of his former friends worried the Count not one jot; in the early eighteenth century considerations of personal advantage weighed far more heavily than any dynastic or national considerations, and for the present the Count was quite prepared to embrace the régime of Philip V. By 1705, as we shall see, he was equally ready to desert the cause of his Spanish masters and join the forces of the Emperor.

Several years previously the Count of Mérode-Westerloo had succeeded to the command of his father's old regiment (*vice* M. d' Ennetières)—which he proudly asserts was 'the oldest in the army' (of the Spanish Netherlands). Indeed, William III had publicly recorded the debt he owed to the former Baron of Mérode and his regiment, on which he claimed to have modelled the reconstruction of the Dutch infantry after 1672. When the Count assumed command at Ostend early in 1698, however, the regiment was in sorry shape, consisting of merely 160 men, mostly riff-raff, but with a leavening of experienced officers. Nevertheless, once the French alliance became operative, this state of affairs was rapidly remedied. The overall size of the Walloon army was more than trebled, and the conditions of service were greatly improved. As part of this period of military expansion, we find the Count being invited to raise a second battalion of his regiment early in 1702, which in due course he entrusted to his half-brother, the Duke of Holstein. He then served for a period as an officer of the garrison of Liège under General Count Ximenes—an occupation he found extremely tedious despite the presence of his admired wife to provide conjugal comforts.

Accordingly the Count was delighted to receive orders in 1702 to take himself once again to North Italy, there to serve under Marshals Vendôme and Marsin against the Imperialists of Prince Eugène. Soon after his arrival he was promoted from *mestre de camp* (or Colonel) to

Brigadier-General. He proceeded to distinguish himself in a tough skirmish on 26 July near Santa Victoria, capturing Colonel Count d'Arberg of the Regiment of Darmstadt in single combat, together with a cavalry standard and a pair of kettle-drums at the crossing of the Cristolo. On 15 August following he fought at the sanguinary battle of Luzzara, commanding Vendôme's reserves. Warfare still held some chivalrous traditions—at least where senior commanders were concerned. At one point in the fighting a horseman rode forward from the Imperialist lines to reconnoitre the French and Spaniards at close quarters. 'I recognised him as the Prince de Commercy by his bearing. Several Spanish soldiers were already aiming their muskets but I prevented them firing.' The Prince's reprieve proved but short-lived, however. 'After he had gone on about 200 yards down the dyke to our left I heard four or five carbine shots—and saw his riderless horse trot back towards their army.'[1] The battle raged on fiercely, but ended inconclusively in a stalemate, for Prince Eugène refused to quit the field. As a result 'we stayed encamped on the field of battle for 82 days', and soon severe epidemics were decimating both armies as the rotting corpses tainted the air in the hot Italian summer. 'We lost more than 24,000 men in the hospitals that year,' our eyewitness recorded.

The news from other fronts was mixed. The Elector of Bavaria's defection to the French cause and capture of Ulm was joyously saluted with three cannon salvoes, but at sea the fleets of Spain suffered a defeat at the battle of Vigo Bay, in which one-third of Mérode-Westerloo's wife's dowry (on its way from the Indies) went to the bottom. This personal blow made the Count more quarrelsome than ever and perhaps accounts for his falling out with Marshal Vendôme over a dispute between their servants. 'From that day I never once called at his quarters, where this prince was insolently wont to receive all the *monde* seated on his "*chaise-percée*" all bespattered with tobacco, and wearing a shirt which he would only change once a week.'[2]

This disagreement did not prevent the Count from serving at the siege of Guastalla (which surrendered on 9 September). A little time later, however, Mérode-Westerloo sought and gained permission to return to the Netherlands—'I wished to see my wife again'—to spend

---

[1] Mérode-Westerloo, vol. I, p. 236.

[2] The Duc de St Simon elaborates on this story of Vendôme's crude habits. (See *St Simon at Versailles*, ed. D. Flower, London, 1953, p. 136.)

the winter there, the Count promising to take himself to Spain before the opening of the next year's campaign. 'I reached Brussels with all the speed of an amorous man,' he recalled, 'and found my new-born son hale and hearty.'[1]

So ended the year 1702, and at this point in time the main extract from the Count's Memoirs opens, and we can leave his description of much of what befell him over the next decade to his own lively pages.

There is only space here to summarize the Count's colourful career following the end of the War of Spanish Succession. When a coveted appointment as Governor of Luxembourg was awarded to another in 1715, the prickly Count regarded his Imperial masters with as much ire as he did his former Spanish rulers. He was somewhat mollified the following year, however, when he was offered the appointment of Vice-President of the *Hofkriegsrath*, or Viennese Council of War, with the rank of Field-Marshal and the additional honour of Captain of the Trabans (part of the Emperor's personal guard). For almost a year he played 'hard to get', pretending to regard these offers with complete disinterest, but in 1717 he allowed his wife and other friends to persuade him to accept 'against my personal inclinations', and accordingly transferred his household to Vienna in July 1717. His wife died of smallpox at Brussels on 9 August 1718, and Mérode-Westerloo found himself a disconsolate widower.

A combination of private grief, hurt pride and a conviction that all the world was against him eventually induced the Count to resign all these distinguished appointments and retire again to his estates. The desire to produce an heir for his titles induced him to enter the realms of matrimony for a second time, and in June 1721 he married Princess Charlotte of Nassau-Hadamar, who in due course presented him with two sons. The family succession at last assured, the Count continued to reside at Westerloo, writing his memoirs and striving to pay off the load of debts that he had accumulated over the years, being forced to pledge his plate and precious stones. Nor were these his only worries; an unfortunate feud sprang up between Mérode-Westerloo and the Governor-General of the Netherlands, the Marquis de Prie, who persecuted the Count mercilessly. In an attempt to gain justice, the Count set off for Vienna to lay his case before the Emperor Charles VI, but he still had powerful foes at Court and his mission failed—indeed, he was imprisoned at Vienna for almost a year before being permitted to return to the Netherlands.

[1] Mérode-Westerloo, vol. I, p. 255. This son died in 1704.

These setbacks probably account in no small measure for the acid tone of so much of his writings, and they may even have hastened his death in his fifty-ninth year. He was actually engaged in writing his memoirs in his study at the Château of Mérode when he was attacked by a fatal apoplectic seizure. By a strange coincidence his last paragraphs were describing this very illness. 'I stayed [*the autumn of 1723*] in the silence and repose of Westerloo, giving no manifestation of life, ignoring the coronation at Prague, neither writing to Court nor receiving any letters from there, and not even setting foot in Brussels, thinking of nothing but ways of paying off my debts and means of improving and embellishing my lands in the hope of living in peace; this is no easy thing today on account of the low price of grain, which presents me with grave difficulties.

'At the time about which I write, on 2 December 1723, Philip, Duke of Orléans, the celebrated Regent of France, died suddenly of apoplexy to everybody's surprise. A few days previously news had arrived of the deaths of the Grand-Duke of Tuscany and of the Elector of Cologne, the first at the age of 82, the second (who had spent his life writing spiritual comedies) aged 52. As for the Regent, he was six weeks younger than myself. . . .'[1]

Here the narrative abruptly breaks off as the Count in his turn is taken by a violent apoplectic seizure, shortly after midnight on 12 September 1732. He never recovered consciousness, but passed away after the administration of the last sacraments. Yet he, like Robert Parker, has achieved a measure of immortality through the medium of his lively writings, which, however biased they may be, provide a fascinating insight into the life, thoughts and earthly tribulations of a distinguished member of the Flemish *grande noblesse*, who devoted the best years of his life to following the drum.[2]

---

[1] Mérode-Westerloo, vol. II, p. 298.

[2] For further biographical information see E. van Elewyck's article already referred to in the *Revue de Belges* (November 1876), pp. 292–310, and the entry in the *Biographie Nationale de Belgique (Brussels 1894–5) Vol. XIII* by E. Duchesne (pp. 539–45).

I

The Campaign of 1703:
The Battle of Eckeren

When the campaigning season came round I decided to spend it in the Low Countries instead of going to Spain.

That year (1703) the Emperor declared his second son, the Archduke Charles, King of Spain, heedless of the fact that the Duke of Anjou[1] had been in complete possession of the country for two years. All the same, he sent him off to take imaginary possession of Spain, without money or men, and with a most wretched entourage. The Emperor should not have wanted to send him there, for he surely must have been certain of the outcome, and in the end everything worked out most disadvantageously for him. But off he went through the whole of Germany as titular King of Spain, and was hailed and received as such in both Holland and England, although both powers had formerly recognized the other claimant to avoid their troops being interned in our towns.[2]

While this prince was in Holland embarking aboard the great fleet which the two maritime powers had put at his disposal for the journey to Portugal, we opened our campaign, divided into two armies. The larger, commanded by Marshal Boufflers, quitted our lines near Tirlemont; the smaller, under M. de Bedmar, was in the vicinity of Antwerp for the purpose of covering the district of Waes, a place of great significance for our country. We had a bridge at Antwerp over the Scheldt, linking Tête de Flandres to the city, and all our positions in

---

[1] Philip of Anjou—grandson of King Louis XIV—claimed the Spanish throne through his great-grandmother, Anne of Austria. The main rival claimant was the Austrian Archduke Charles.

[2] The Count of Mérode-Westerloo was by birth a nobleman of the Spanish Netherlands (today Belgium). This region, like Spain itself, found itself faced by a 'reversal of alliances'; during the Nine Years War (1688–97) both countries had fought alongside England, Holland and the Empire against France. Now, from 1701–13, Spain and her satellites found themselves fighting their former allies.

the district of Waes as well as in Brabant were well furnished with troops.[1]

These lines, which were of prodigous extent, stretching all the way from the Meuse to the Scheldt and thence to the sea, were to my way of thinking more profitable to the purses of the engineers who built them than for the country they were supposed to protect; they really represented a scarecrow for little birds, providing a pretext for those who wished to halt and do nothing. How could anyone guard such an extended system of defences? If you possess a large enough army you have no need of lines, and if you have not the enemy can make twenty feints and get straight through, knowing that your men cannot be everywhere; alternatively he can simply force them using his superior force. I have always noticed that a soldier behind such a line has no feeling of confidence, no matter how far the enemy may be from breaking through; and once a hostile battalion does penetrate, the soldier loses all confidence and thinks only of flight. On the other hand a short line, well built and designed to cover an area of advantageous ground, can be extremely useful.[2] But the fortifications we are speaking of, which made Verboom's fortune and cost the country immense sums of money, were expected to serve in this campaign as a scarecrow to frighten off the seven-headed beast of the Allies, who enjoyed a numerical superiority over our forces. In the event they easily forced them in the Waes district close to Stekem, and this must have made them realize how little they needed to fear them.

At the opening of the campaign the Duke of Marlborough, accompanied by the Dutch Field-Marshal Overkirk and the Deputies of the States-General, marched their main army from the direction of St Trond. At the same time M. Opdam, with their other generals, including Paymaster-General Hope, drew close to our lines near Antwerp, and eventually encamped a bare league away at Eckeren. Meanwhile Koehorn [*Coehorn*] and Sparre approached our defences on the opposite bank of the Scheldt. This caused us to run to and fro over the river for some little time, constantly crossing and recrossing and passing through Antwerp in order to keep them under observation with M. de Bedmar's small army. Sometimes we camped near Burcht; at others amongst the Jesuit farmhouses close by Berchem.

[1] See Parker, pp. 26–8 above, for an Allied view of this campaign in the Netherlands.

[2] The lines of Stollhofen, guarding the gap between the Middle Rhine and the Black Forest, is one example of a useful 'short' line; the fortifications dug by Villars's forces to cover their centre at Malplaquet represent a second, tactical form.

After carrying on in this fashion for some time, we eventually thought up an enterprise against their camp at Eckeren. This was cleverly planned, well concerted and satisfactorily executed during the march until the moment of climax, when Fate turned against us.

We were in camp at Borgerhout, within our defence lines, when one early morning we were told to stand to arms. Shortly afterwards a large detachment from the main army joined us under Marshal Bouf-flers, after making a remarkable all-night march. Reinforced in this fashion, we found ourselves three times as strong as the enemy, and we set out secretly through our lines at three points, making no noise, the time being about five in the morning [*30 June*]. I was lodged near my brigade in a small Jesuit farmhouse, close by one of the barriers we used for our exit. The Marquis of Bedmar accompanied our main body, the Duke of Bisaccia travelling with the other. We marched for a long time, making a long detour in order to avoid the marshes and at the same time to take the enemy in the rear. After we had reached the large heath of Braschaet our generals drew us up in order of battle; we then continued our march in excellent order.

Before passing through the barrier earlier that morning, I noticed the arrival of the Count of Brias's Regiment, and this infantry halted at the head of my brigade. Some little time later, as they were in my way, I sent a message to the Count asking him why he had planted his men there? He came back in person to tell me that he had orders to join my brigade, which in terms of effective strength only consisted of the second battalion of my regiment[1] and one from the French Vexin Regiment. So I told him to follow my men. His formation was, in fact, an experienced German unit.

We continued on our way. I rode with my brigade at the right of the second line, and all at once we arrived at a windmill near some hedges and houses. From the top of this we could easily espy the enemy's camp, which lay between some dykes with the Scheldt to its rear. Our first line then stormed over the dykes on the left, and from the beginning pushed the enemy back. I was sent off with my brigade —the advance guard and right flank of the second line under the over-all command of a M. de Guiscard—to attack the enemy from the rear, that is to say at the single spot through which they could retire towards Lillo and Kruysschans—the village of Oeteren. There they had drawn

---

[1] The Count had succeeded to the command of his father's infantry regiment late in 1697, it being 'the oldest in the army', as he was proud to boast.

up the battalions of Fagel and Friesheim and some other detachments under Major-General Count Dohna.[1]

The village cemetery was a good position, and in front of it they had sited four cannon. I moved forward along the dyke, and although the French wanted me to march under cover I rode along the top, completely exposed, my hautbois playing at the head of my men. To instil confidence and to avoid tiring the men to no purpose I advanced at a slow pace. When we reached the small sluice near the bend in the dyke which leads away towards Wilmerdonck, I met Countess Tilly, who had just been captured in her six-horse coach by our dragoons as she tried to make good her escape. The enemy's musket fire became heavy as I busied myself paying my compliments at her coach door, and this frightened her, with the result that she returned me only a short salutation.

By this time the head of my battalion had reached the coach, and so I marched on again, descending into the dyke close by a small sluice, which I left in front of me. Forty paces to the right I found M. de Guiscard whom I had never seen before nor since—I was not even sure he was my commander—standing at the bottom of the dyke. He told me to lose no time in driving the scoundrels out of the village, but then rode off without making any other dispositions. Personally I wanted to make a reconnaissance of the ground first, as I should have done: but, considering the *élan* of the French, and the poor opinion they held of us, and fearing that the short time I required to carry out the business of a sensible man and true soldier might possibly be interpreted as a failing of heart, head or resolution, I decided to go along with them and act after their fashion. So I made no plans except to order the Sieur de Beauregard, a veteran officer from my old battalion whom I had appointed Captain of Grenadiers in my new one, to take all the brigade's grenadiers and with them attack the front of the village along the main road; at the same time I instructed the battalion of the Vexin Regiment to attack on the left, and that of Brias to the right of the main road, together with my own battalion, which was in the process of forming up.

Unfortunately this evolution was still incomplete—nor were the other units any more ready—when, after sallying forth from the village to meet us and drawing up in a large cornfield, the enemy fired

[1] Bodart (p. 131) gives the relative strengths as follows:
Franco-Spanish forces—28 battalions, 48 squadrons = 19,000.
Anglo-Dutch forces—24 battalions, 23 squadrons, 48 cannon = 15,000.

a volley at us. This happened at the very instant that I had gone back to form up the Regiment of Brias before dismounting to place myself at the head of my own men for the advance against the foe. This unexpected volley, fired at point-blank range into a newly raised battalion which was still unaccustomed to fire, would not have caused all the havoc it did, in fact, had not my major, mounted on a skittish horse, been shot down amidst the right wing of the battalion's musketeers, thus throwing them into confusion. Upon this the whole battalion, without orders from anyone, fired their muskets—mostly into the air—and turned and fled, most of them throwing away their weapons. Fortunately the Regiment of Brias stood firm, as did my grenadiers, who continued to endure the fire of the four enemy guns at no more than fifty paces. This enabled me to remount my horse and spur towards the last fugitives of my battalion. After shouting and beating them, pointing out the shame of their conduct and jumping down amongst them with my drawn sword, I succeeded in rallying some 300. Next, while the men around me were all in desperate confusion, pikemen picking up muskets and musketeers laying hold of pikes,[1] I set out, head down and feeling desperate, to attack the enemy battalions, being followed by the colours, my brother the Duke of Holstein (whom I had made lieutenant-colonel of the second battalion), two captains and as many sergeants. After penetrating into the very midst of the foremost unit in spite of their fire, we soon put them into confusion, and sent them reeling back on top of the second, and this good fortune enabled me to press them so hotly that, when they tried to fall back into the village, I entered pell-mell with them.

While my battalion was fleeing, the Count of Brias was hit in the head by a musket-ball which laid him out cold—a sad loss. Then, as the enemy were trying to get back into the cemetery, where they still had plenty of reserves, and I hot on their heels some ten yards behind, I tripped over the body of a dead man in the passageway between two houses (which ran from the dyke to the church) and fell without being wounded, thus occasioning the rumour that I was slain to run throughout the army. Four or five of my soldiers promptly trod on me one after another, forcing me back into the mud as I tried to struggle to my feet. In fact, I was rather fortunate to be flat on my face at this juncture, for the enemy, now safely within the cemetery, were firing hotly at us at point-blank range, killing and wounding plenty of men around and behind me, while I was still on the ground.

[1] Proof that some battalions still had a proportion of pikes as late as 1703.

Getting up at last, I made my way into the cemetery through a small breach that I happened to notice, followed by a confused crowd of about a hundred men. Then, after forcing our way into the very midst of the enemy, the men of my brigade—joined by the Dragoons of Richebourg, who had come on dismounted from the back of the dykes, charged the enemy on all sides. This went so well that the enemy abandoned the cemetery, village and all four cannon, and fell back in dire confusion towards their main body. I had the four guns turned upon their camp and made some officers and musketeers fire them, but they proved poor gunners.

While all this had been taking place on my side (where I was supported by the Marquis of Deynse's brigade, of which only the Regiment of Mortemart, and the Marquis himself, acquitted themselves well), the enemy, who had been so vigorously charged at the beginning of the action, somehow managed to repulse the whole of our army. Their Major-General Hompesch and forty Dutch cavalry routed 1,500 drawn from the best French cavalry regiments (and our dragoons into the bargain) on the top of a dyke, and pursued them closely for almost half a mile. Our infantry, despite its superiority of number, received much the same treatment from their foot, which was better trained. De Capra's brigade was meantime sent to my assistance, but its commander, whether from knowledge that things were going badly, or just plain, simple prudence, kept it well behind the dyke and never came forward into the village, despite my repeated pleas for him to do so. I even sent my brother, the Duke of Holstein, over to see him, but all to no avail.

After repelling our army, the enemy's only thought was to escape from the cul-de-sac they had placed themselves in. This, however, they could only do through the village I had chased them out of. I would dearly have liked to entrench the place had I possessed picks and shovels, but as it turned out they came down upon me with their whole army at a time when I had barely a quarter of my men under control. For, besides the killed and wounded, the great heat of the day and the fatigues of combat had induced many more to take shelter in the village cellars. Some soldiers were drunk with excitement; others scattered far and wide, and so I was left with barely 600 men when the foe, newly emboldened by the repulse of our army, launched attacks against my front, flanks, and indeed from every side. I conducted the best defence in my power, but weight of numbers eventually told. I continued fighting in the cemetery, but eventually it proved necessary to pull out and fall back behind the dyke after they had set fire to some farms to throw some light on us. There I found M. de Capra who, after firing a single volley into the air, immediately marched off in retreat, although he had the dyke between him and the enemy. I retired step by step at the rear of our troops, and managed to have one of the four guns I had captured flung into the sluice.

An astonishing thing! I never saw a single general officer during all this affair, which for me lasted from three in the afternoon to ten at night. The foe fell back during the night to Lillo [*and towards Breda*], only too glad to find their passage unopposed. Our main body had already been enveloped in a thick fog for some time when it heard the attack on the village and saw the gun-flashes. Bedmar was very troubled by this, and believed I was both surrounded and lost. As I retired but slowly, I only rejoined the army one hour after midnight—feeling very disgruntled with them all, and quite voiceless on account of the heat and my shouting.

We lost more than 2,000 killed and wounded,[1] although, in fact, we might have made the entire Dutch army prisoners of war for a loss of less than a hundred had we only occupied the line of the dykes and then pounded them to pieces with cannon fire or starved them into surrender. But French foolhardiness and I don't know what besides made us muff the opportunity, and all we gained from it was what the foe cared to leave on the field of battle. Indeed, it was only next morning that we truly knew that they were not still in position, and set out to seek what they had forgotten to take with them. And so, two days later, they fired a salvo from all their forts [*claiming a victory*] with more justice than ourselves.

At daybreak I sent off a messenger to tell my wife that I was unharmed. I had induced her to come so close in order to enable her to pay some visits to our camp. She had left my son in Brussels, and was at that time carrying my daughter, the Countess of Czernin. No harm had befallen her, although she heard all the firing from the Jesuit church to which she had repaired when some fool of a Frenchman had imprudently told our governess, accompanying her in the coach, that we were all in the enemy's hands—tidings which the governess had sense enough to conceal from her. In the meantime rumour throughout the army had it that I was dead. Bedmar believed it until the next

[1] Bodart (p. 131) puts the casualties as follows: Franco-Spanish force: 141 officers and 2,300 men; Anglo-Dutch forces: 137 officers, 3,300 other ranks killed and wounded (including 800 prisoners), and 48 cannon abandoned on the field.

morning, when he found me asleep beneath my colours as he passed along the line with M. de Boufflers. A sergeant of my Regiment had captured a colour from the Regiment of Fagel during the mêlée, and then, after bringing it to me, had stationed himself in front of me in the midst of our enemies, receiving a musket-ball through his body that was meant for me. He didn't die of it, however, so I gave him a company.

The Marquis of Bedmar and Marshal Boufflers could hardly think of enough compliments to pay me, although I remained distinctly aloof throughout. The former compelled me to leave my brigade on the march and return with him to the camp, where I spent a deal of time. While we were riding through the mist we suddenly came across a pond of water. I was wearing gaiters and riding one of my best Spanish horses at the time. As I was about to enter the water, I reined in my horse for a moment to allow the Marquis to pass without being splashed. One of my pages, however, pressed forward into the gap, riding ahead of me; meantime my horse, which, like myself, had neither eaten nor drunk for eighteen hours, seized the opportunity to refresh himself, and lay down at full length with me still on his back, and then, after having lain on his belly, proceeded to roll from one side to the other, soaking me to the skin in the process. The heat he had suffered had been extreme, for it was 30 June 1703 [*more probably 1 July*]. I was extremely annoyed about this incident, which took place in view of the whole court. The page was roundly sworn at, but I suffered no real inconvenience. So we returned to our lines, where my wife, coming out to meet me, through the imbecility of her coach-man, narrowly avoided being carried off by the enemy for exchange against Mme de Tilly. She would have been driven straight into their hands had she not met the Marquis of Lède at the head of some troops. He brought her to my quarters, and the same day I took her back to Antwerp, travelling all the way in her coach, to persuade her that I was not dead.

Following this combat we did nothing for the rest of the campaign except march and countermarch. The main army, which had observed the enemy's [*i.e. Marlborough's*] movements beyond the lines, considered itself in danger of attack from the direction of St Job-in-T'Goor and West Osostmal. It consequently fell back somewhat precipitately into our lines. A short time later, when this same force had marched back again towards the lines of Tirlemont and Léau, I was detached from M. de Bedmar's camp to join the main body with twelve battalions. Leaving Antwerp, we camped the first night at Malines, the second at Louvain, the third at Tirlemont. But when we had camped near Léau I fell sick with a fever, which forced me to return to Brussels. Following my recovery, I again rejoined the army at Antwerp, whence I was sent to camp in the lines running through the district of Waes at Stekem; then I was again sent to join the main army, making several forced marches to meet it near Wasseige, marching by day and night without any baggage. At one moment we thought we would have a battle on our hands near the tombs of Ottomond [*destined to be the site of the last stages of the Battle of Ramillies in 1706*].

For the first march from Antwerp I took my wife with me as far as Malines; then, after dining with her, I packed her off back to Brussels, where she found my son already rather ill.

When I in due course returned to Brussels, I was told as I entered my house that my wife had just given birth to a daughter—tidings that made me very disappointed on account of the critical nature of my son's illness. Thus my daughter, the Countess of Czernin, came into the world at Brussels on 13 October 1703. I stayed there all winter that year, and from the start there was talk of promotion. Nevertheless this was held up until the spring, when I was appointed Major-General [*Maréchal-de-camp*] along with a great many others; but I was amongst the most senior.

II

The Campaign of 1704:
The French Advance to the
Danube

It was no more than a month after my promotion to the rank of general that I called on M. de Bedmar at his house about midday— the hour he was accustomed to receive visitors. My preparations for the campaign in the Low Countries were well advanced, but as I was taking my leave after being shown round his home he called me aside, and drawing me along with M. de Villeroi into a window alcove, he asked me if I was willing to undertake a special service. I at once replied that I had not the least idea what he had in mind, but that it was my obvious duty to obey any order compatible with the honour of a gentleman. He at once reassured me on this point and told me that he would come to my house that evening after dinner to take a stroll with me. He arrived in good time, and sitting in his coach I heard what my employment was to be: I was to relieve the Prince de Hornes, who had been sent into Germany in command of the Spanish forces after the loss of the Province of Gelder, where he had formerly been governor. They had seen service at the siege of Brissac [*Breissac, 15 August–7 September 1703*] under the Duke of Burgundy and were later present at the battle of Speyerbach [*15 November*] (the action where M. de Pracontal, commanding the detachment sent from my homeland of the Low Countries, met his glorious death at the supreme moment of winning the battle for the French).[1] This led to the reduction of Landau which Marshal Tallard had besieged. The expense of all this active campaigning had proved rather too much for the canny Prince de Hornes: and as a result the authorities had at once thought of sending me to take his place, especially after receiving news that the

---

[1] At Speyerbach the French fielded 34 battalions and 66 squadrons (or 18,000 men); the Allies, 28 battalions and 54 squadrons (22,000 men). The respective casualties were 4,000 French (including seven generals) and 6,000 Allies (including eight generals and 150 officers); the Allies also lost 23 cannon and 50 colours. (See Bodart, p. 134.)

Duke of Marlborough with the English troops had crossed over the Rhine and advanced into Germany. Replying to the Marquis de Bedmar, I said I would make a last effort to perform this service, in spite of the fact that all my property had been confiscated or ruined, with the sole exception of my Westerloo estate, which had somehow escaped the attentions of the two armies in its proximity. He promised he would give me more troops, greater seniority and higher authority than the Prince de Hornes had ever enjoyed, and asked me how long it would be before I was ready to leave. I replied that I would need three weeks to prepare my equipment. This request he thought extremely reasonable, and he paid me many compliments on the good grace I always displayed.

[*The Count's period of preparation for the campaign was saddened by the death of his only son, aged eighteen months, on Easter Day. At the same period his half-brother, the Duke of Holstein, quarrelled with the Count and took himself off to Paris, where he married Mlle de Mérode, Marquise de Trelon. This match did not have the Count's approval, and we gather he had nothing further to do with his half-brother.*]

While I was making all the necessary arrangements I received my instructions and letters of authority; these I insisted should be written and signed by de Bedmar and de Bergeyck in person, for I wanted them clearly and fully set down. My rank was to be Commander-in-Chief of all His Spanish Majesty's troops—horse, foot and dragoons—stationed in Alsace and Germany; I received the rights to inspect and review, to cashier officers who deserved it, and to appoint others to the vacancies in all arms of the service; I was also authorized to commute death sentences and to hold Councils of War at my discretion: all in all a very broad authority—and I was only placed under the French Marshal's orders in a very formal fashion. I was given permission to correspond directly with the Courts of Madrid and Brussels and with the Elector of Bavaria, who would choose my colonels from short lists of three nominated by myself—as and when I wished. Indeed, I do not think there was ever a broader commission than this.

I set out at the end of May, having sent my suite on in advance; it consisted of more than a hundred horses and mules. I travelled by way of Charleroi and Malines and then on through Philippeville, Charleville, Mezières, Sedan, Metz, Pfalzburg to Saverne, until at length I joined M. Tallard at Lauterbourg. He sent me into quarters with several battalions at Kronweissenburg, and also put under my orders Flavacourt's regiment of Flemish Dragoons. However, the incurable murrain this regiment contracted whilst sharing winter quarters with the French Sommeri Regiment had already put most of the troopers on to their own two feet before I arrived—and shortly afterwards this contagion spread to the whole army under the name of the 'German sickness' for want of a better diagnosis [*probably glanders*].

We spent at least a month, if not longer, at this place; I diverted myself as best I might with the French officers there by paying court to the very pretty and delectable Mlle de Vitzthum, who claimed to be related to the Comte d'Autel, perfectly justifiably in my opinion. One day we accompanied M. Tallard and all the French generals on a reconnaissance along the Rhine, and we were actually fired upon from a fort the enemy then held on the Island of Dalhunt; several cannon and musket shots were fired at us, narrowly missing the Comte de Verue.

A few days later M. Tallard ordered me to march to Strasbourg by way of Sulz and Hagenau and then on to Kehl, taking my battalion and several others that joined me. This I duly carried out and arrived at Kehl slightly behind the rest of the army. Flavacourt's regiment I had to leave in Alsace owing to the horse-sickness, and de Neufville's and the Ceretani infantry at Brisach and Kehl respectively; these three units—out of my whole command of twelve battalions and thirteen squadrons—gave me more trouble and headaches than the control of fifty thousand men, what with their courts of inquiry and continual squabbles between the colonels and their subordinate officers.

After seeing my men into camp, I returned to Strasbourg for some relaxation and a number of officers followed me. I went to dine at the best hotel (the one near the bridge). As I dismounted Madame the Marquise de Trazegnies, who was watching from a window, sent me her regards, and I went to pay her a visit. I declined her invitation to dine with her, as my retinue was too numerous. She told me that she had been waiting two whole months to cross into Bavaria to take up her post as Mistress of the Robes to the Electress of Bavaria. She begged me to ask M. Tallard to allow her to travel with us; this I duly did, but the Marshal was against it, as our march was likely to be beset by numerous difficulties and uncertainties. If it had been up to me to decide, I do not think I would have been so prudent; I had even offered the Marquise shelter in my household for the duration of the journey—and she had accepted. After dinner she had taken me sightseeing around the town in her coach, as my horses were badly in need of rest.

M. Tallard, who was always most obliging to me, had asked me if I wanted to cross into Bavaria. I had answered in the affirmative, although the heavy expenses of the campaign, which alone had already cost more than 25,000 crowns, and the charges of my wife's household in Brussels (which was both large and costly due to her overgenerosity and general lack of experience) had sent my financial affairs in the Low Countries from bad to worse; especially as the greater part of my property was confiscated or ruined. The Marshal then asked me to take only four battalions and six squadrons of the Spanish troops with me. I chose the two Milanese and the two Montfort battalions and added to them the cavalry regiments of Heyder, Acosta and Gaetano, all of which were in excellent condition. The remainder stayed in Alsace.

After making a feint attack on the lines of Stollhofen, we left the fortress of Kehl [*1 July 1704*] and entered the Black Forest down the Kintezingerthal valley. Before we did so M. Tallard formed us into battle order, giving me the choice of a cavalry or infantry command. I chose the former, and was placed on the right of the second line.[1]

First a detachment was made to dislodge General Bibra from his position at Rozberg—and I was sent with it. We toiled upwards along narrow, difficult roads, camping one night at Haslach before continuing up the steep tracks amidst the pine forests (so typical a feature of the Black Forest) for a distance of more than two leagues. Then at last we came to Rozberg, surrounded by entrenchments, palisades and redoubts on the very top of the mountain; barricades of fallen trees were in place in front of the trenches. On the side of our approach the foe only needed to roll down boulders to ward off an attack—indeed, some people thought that an assault was out of the question. One narrow road—a mere three yards wide—wound its way towards the enemy lines.

Our force of twelve battalions, three dragoon regiments and four guns [*about 8,500 men*] was gazing at this formidable position when a captain of hussars[2] informed me in German that the foe was very vulnerable from the rear. I passed this information on to the lieutenant-

[1] On the subject of the allocation of commands at this period, see p. 37 n. above.

[2] This form of light cavalry—Hungarian in origin—was only just being introduced into the French forces through the medium of their Bavarian allies. The Imperial armies had employed hussars for some considerable period. They were not regarded with much favour by many contemporary soldiers; de la Colonie, for example, calls them 'properly speaking nothing but bandits on horseback' (p. 159).

general commanding the detachment; he at once asked me to make a personal reconnaissance of the enemy position. I suggested that he should continue with preparations threatening an attack on his side to keep the enemy amused, and I also requested that he would spare me two of the four cavalry regiments to support me if the need arose. He agreed to all this, and off I set with my hussars and the two cavalry regiments. We slipped around the side of the mountain, slowly climbing up narrow paths in single file, and at length came out on to the summit of a hill overlooking the rear of the enemy—divided from us by a single valley.

I at once perceived that all their attention was concentrated to their front, and informing the general of this I begged him to send me the other two cavalry regiments and to mount a diversionary attack when I gave the signal. I also told him I was quite prepared to take full responsibility for the entire venture. Waiting for his reply, I made my preparations for crossing the intervening valley, which was fairly broad, and ordered my dragoons to dismount. Then at last the enemy spotted us, and at once their baggage train began to move off to their right. Noting that the reinforcements were on their way, I decided to wait no longer. Leaving them orders to dismount and follow in my support, I ordered an advance downhill, covering as large an area as was possible. This was enough to persuade the foe to abandon his position—and by the time I had crossed the valley and climbed the far side I found his camp empty and not a soul in the entrenchments. These I at once occupied, and, passing by a number of cooking fires, my men flung down the barricades blocking the approaches. I sent word to the general of our success, and at once the infantry began to march up to find us in full possession of the enemy's camp without a single casualty suffered or one shot fired. Our baggage, left in the rear, was at once summoned, but it was midnight before it arrived—and then only the mule train. Owing to the easy capture of this important position, the main army was able to march on towards Freiburg and Hornberg the very next day. It was on this operation that I made the acquaintance of Brigadier-General de Saint-Ségond—a good fellow— who was in command of a first-rate Italian regiment in the French service. We spent one whole day up in our mountain, and then marched down to Hornberg after burning the forts and other defences —all of which were constructed of revetted branches and boughs.

An amusing incident tickled our soldiers' sense of humour whilst we were still at Rozberg. There were three great buildings in the camp, each easily capable of holding a hundred men. The inhabitants lived in the downstairs part, whilst the granary and stables were on top—and even fully laden carts could enter with ease. A bridge, the whole length of the house, connected this upper storey with the mountainside on which the whole building hung. All of us—that is to say all the senior officers at least—brought our food and wine into one of the houses to make merry. It was whilst we were looking it over (incidentally, not a single iron nail had been used in its construction) that I found a great brass alpenhorn. Try as I might I couldn't get a sound out of it. Eventually everybody had a go, and at last one of them with stronger lungs than mine got the thing to work. So well did he trumpet that a moment later we heard the lowing of cattle all around in the woods, and out they came, trotting from the trees towards the fort, obeying our horn. The soldiers regarded this as manna from heaven, and in no time at all the camp resembled a slaughterhouse. However, this droll incident had one unfortunate repercussion; it encouraged the troops to scatter into the woods and hills—we could do nothing to stop them—and a few regrettable incidents resulted. The enraged peasantry eventually killed several thousand of our men before the army was clear of the Black Forest.

We reached Hornberg at the same time as the rest of the army, to find the fine château abandoned, and the small town sacked by our marauders before we arrived. There we camped and rested the space of one day, to await the arrival of the head of a huge convoy (made up of more than eight thousand wagons of bread, flour and biscuit). Moving on, we next deployed on to the heights above Villingen, and duly invested the town the next morning [16 July], as we wished to take the place and use it as our forward-depot. In the meantime the convoy creaked out of the Black Forest's passes, taking almost eight days to complete the journey, even though they travelled day and night. However, in spite of our opening trenches and mounting mortar and cannon batteries, we were eventually forced to abandon the siege [22 July], after wasting much valuable time and material; for the townsfolk and the small garrison defended the puny place so well— even though it only boasted a single ancient wall—that we had no option but to move on and join the Elector of Bavaria.

This prince was harassed by two armies: the first was the English force of the Duke of Marlborough, which had travelled all the way from the Netherlands by long marches to join the second army, that of the Emperor.[1] These troops were burning and plundering the countryside. Earlier in the campaign the Emperor had attempted to offer the Elector favourable terms—but these he had haughtily rejected on receipt of definite news that we were on our way through the Black Forest. This information was brought to him by a messenger carrying a microscopically written letter on a tightly rolled piece of parchment.[2] The man had been minutely searched by the Imperial generals, who had every scrap of clothing off his back, but they never found it. M. Tallard showed it to me on a later occasion. Meanwhile we marched on to Ulm from Villingen, under observation all the time by Prince Eugène's powerful cavalry force. This forced us to move slowly, thus ensuring the safe arrival of the convoy at Ulm [29 July], since Villingen had evaded our grasp. Leaving Ulm, we took the road to Augsburg, where the Elector was camped in company with M. Marsin, watching his country burn on the further side of the River Lech. As we approached the city we saw clouds of smoke drifting to the skies. At this stage Prince Eugène joined the Duke of Marlborough and the Elector of Baden after shadowing us all the way from Rothweil. Our camps en route were at Weissenhorn and Kirchberg, but at last we arrived late at night within six miles of the city.

Before I continue my narrative, I wish to recount a conversation Marshal Tallard held with me eight or ten days earlier. We had camped at a place called Moesskirch after giving up the siege of that frightful place Villingen—an ill omen for the future—and there the Marshal took up his quarters in the fine old castle belonging to the Fürstenberg family. When the army resumed its march on the morrow he happened to be standing at the gate as the column I was leading passed close by. I noticed that the sound of our troops gave back a fine echo, and I halted for a moment to give the echo a second try. The Marshal recognized me, and invited me in to share his breakfast chicken. He was very partial to the fine martial air imparted by receiving from a page a chunk of cold meat or a smoked tongue merely wrapped in a napkin with a hunk of bread; he would, on occasion, however, entertain anything up to a hundred officers at a time during the first or second halt of the day's march, keeping two mule trains laden with good things to eat—and wines too—at the head of the army for this very purpose. Although it was my normal practice never to eat or

1 See Parker, pp. 31 et seq. above.
2 Probably concealed in a button.

drink in the morning, I accepted his offer, thinking it tactful to do so. We were standing before a window devouring chicken and watching the army roll by beneath, when he suddenly emerged from the pensive mood that had gripped him for some time and remarked, 'Unless I am very mistaken, there will be a battle before three weeks are out; if one does take place—it will be a very Pharsala.'[1] In this he was quite correct, for the Emperor would have lost his throne had we won the battle of Blenheim. He was already hard pressed by Rakosi and the Hungarian rebels on one side, whilst the Elector of Bavaria, already master of Passau and all Swabia, was menacing him on the other.[2] In the event of our victory at least the fate of the Holy Roman Empire would have been decided; but this would not have been on quite the scale of the results of Pharsala which altered the fate of the whole world.

We spent three days near Augsburg—but never went closer than two leagues from the town. Two separate armies then set out [*9 August*], the Elector's close to the River Lech and ourselves rather farther to the westward, but both marching equal distances. During the second part of the march, we halted for an entire day. The army was drawn up in battle order, wearing its best uniforms (well powdered for the occasion), to be reviewed by the Elector. In due course he made his appearance, and began to inspect the right wing—where I was stationed. I saluted him at the head of my squadrons before following him round. Perhaps I should mention here that, on the Elector's orders, I had left my two Milanese battalions under the command of an excellent officer, M. de Waha, as part of the garrison of Augsburg.

The following morning we marched away to the westward, for we were now close to the Danube. At this juncture we learnt that the enemy had invested Ingolstadt, the only real stronghold left in Bavaria. Next day I was the general on duty, and drew up an immaculate and well-proportioned camp at Aislingen, a residence belonging to the Bishop of Augsburg. While I was busy about my duties, M. Tallard passed by towards Lavingen, almost unattended, after holding a council of war in the main army. I followed him, and, crossing the Danube and skirting the town, the Commander-in-Chief mounted a

[1] The battle of Pharsalia (or Pharsala) took place in August 48 B.C., in Thessaly, Greece. Caesar's triumph over Pompey left him virtually undisputed master of the Roman world.

[2] A further threat to Vienna was currently being mounted by Marshal Vendôme from North Italy.

high hill bearing traces of an old camp. He ordered a new camp to be made there, himself drawing up the limits of a very compact position. It was already later than ten in the evening when we arrived, and as there was neither pick nor shovel in the arsenal of Lavingen we returned to my original camp. However, I enjoyed hardly a wink of sleep, in spite of my most comfortable lodgings in the castle on the mountain, for we were on the march again at one in the morning, reaching the Danube at daybreak [*10 August*]. The army crossed at once, and marched away to the east in two long columns towards Dillingen.

It was during this march that the two armies joined up. We marched past the fortress of Dillingen, but although it was still holding out at that time—and indeed its shot almost reached my squadrons—it soon fell and its garrison became prisoners of war. Our force comprised the right wing of the army with the village of Steinheim as its focal point; I set up my headquarters there. The Elector, commanding the left wing, occupied the ruins of the very same works he had held during the Donauwörth affair [*the Schellenberg, 2 July 1704*], which took place before[1] our army had entered the passes of the Black Forest. On that date I had again been general-officer of the day; and whilst I had been busy marking out a camp in a wood that blocked our view of the city of Freiburg, I heard a number of salvoes fired by that fortress about the hour of midday. I reported this to the Marshal, who informed me he had no idea of the enemy's motive for this. Next day he was able to tell me, for the demonstration was caused by the Elector of Bavaria's decision to abandon the sieges of Dillingen and Lavingen in order to retire to Augsburg; there we duly found him, as I have already related, after hastening our march on the receipt of this news.

One thing is certain: we delayed our march from Alsace far too long and quite inexplicably, for it was contrary to the usual diligence, promptness and vivacity of the French.

The army passed a complete day in the camp, but on the 12th marched at break of day. Our next resting-place was sited on the plain, about one and a half miles beyond the little town of Höchstadt. Our right wing was on the left bank of the River Danube with the village of Blenheim some two hundred yards to its front. All the generals of the right wing had quarters there. In front of this village ran a small stream [*R. Nebel*], running from its swampy source a

1 See Parker, p. 32, above for a description of this celebrated engagement; also p. 33 n.

mile or so away to the left. The camp main guard was posted beyond the village of Blenheim, but in my opinion the left was a trifle over-extended: of course, this was due to the usual French desire to appear imposing. The Elector and his men held a position reaching as far as the village of Lutzingen, which contained his headquarters, with the woods stretching away towards Nördlingen to his front. Before this position was an area of marshy ground, a few hamlets and one or two mills along the little stream. Blenheim village itself was surrounded by hedges; fences and other obstacles enclosed gardens and meadows. All in all this position was pretty fair, but had we advanced a mere eight hundred or a thousand paces farther to our front we could have held a far more compact position, with our right still on the Danube and our left protected by woods, and our centre more concentrated. There we could have drawn up three if not four lines of infantry, one behind the other, with our ninety-four guns to the fore, and three or four lines of cavalry to support them in the rear.

Following our arrival, we camped in two long lines in order to cover the vast front selected. We soon saw that our advance guard and outlying pickets were in contact with the enemy's patrols along the edge of the woods a mile away in the direction of Münster. A brisk skirmish took place. All this activity was due to the plots and machina-tions of the Duke of Marlborough and Prince Eugène, who were determined to deprive the Margrave of Baden—in fact, the senior commander—of the distinction of giving us battle. They managed this by sending him off [9 August] to amuse himself by besieging Ingolstadt, which kept him fully occupied, whilst they pretended that their operations were solely designed to cover the siege and keep our army under observation. Indeed, nor were the French Marshals or the Elector of Bavaria expecting a battle—in spite of the strong indications provided by the enemy's movements: for whilst we were advancing to our position, they, too, were moving up, and in due course they camped in an area stretching from the Danube on their left, through Münster and into the woods on the right.

So both armies made camp for the night, separated by little more than three miles. The allied army consisted of 182 squadrons, 63 infantry battalions and 60 guns; our force totalled 84 battalions, 140 squadrons supported by 94 cannons.[1] But let me hasten to point out that their battalions were up to one-third stronger than ours in respect

[1] Compare with the figures given by Parker, p. 37 above. See also the footnote on that page.

of soldiers, and as for our squadrons, not one was at its full establishment of one hundred troopers—most containing only seventy or
eighty. The Bavarian forces and my own troops were in point of
fact the strongest units; the average French battalion consisted of a
mere 350 men.

I arrived in the camp during the skirmish I have mentioned and as
a precaution ordered my horse to be left fully saddled in case of an
emergency. Filled with curiosity to discover how events were faring,
I rode out beyond Blenheim village into the corn-filled plain—taking
good care not to get too far away from my escort, which I might well
have needed. When I saw our troops falling back I also returned to the
camp, and sat down to a good hot plate of soup in Blenheim along
with my generals and colonels. These included Messieurs de Courtebonne, de Sainte-Hermine, de Saint-Pouange, de Ligondes and de
Forsac, together with the old and brave officer commanding the
Orléans Regiment whose name escapes me;[1] old Heider was also at
the supper party. I was never in better form, and after wining and
dining well, we one and all dispersed to our respective quarters. I had
placed my Spanish troops under the Duc d'Humières away to the left,
slightly in rear of my position. I was personally in command of the
right wing of the second line. I don't believe I ever slept sounder than
on that night, and the rest certainly did me good.

[1] It is possible that this officer was the Colonel de Brancas who is known to have commanded the Orléans Infantry Regiment between 1699 and 1706.

III

The Campaign of 1704:
The Battle of Blenheim

Upon my orders, the valet had set up my camp bed in a barn—and there I spent the night, whilst my servants lodged in the main farm building. I slept deeply until six in the morning [*13 August*], when I was abruptly awoken by one of my old retainers—the head groom in fact—who rushed into the barn all out of breath. He had just returned from taking my horses out to grass at four in the morning (as he had been instructed). This fellow, Lefranc, shook me awake and blurted out that the enemy were there. Thinking to mock him, I asked, 'Where? There?' and he at once replied, 'Yes—there—there!' --flinging wide as he spoke the door of the barn and drawing my bed-curtains. The door opened straight on to the fine, sunlit plain beyond—and the whole area appeared to be covered by enemy squadrons. I rubbed my eyes in disbelief, and then coolly remarked that the foe must at least give me time to take my morning cup of chocolate. Whilst I was hurriedly drinking this and getting dressed, my horses were saddled and harnessed. As my lodging was situated in the very last house in the village and thus nearest to the enemy, I ordered my servants to pack my kit with all speed, and to watch Marshal Tallard's retainers and do with my belongings exactly what they did with his; but first of all to get everybody and everything clear of the house. Jumping on to my horse I rode off towards the camp, accompanied by my two aides-de-camp and taking all my thirteen spare chargers with me.[1]

There was not a single soul stirring as I clattered out of the village: nothing at all might have been happening. The same sight met my gaze when I reached the camp—everyone still snug in their tents—although the enemy was already so close that their standards and

---

[1] This may seem a generous provision for one general officer, but we know from the narrative that follows that at least three were killed and two more wounded during the day's fighting; indeed, the Count places his total loss on the 13th at thirteen horses (p. 181 below), but presumably some of these were captured or went astray.

colours could easily be counted. They were already pushing back our pickets, but nobody seemed at all worried about it. I could see the enemy advancing ever closer in nine great columns of cavalry and deployed battalions, filling the whole plain from the Danube to the woods on the horizon. I could even make out that they were organized in alternate pairs of columns, two of horse and then two of foot. I still had received no instructions, but I ordered my cavalry regiments to mount by way of precaution; I went in person to the standards of each squadron to give them this order, making sure that the trumpeters did not sound 'Boot and saddle' or 'Mount'. Soon everyone was on his horse, and I kept them all drawn up at the head of their tents, and then—and only then—did I notice the first signs of movement in Blenheim village.

A little later Marshal Tallard galloped past the head of the second line of battle. Pausing to compliment me on my wise precaution in mounting my men, he asked me to sound 'Boot and saddle' and 'To horse' repeatedly, and to send an aide-de-camp to the artillery to order the two signal salvoes fired for the recall of the foragers. He told me he was going over to the left, but that he would soon return. My trumpeters were immediately ordered to sound the two calls time and time again, one after the other, and they were repeated all the way down the line. My aide-de-camp with noteworthy rapidity got himself recognized and obeyed by the gunners, and we soon heard the 24-pounders fire the two salvoes. There were in all four pieces of this calibre.

Whilst all this was going on, I saw the baggage escaping precipitately and noisily out of Blenheim village, and everything rushed to the rear through the intervals between my squadrons.

A moment later we saw two columns of the enemy filing along the edge of the woods, away on their right, and this made the French experts declare that the enemy were in full march away towards Nördlingen.[1] This made me smile, for, of course, it was Prince Eugène marching up to form the right of their line of battle in order to attack our left whilst their opposite wing made all its preparations to assault us.

---

[1] Tallard, of course, had already written in this vein in a dispatch to Versailles about seven o'clock that morning. 'Rumour in the countryside expects them at Nördlingen.' (See Churchill, Book One, p. 847.) He was to be speedily disillusioned. However, Mérode-Westerloo can fairly be accused of 'wisdom after the event' in the criticisms that follow.

At this stage I saw two lines of our infantry forming up behind the village of Blenheim, with their right flank on the Danube's bank. If only they had stayed there, and left the defence of Blenheim's gardens, hedgerows, houses and barricades to smaller detachments—constantly reinforced or replaced as the need arose—things would have gone much better. However, the whole formation was eventually drawn into the defences.[1]

It would be impossible to imagine a more magnificent spectacle. The two armies in full battle array were so close to one another that they exchanged fanfares of trumpet-calls and rolls of kettle-drums. When ours stopped, their music struck up again. This went on until the deployment of their right flank was completed, their left preparing to attack the village. The brightest imaginable sun shone down on the two armies drawn up in the plain. You could even distinguish the uniforms of each successive unit; a number of generals and aides-de-camp galloped here and there: all in all, it was an almost indescribably stirring sight. But a moment later other considerations came to the fore in our minds as the enemy artillery, brought forward and drawn up at the head of their army, loosed a terrible bombardment upon us;[2] our guns at once replied with a similar devastating effect, whilst the French, following their usual deplorable custom, set fire to all the villages, mills and hamlets to our front, and flames and smoke billowed up to the clouds.

This great and magnificent prelude lasted another two hours. We maintained our position at the head of our camping area, where the tents were not yet struck. Trumpet call answered trumpet call; cannon balls inflicted grave disorder on my squadrons. These circumstances made the proceedings even more impressive than any distant view from the safety of a church tower. I was riding past Forsac's regiment when a shot carried away the head of my horse and killed two troopers; another of my Spanish mounts was killed behind one of the Orléans squadrons, whilst yet a third received a hit which carried away the butts of my pistols, the pommel of the saddle and a piece of flesh as large as the crown of a hat. He recovered from this wound, however, without any disfigurement, and years later I gave him to the Duke of Wolfenbüttel.

[1] This error was due to the sector commander, M. de Clérembault, who eventually insisted on packing at least twenty-seven battalions into the village.

[2] It is more probable that a French detachment of six guns sited slightly to the north of Blenheim village was the first to open fire at about ten o'clock.

Following this lengthy prelude, the English infantry, who had waited for the Imperial forces to join battle on the right, at last attacked the village of Blenheim; shortly after midday, I think it was. The first volleys in this attack had hardly been fired when the two lines of our infantry, some twenty-seven battalions in all, whose orders I believe had been to support the position, entered the village most prematurely and ill-advisedly. What is more, a further twelve regiments of dismounted dragoons were also sent in. Why!—a mere ten battalions would have been capable of defending the place in far better fashion, and all the remainder of this veritable army could have been far more usefully employed elsewhere. The men were so crowded in upon one another that they could not even fire, let alone receive or carry out any orders. Not a single shot of the enemy missed its mark, whilst only those few of our men at the front could return the fire, and soon many of these were unable to shoot owing to exhaustion or their muskets exploding from constant use. Those drawn up in the rear were mowed down without firing a shot at the enemy; if they wanted to reply they could only fire at their own comrades or indiscriminately without aiming. To make things even worse, the village had been set on fire by the French troops, and our poor fellows were grilled amidst the continually collapsing roofs and beams of the blazing houses, and thus were burnt alive amidst the ashes of this smaller Troy of their own making.

The fire of both attack and defence remained heavy and prolonged. Half an hour after it had started the Gendarmerie, situated directly in front of me in the first line under the command that day of Lieutenant-General de Zurlauben (a Swiss-born infantry officer), charged the enemy cavalry stationed on the right of the attacking English infantry. This force was drawn up in five lines, one squadron behind the other. Our charge went well and the Gendarmerie flung their first line on to their second, but since the troops to the Gendarmerie's left did not ride forward with equal dash, if indeed they charged at all, the Gendarmerie found itself unsupported facing fresh enemy squadrons which charged and in their turn flung them back in rude disorder.[1]

During this period the engagement spread over the whole field of battle, and firing broke out everywhere from one end of the armies to the other. Not only did Prince Eugène attack the Elector, but the

---

[1] One of the most celebrated cavalry engagements of the day was between five English squadrons, led by Colonel Palmes, and eight squadrons of the Gendarmerie. See Parker, p. 40 above.

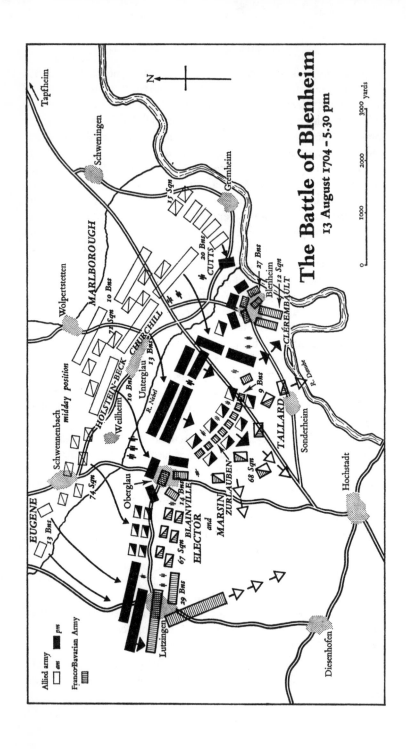

The Battle of Blenheim

13 August 1704 – 5.30 pm

Allied army
□ am
■ pm
▨ Franco-Bavarian Army

N

0   1000   2000   3000 yards

Dutch and Hessians attacked the two hamlets Oberglau and Unter-
glau, which were situated in advance of our centre, and the enemy
began to cross the marsh which we had considered impassable, leading
their horses by the bridles. So they were allowed to get over and
remount right in front of our positions, and then calmly charge and
attack us as if we were babes in arms.

Our senior generals had been pleased to leave too great an interval
between our first and second lines. When the enemy attacked Blenheim in two-column strength, and the Gendarmerie charged over the
stream as already related, I wanted to advance with the second line
to support them, but this the French high command would not allow.

In spite of this I did march forward when I saw the Gendarmerie
break and retire in confusion, hotly pursued by the foe. The broken,
disordered cavalry poured through the intervals between my own
squadrons; the Gendarmerie was undoubtedly soundly beaten, and
the gallant Zurlauben received several grave wounds which caused
his death two days later. I came face to face with the enemy after he
had passed the stream, and my fresh, well-ordered squadrons charged
and flung them back, right over the Nebel; following them up, we
then attacked their second line, which also crumbled; but then we came
up against a third, untired force, and my squadrons, disordered and
blown by their exertions, were themselves defeated and pushed back
over the stream.

A few of the Gendarmerie, who had rallied and reformed, and the
Regiment known as the '*Royal Étranger*', who remained drawn up
in a sort of line, caused the enemy to rein in their horses when they
saw them. This respite gave me time to rally the greater part of my
squadrons; I had it in mind to counter-attack, although I knew there
was no longer a second line to support me. Of course, there was not
a single French general officer in sight. But I failed to notice that all
the forces originally stationed on my left, stretching away towards
the centre, had turned about in their tracks and were gone from the
field. They had given ground to the enemy, who were pouring over
the stream and forming up on my flank in the very midst of our army,
the centre of which was now under the command of the Duc
d'Humières, conspicuous in his fine gilt cuirass.

Notwithstanding, I charged with all the men I could rally, and I
had the good luck to defeat my adversaries and push them back to the
brink of the stream—but I had no wish to recross it, for I could see
they still had five lines of cavalry. However, I failed to notice that

they had brought their infantry well forward and they killed and wounded many of our horses at thirty paces. This was promptly followed by an unauthorized but definite movement to the rear by my men—and I, too, would have been obliged to accompany them had not two musket-balls killed my horse beneath me, so that he subsided gently to the ground and I with him. I really do not understand why there was not a single enemy grenadier with charity enough to come forward and give me a hand to my feet, for I was no more than fifteen paces from the stream, and they were drawn up all along the bank, supported by cavalry, five lines deep in all. Luckily, however, one of my aides-de-camp and a groom came up with yet another horse after observing my fall, and they soon had me hoisted on to horseback again.

I then re-formed some sort of a line, and placed four pieces of artillery in front of my position—I had noticed them trying to sneak off and promptly commandeered them.[1] Whilst these guns were being sited I rode over to Blenheim, wanting to bring out a dozen battalions (which they certainly did not need there) to form a line on the edge of the stream supported by the cannons and the debris of my squadrons. The brigades of Saint-Ségond and Monfort were setting out to follow me, when M. de Clérembault in person countermanded the move, and shouting and swearing drove them back into the village. However, I firmly believe that my proposed move would have been the only way to avert the disaster that ensued.

Whilst all this was going on over on my side, the enemy had cut to ribbons seven[2] newly raised French battalions after their easy deployment over the marshes. These unfortunate battalions had found themselves completely isolated in the centre, and died to a man where they stood, stationed right out in the open plain—supported by nobody.

Over on the Elector's side, Prince Eugène and the Imperial troops had been repulsed three times—driven right back to the woods—and had taken a real drubbing. There were some places in the centre, too—for instance, those areas held by de Vaillac and my Walloon cavalry—where the foe was also defeated three times, and indeed in the case of the men of Flanders the success was gained without the interference of a single general. Thus from a church tower you would have seen

---

[1] Almost all armies at this period employed civilian drivers for their gun-teams and convoys. These non-combatants were notoriously unreliable under fire, and often deserted.

[2] Most accounts say nine battalions; a few say ten. (See Parker, p. 43 above.)

the enemy repulsed on one flank and we on the other, the battle rippling to and fro like the waves of the sea, with the entire line engaged in hand-to-hand combat from one end to the other—a rare enough occurrence. All this took place under a deadly hail of fire from the infantry, especially during the various attacks on the villages and hamlets, as well as on Blenheim and the other sectors under attack in the centre. This spectacle, lit by bright sunlight, must have been magnificent for any spectator in a position to view it with sang-froid.

Compelled to abandon my plan, I returned to my cavalry, which now mustered only thirteen troops—I really could not call them squadrons. One or two still possessed their standards and kettle-drums. I could not help but notice at this moment that the enemy was forming up a complete battle array at his leisure in the very centre of our army. After Vaillac and five more troops had joined me, I resolved to charge once more. This we carried through so vigorously that we routed the Prince of Hesse. I was joined by the five remaining troops of the Walloon squadrons who had already performed more than their duty, two more from both Acosta and Heider, and the second Gaetano squadron under their Lieutenant-Colonel, Jobart. By this time the Prince of Hesse had rallied his forces and counter-attacked—but we soundly beat him again. However, in the meantime hordes of the enemy were pushing round our flanks, and we soon found ourselves faced by numerous enemy squadrons on no less than three sides—and we were borne back on top of one another. So tight was the press that my horse was carried along some three hundred paces without putting hoof to ground, right to the edge of a deep ravine [*near Sonderheim*]: down we plunged a good twenty feet into a swampy meadow; my horse stumbled and fell. A moment later several men and horses fell on top of me, as the remains of my cavalry swept by, all intermingled with the hotly pursuing foe. I spent several minutes trapped beneath my horse.

While all this was going on the Elector and Marshal Marsin conceded that the day was lost when they saw the enemy in possession of the centre. They ordered a retreat, which was carried out in good order; but I believe they would not have escaped so easily but for my men keeping the enemy's attention fully occupied. Otherwise the foe could have attacked the head and flank of our left wing as it retreated towards Lavingen. As things turned out, however, our entire left got safely away.

Meantime the enemy sealed all the exits from Blenheim at their leisure, and the general commanding the village [*Clérembault*] rode straight into the Danube and was drowned, instead of organizing the twenty-seven battalions and fourteen dragoon regiments into a square to fight their way out. Good infantry, well disciplined and highly trained, could easily have done this. As it turned out, however, these forces fought on until after seven o'clock, bereft of an experienced commander, and then surrendered as prisoners of war when they saw the enemy bringing up all his artillery.

The French lost this battle for a wide variety of reasons. For one thing, they had too good an opinion of their own ability—and were excessively scornful of their adversaries. Another point was that their field dispositions were badly made, and in addition there was rampant indiscipline and inexperience displayed in Marshal Tallard's army. It took all these faults to lose so celebrated a battle. As regards casualties, I believe these were practically equal on both sides if we discount the prisoners. I calculate that the enemy lost twelve or thirteen thousand killed and wounded on the field of battle and we about the same; but, of course, the foe also captured the entire Blenheim garrison and other captives during the course of the different actions and the pursuit. M. Tallard was himself taken prisoner. They also took fifty-two guns, but the other forty escaped.[1]

Everything happened very quickly, and the crowd soon passed me by; I managed to escape from beneath my horse, which was not dead but utterly exhausted, and extricated myself from the pile of dead horses that had fallen on top of us both. I had barely found my feet when a passing hussar fired his pistol at me. The next moment a huge English horse grenadier—a whole head and shoulders taller than I— came up. He dismounted and came forward to take me prisoner in a leisurely way. I noticed his lackadaisical air, and grasped my long sword, which was dangling from my wrist, keeping it pressed well into my side. When he was within two paces I lunged at him, but I then discovered my left knee was injured, so I stumbled and missed my stroke. The Englishman raised his sword to cut me down, but I parried his blow and ran my sword right through his body up to the hilt. I wrenched my blade free, but as he fell he slashed at me again, but only succeeded in cutting the thick edge of my boot, which did me no harm. I put my foot on his head and plunged my sword through his throat. My blade penetrated into the soft earth and

[1] See Parker, p. 44 above, and the footnote on the same page.

snapped under the excessive pressure, leaving me with only the hilt.

This left me in a sorry state, but I snatched up a pistol from the ground, though I had no idea whether it was loaded or not. Who should then happen to ride past but my valet, gazing around in terror. He recognized me stretched out on the ground, and dropped something heavy on my face—a pistol butt, I believe it was—making my nose and teeth bleed. 'Is it really you, my Lord?' he asked. I replied in no uncertain terms that it was, and he at once jumped down from his horse and hoisted me on to its back: I was unable to do this unaided because of my damaged knee. Once I was firmly in the saddle, I told him to get up behind, but he refused. 'But what on earth will you do, then, my poor Leblond?' I queried. He never had a chance to answer, for at that moment he fell riddled with shots fired by some passing soldiers. I lost no time in riding off the way I had come, planning to swim across the Danube: the greater part of the cavalry survivors had already attempted this.[1]

As I rode on my way I removed the white cockade from my hat, and rode straight up to a large body of formed cavalry drawn up with their backs to our camp. I reached a large squadron, made up from the debris of two others. As I speak several languages, I was not interfered with as I rode up, and seeing that nobody took any interest in me I resolved to ride straight through the gap in their midst. Finding myself between two of their lines, I rode off to the left to find a path I had followed the day before, coming from Höchstadt. Eventually I found it, and rode off, passing again between two more enemy squadrons. They never challenged, so I slowly went down my path, speaking to this group in German and answering others in the language they addressed me in. When I reached some windmills on a small stream, not far from Höchstadt, some of these soldiers advised me not to go any closer, as the enemy were still in possession of the town. I replied that we would soon have them all in our clutches, and pretended I was going closer for a reconnaissance. The others stayed behind. As I approached my objective, someone fired several shots at me, but I got past and into the town. Reaching the barrier, I walked my horse for a short distance before being challenged: 'Who goes there?' 'French general officer!' I replied. An officer then let me enter. I went into the square, where I found several French generals who had the nerve to tell me I was pretty late. I retorted that they, for their part, had arrived too soon. We then all had a drink at the fountain.

[1] With varying success, we might add. (See p. 42 n. above.)

IV

The Campaign of 1704:
The French Retreat and the
End of Operations

I visited the castle to see Zurlauben, and found him very ill, though still able to recognize me. After spending a short time with him, I climbed the tower in an effort to verify whether the town and castle were indeed cut off by the enemy, as some were saying. I decided that this was not the case and my finding was confirmed by the arrival of Lefranc from outside. I went to inform Zurlauben of this and advised him to have stretchers made and to allow himself to be moved on his bed. I passed this idea on to his retinue and they made four or five hundred stretchers which carried a very large number of wounded officers. I said farewell to Zurlauben, urging his attendants not to rush his evacuation, and left the castle. I passed through the little town and came out on to the ridge behind the marsh, and there I found all the debris of our cavalry in indescribable confusion.

It was almost eight o'clock when I reached them; I at once settled down to work, as nobody else was doing anything about the disorder. First I posted a troop of twenty or thirty Gendarmerie on the road which I had followed to Höchstadt: it was only a narrow lane, but it offered the enemy the only approach to the town. One hundred yards back I drew up a second troop, and then another and another and so on all along the ridge, thus forming a line of small troops. A few still had their standards with them and men from other formations attached themselves to them. This had two good effects: first, fugitives at last began to look for their units; secondly, the foe, who had made his appearance on the farther side of the marsh, was taken in by what appeared to be a rapidly reinforced body of cavalry. A few French generals at last made their appearance, but they were somewhat shamefaced and didn't interfere in any way. All the officers took their orders direct from me.

Night fell. Under cover of darkness I marched my men back over the stream which led away towards Steinheim, as I had noticed the day before. I crossed near a water-mill, making no sound. Taking Vaillac's advice, I then resolved to continue my retreat to Dillingen, although at this stage I had no idea that Marshal Tallard was himself a prisoner and I did not know what was happening. I hoped to get between Dillingen and Lavingen before daybreak. I was still a mile from the former when my advanced guard was challenged. Word was sent back to me that we had come across some of our own Party; so I rode forward to find a mere handful of soldiers. 'Who are you?' I asked. Someone replied that he was the Count d'Arco.[1] I identified myself, and he asked where I had come from so late at night. I replied that I was at the head of some thirty-six cavalry troops. Then in a few words he explained to me that the Elector had sent him out to reconstruct the old entrenchments—which had been destroyed by the enemy. He complained that he was without picks, shovels or pioneers, and that in consequence he could do nothing until daybreak, it then being past eleven at night. The Elector was at Dillingen, he thought, and the infantry was in camp there. I asked him if there was anything I should do, and he offered to send a messenger to the Elector to find out. Marshal Marsin was busy all night building two bridges, and all the baggage had been held up the whole day outside Lavingen because the town commandant had closed the town gates, and the column was only just starting to cross the river by the town bridge. It was a physical impossibility to get everything over a single bridge and there was complete chaos at its head as well as elsewhere.

Eventually the aide-de-camp came back bringing with him my sole surviving aide: the other, young Clermont, had been killed in action. Between them they recounted the points I have described above, and added that for these reasons his Excellency begged me to lose no time in marching on towards Ulm by way of the north bank of the river, by-passing Lavingen without getting embroiled with the infantry and equipment crossing there. He also placed all his cavalry under my orders. He said he hoped to get all the infantry and baggage away over the two bridges that were being constructed, but that if this failed he would set fire to all the latter.

I requested d'Arco to inform the Elector that I would comply with his orders, in spite of the fact that I was suffering from three wounds, but that I could not hold myself responsible for what might happen

[1] Presumably the defender of Donauworth and the Schellenberg Heights on 2 July. See Parker, p. 32–3 above.

if we came within a mile of Prince Eugène, for the troops in their present nervous condition were likely to bolt if a hare got up. I then marched on: midnight tolled from Lavingen as we passed by. There the Elector's cavalry caught up with me. We pressed on in complete silence until daybreak, when I calculated we had put some eight miles between ourselves and the enemy, after passing very close to his right wing. At nine in the morning we halted on a beautiful, grain-filled plain. We fed the horses half at a time, the remainder standing guard fully bridled. About eleven we set off again, and made one more halt at three. At last we reached Ulm about seven in the evening and marched into the town, trumpets and kettle-drums playing.

The day's march had been no less than forty-two miles; I lost no time in camping my men after crossing the Danube and posting sentries. I soon found some French generals. I told them I could do no more through fatigue and my wounds. M. Descartes, the commissary —an old acquaintance of mine and the last person I expected to see— allotted me a quarter in the town. There I went to rest, after being in the saddle for thirty hours with neither sleep nor food and only one drink of water. My knee had swollen to the size of a man's head; although a bullet had been fired at me at point-blank range, it had failed to penetrate thanks to my strong thigh-boots with thick flaps down to the knees; beneath these I had worn a pair of stockings to keep off the flies, and my underwear. The bullet had got as far as my stocking, but had penetrated no farther.

Whilst I was undressed and was having my wounds attended to, I dictated from my bed a letter to the Marquis de Bedmar giving an account of the battle; my secretary Laclos took it down. I sealed it in a letter to my wife, placing this within another cover addressed to Gent (my neighbour at Petersheim) at his Maastricht home, and this package in yet another envelope made out to my steward Steinhausen at Wetzlar. In spite of all these precautions it failed to get through, for M. le Comte de Loewenstein intercepted it. I sent it off to the post before going to sleep that very day—14 August 1704.

On my third day at Ulm, I learnt that the Elector had arrived with the infantry and baggage and that my belongings were saved, being the very last allowed over the bridge. By sheer good fortune, Marshal Marsin was supervising on the spot, and was about to order my baggage fired when one of my servants told him that it was all I possessed, and so he let it through; everything behind was set alight. At Ulm, the Elector lodged a short way outside the city at the Abbey of Weillingen and the reunited army rested three or four days in the neighbourhood. On the second day I went to visit the Elector, invalid though I was. He issued his orders for the day and I listened with the rest. Then he went on to pay me a very fine compliment, far more than I deserved. He ended by saying that he would personally write to the Kings of France and Spain to tell them that I was the only man who had come out of the sad battle well—and that I could rest with an easy mind. I was most confused at this, but managed to reply that his words were most generous. I had done nothing but my duty, and if anyone thought I had done more I was already excessively rewarded by his kind words. He said all this to me in the presence of the other generals, and I received the congratulations of Marshal Marsin and the rest, though I could tell they were inwardly seething with jealousy.

Indeed, throughout the campaign I received nothing but praise from the Elector. Whilst we were in Bavaria, I always took precedence at table immediately after him; as soon as I arrived he had begged me to dine with him; and placed me at his side in the place of honour. He drank my health first on every occasion. When I arrived at Augsburg I had informed him that I considered my commission to be at an end, after showing him my orders, and that I expected no favours. 'No,' he had replied, 'far from depriving you of any authority I will augment the powers you hold if it lies in my power.'

As we prepared to march I came across a number of wounded Spanish and Flemish officers from my cavalry in a penniless condition. They were doomed to stay in Ulm. It appeared that our pay office had no funds to deal with any unusual needs or accidents. I thought of going to see the Elector, but I knew he had enough on his hands by way of troubles and anxieties. So, poor though I was—with almost all my property confiscated and with the large household in Brussels to maintain, not to mention my equipment, military entourage and all the rest—I had stretchers made for them, engaged good surgeons, had their soup and food cooked in my kitchens and finally had them brought into the quarters assigned to me all the way to Strasbourg, whilst I myself lived in a tent. Once we reached our destination, I gave them between 20 and 50, even 60, pistoles each according to rank, before I departed. Luckily my wife had the foresight to send 600 pistoles to Strasbourg to await my arrival.

Those of our officers, including the Comte de Monfort (now Prince of Rubempré) who had fallen into enemy hands, sent an enemy trumpeter to me under a flag of truce to ask for their personal effects. The Elector allowed me to send their baggage to them. At this time we heard of the fall of Ingolstadt [*21 August*] and of Prince Louis's [*of Baden*] rage when he learned of the trick Prince Eugène and the Duke of Marlborough had played him. It is quite certain that there would have been no battle had the Prince been with them; he was not the sort to risk all to gain all. If no battle had taken place, the English could hardly have wintered in Germany, and I don't know what might have befallen before they could have returned, as we would have enjoyed superiority of numbers. Moreover, the Elector had in addition a large corps of well-trained soldiers scattered about Bavaria who remained there and were lost to us as things turned out.[1] Had these men been with us on the battlefield, the issue might have been different despite all our mistakes.

When we learnt that the enemy was on the march after the capture of Ingolstadt we left the neighbourhood of Ulm. If the foe had been quick enough, not one of us would have escaped.[2] Had they only massed all their dragoons together and sent them ahead of us to occupy the lines near Moesskirch, we would have been utterly unable to march past, taking into consideration the shaken morale of our army; then, if the remainder of the enemy had come up behind us, we should have been forced to lay down our arms.

The march to the lines of Moesskirch was made in long stages. The fires and clouds of smoke rising from the villages and châteaux along our route bore witness to the indiscipline of the army. Our people burned and pillaged and committed some frightful atrocities, but no one could restore order—or even seemed to want to. If the foe had been served by good spies, our entire march could have been followed by looking for these signs.

A good-sized garrison was left in Ulm with all the wounded who had managed to reach the town. At last we came within half a day's march of the Moesskirch position. A strong detachment was formed to force the lines if the enemy was in possession, as we feared was the case. All the Elector's finest troops—his grenadiers—were selected for this duty, and I was ordered to command the advance guard: the

[1] These detachments had been made during July in an attempt to protect the Elector's estates from being ravaged by the Allies.

[2] The administrative complications caused by the need to pursue the French towards the Rhine—and provide for some 20,000 prisoners—accounts for the slowness of the Allied advance.

Elector told me that the fate of the entire army rested on the presence, or absence, of the enemy in the entrenchments. I made my plans, but I felt instinctively that we should find the place empty. I sent forward two grenadiers to make a reconnaissance. I gave each one a crown and promised them ten more ducats apiece if they could penetrate the lines and bring back some clear and positive information. Off they went and eventually one came back to say the way was clear. I then sent forward fifty grenadiers under a captain to make quite sure. I followed close behind, silently. It was after midnight, and he sent me a sergeant and five men to announce that we only had to march through the barrier, which was now wide open. I at once advanced, and occupied the position, sending word to the Elector. He marched before daybreak and passed the lines at a distance of two leagues. I formed the rearguard, responsible for escorting the baggage—a rotten and irksome duty.

I should have mentioned that the moment we left Ulm all the heavy baggage and carts were set on fire in the interests of mobility. Three great waggon-parks were formed in the countryside, and we had the sorrow of watching them burn as we marched away. I, like all the others, lost in addition to my carts all my field furniture, chairs, tables, beds, utensils, field ovens—the lot. I was fortunate to keep my two dozen mules which carried my most vital possessions. I lost still more horses through the ravages of the so-called 'German sickness' which put all our cavalrymen on their feet. The disease started in my stable the day of the battle. From the time I lost my first horse, besides the thirteen that were killed or injured on the battlefield, one or two fell sick every day, dying forty-eight hours later. Thus between Blenheim and Brussels I lost ninety-seven horses and all their harness had to be left behind, too. The mules alone were not subject to this plague, but one slight consolation was that the enemy also caught it after camping on some of our vacated sites.

We rested two whole days at Duttlingen—not before time. We could take no more rest for we heard that the enemy was marching along the northern banks of the Danube in force, leaving a mere detachment to besiege Ulm [23 August–11 September]. On this news the Elector, acting on Marshal Marsin's advice, asked every general to give his opinion in writing—without holding a council of war or suggesting any course of action. Marshal Marsin's aide-de-camp came to ask me for my appreciation, and left me some fifteen other original opinions. I was not a little startled at the method adopted, all the more as I had learnt that Mme the Electress had advanced as far as Memmingen, only one day's march from Ulm, but that the Elector had ordered her to turn back. In any case it was now too late, events having taken the turn they had, to adopt any other course of action than those I read. I was ignorant of what forces the Elector still possessed in Bavaria; I did not know their positions nor what assistance they might afford. But I did know by bitter experience the disorder rampant in a defeated French army. Therefore I wrote that, taking into consideration our present situation, my advice was to retire towards the mountains of the Black Forest—to await tidings of the Army of Alsace[1]—and then to take whatever measures appeared most advisable. And that was, in fact, what happened.

I had always evaded the man Vaillac socially, for I knew he was a fearful drunkard. He had, however, borne himself with so much courage at the battle that I embraced him in the open street the first time I saw him thereafter. He asked if he could dine with me, and I could not really refuse, even though all my table appointments had been destroyed. He brought with him the Chevalier de Cronsi, the Marquis of Torcy's brother, and several more; and although we did not enjoy as good a dinner as I could have wished, we certainly drank plenty of champagne, 'rosolis' and other wines—and in the end we were all pretty merry: several indeed, ended up beneath the table. I fared best of our company—but by eleven o'clock we had dispatched forty bottles of wine and nine of 'rosolis'. At that stage I staggered off to attend the Elector's general orders, and there was no disguising the fact that I was drunk—an extraordinary occurrence, let me hasten to add. He inquired where I had dined. I replied at home, but that I had entertained de Vaillac, whom I had left under the table. This the Elector thought very funny, and he roared with laughter, as did Marshal Marsin. I then solemnly informed them that I thought I had better go and lie down—and so I did. The result of my potations was a 'fever' that plagued me for four or five days of the retreat.

Next we reached Donaueschingen, the seat of the Prince of Fürstenberg. In the lower courtyard of the château are two springs called 'Donau' which provide the source of the Danube. A little way from the castle a broader stream from the direction of Villingen makes a confluence and loses its name, thus forming the Danube proper: really just a broad stream at this point. We camped rather higher up the heights in the general direction of the Black Forest near the Abbey of

[1] Marshal Villeroi and General de Coignies acting in conjunction.

St Blaise which, incidentally, Marshal Tallard originally had promised me for my winter quarters. In addition I would have been authorized to draw the equivalent of three hundred rations in local contributions; other generals at Augsburg and in Swabia had been awarded a rate per ration of thirty French sols a day. All in all, when this considerable sum was added to the other perquisites of a general officer, it would have put some 80,000 crowns into my pocket. This would have done my affairs a lot of good, especially as the lands of Württemberg were on my doorstep and had never yet been put under contribution. But the outcome of the great battle and my ill-fortune, which so often made me arrive too early or too late for the pickings, had let me down once again, and I was deprived of these fat prizes which would have meant so much to me, although I was never a pillager—nor ever would be, thank God.

It was while we were at this camp that Marshal Villeroi came to visit the Elector. He had come down from the Low Countries and advanced as far as the Heights of Villingen, securing all the passes we had marched through.[1] The fever and my wounds prevented me from quitting my quarters, which I shared with my other wounded officers, but to my surprise one day in walked Grimaldi and several other Spanish officers. They had come with the Marshal's army. They were the first to tell me that the Marquis de Bedmar had, in fact, received news of me. I had written to him several times, but all messages had been intercepted. However, M. de Bedmar had been considerate enough to send my wife Grimaldi's letter by hand of his secretary, concealing the news that I was wounded from her, as she was pregnant.

At this time I also mentioned to the Elector that he might care to replace the officers I had lost in the battle. I drew up a list, consulting the colonel of each regiment in turn, and this was taken to the Elector, who signed it without even a glance, in spite of my requesting him to review my suggestions. The Heider Regiment had lost its colonel— dead, I thought—though, in fact, it turned out that he was grievously wounded and a prisoner. In spite of his great age he survived his injuries, and died several years later, a captive in England—or so I believe.

Once more we were on our way, passing Villingen below us to the right. We re-entered the gorges, finding Villeroi's men in full control of the passes. His army formed our rearguard. When we eventually

[1] Villeroi's strength at this juncture can be estimated at about 25,000 men.

emerged from the mountains I was given leave on account of my wounds to ride ahead of the army, and I reached Strasbourg in one day, passing through the beautiful and fertile plain that separates the Danube from the Black Forest; I consider it even more beautiful than my native Low Countries—and the local peasantry seemed very prosperous.

The army reached Strasbourg three or four days later and there it rested. The Elector was housed in the Governor's residence, built overlooking the river, and there that very same night he was serenaded by the mayor from some boats. I do not think this was very well received on his part.

Several days later I was sent into a rear area with all Tallard's cavalry. I was assigned the town of Höchfeld close by Saverne. There at long last I found enough leisure and spare time to write down my account of the battle. I dictated it to my secretary Laclos, giving all the relevant dates of the campaign, which I think were accurate, as they were still fresh in my mind—and in any case I have checked them since; a great desire to write my *Mémoires* seized me.[1]

While we were at Höchfeld a false alarm took place which amused me not at all. One of my cavalry captains, rather a cowardly knave, was on his way to some rendezvous or other in a neighbouring village when he heard a great noise of horses stamping and snorting in another town. He rushed back to camp to give the alarm, and came to report his suspicions to me at one in the morning, saying that the enemy was upon us. I was completely taken in and jumped into my clothes, pulling on my boots without waiting to put on my stockings. I mounted my horse and rode up to the camp, to find everybody alerted and astir. I kept the men mounted at the head of the camp, whilst I set out for the picket-line with this captain and an escort of 100 troopers. The captain and another officer were riding some yards in front of me when they saw what they thought was an enemy sentry: they both assured me it was, though I couldn't really believe it could be a guard right out in the full light of the moon. I sent two horsemen on ahead to make contact whilst I followed close behind—and all the time the noise of horses could plainly be heard in the distance. The

---

[1] The Count would seem to have composed his *Mémoires* over a considerable number of years, perhaps beginning as early as 1704, as he suggests here. It is also clear that the parts of his writings relating to 1706 were written before 1723 (see p. 195 n. below), although it is also certain that he was working on his *Mémoires* when he was overtaken by his fatal illness in 1732 (see p. 145 above).

'enemy sentry' turned out to be a signpost marking a cross-roads! My advance guard pushed on to the village, and there discovered that all the commotion was caused by the local peasants, who were loading their valuables to move them away to safety. I was speechless with fury. I felt strongly inclined to put the wretch of a captain under close arrest, but I forbore.

A few days later the enemy arrived to besiege Landau [*24 October–28 November*], the Emperor himself hurrying across post-haste to be present at this event. M. Villeroi called up all his men in Alsace, including the garrison troops, and posted himself on the little River Queich in an attempt to daunt the enemy. His announced plan was to cover Landau, prevent the siege and even to fight a battle. But the moment they heard from a sure source that the enemy would without fail attack our position the next day, the army fell back the very same night. In the meantime M. Villeroi, who had refused to believe an enemy attack possible until he received definite intelligence, summoned to his aid all the debris of Tallard's army.

I then left Höchfeld with all speed, and came up with the army near Langenkandel in the act of falling rapidly back from the abandoned position on the Queich. The confusion and consternation that accompanied this manoeuvre had to be seen to be believed: the retreat resembled nothing more than a full-scale rout. M. Villeroi begged me to form the rearguard and to help his rabble by not getting in their way—an unpleasant duty, especially with a panicky lot of soldiers. So I allowed them to flood past me and took up the rear. The last squadrons of my rearguard had just reached the broad stream of Kronweissenburg when I spotted several enemy squadrons. I ordered my squadrons to turn about, and ordered a second line to be drawn up five hundred yards to their rear. The remainder of the rearguard awaited my orders a thousand yards behind the second line. When three or four enemy detachments had passed the stream, I charged them and flung them back to the farther bank in spite of their counter-attack. They followed me when I withdrew, but finding themselves up against a superior force they halted. I soon realized that the foe had only pushed a few detachments forward, and that he was too late to trouble our retreat, and so I ordered the remainder of the rearguard to follow the main army accompanied by the four squadrons which had already been engaged and had suffered some casualties. I then charged with six squadrons of the second line, leaving four in reserve. The enemy attacked us with great vigour, but we repulsed him again and he drew off and let us resume our original position. As my men withdrew, so did theirs—but I took the precaution of covering every stage of my retreat with several squadrons facing the enemy's direction. Quite a few men were killed and wounded during this sharp skirmish; on our side we lost about eighty killed and wounded and many horses.

And so we fell back through Sulz and the woods of Hagenau back to Höchfeld, whilst the enemy settled down to the siege of Landau and the Marshals Villeroi and Marsin began to build the lines of Hagenau.

A few days after the enemy laid siege to Landau, which they undertook with the greatest ease, I learnt that the Elector had set out for Strasbourg *en route* for the Low Countries. As I considered that the campaign was practically over and would end with the inevitable surrender of Landau [*28 November*], I wrote to the Elector asking permission to return to Flanders. Since the battle I had lost more than sixty horses through illness; all my baggage had been burnt; my personal expenditure during the campaign had been frightful; and I just had no idea how I could honour my debts and obligations with so much of my property ruined. To all this I added that I wanted to see my wife again. I sent my application to the Elector by hand of an officer, and he replied at once in most obliging terms and gave me the permission I sought.

I next wrote to Marshals Villeroi and Marsin at Hagenau, enclosing the Elector's letter, to ask their permission. They raised no objections, so I at once left Höchfeld and posted to Saverne, ordering my household to follow. I travelled in a post-chaise, attended by my valet, whilst a cook rode behind. Several days later I reached Sedan, where I purchased some fine pistols to replace the four or five pairs I had lost on my horses at Blenheim. Each horse's holsters, saddle and harness, pistols and other equipment cost me a cool thousand crowns, and I had lost a couple of horses whilst they were held by grooms and had three killed under me. Some days later, to my great joy, I once again reached Brussels and home.

V

The Campaign of 1705:
The Count Quits the Spanish
Service

The following winter [1704–5] I received orders to do duty at Malines. I told Bergeyck that I wanted to spend my period of winter quarters at home for once, especially as I had seen so much service since the outbreak of war. Moreover, the pay was only 600 crowns, and my services throughout the preceding year had brought me a mere thousand pistoles. A brigadier-general serving with his own regiment would be better off, for altogether he would receive more than 1,200 pistoles, even though the regiment itself might be worth only 1,000 crowns. War is like a game of hazard: men of means are ruined, men with nothing grow rich. A man can consume as much as a third of his capital by the time he reaches a high rank with sufficient emoluments attached to maintain himself fittingly from them alone; at least, that has been my experience.

One day I was closeted with Bergeyck, informing him of the true condition of the troops I had taken to Germany, when a letter arrived from Paris, forwarded to me at his house. Opening it in his study, I found it was from a friend of mine who was well placed to know what was in the wind. He warned me not to delude myself, and that no matter what anybody said it was certainly intended to give the commission of General of the Horse to Count Egmont. This was due to the influence of the Princesse des Ursins, who had returned to France in greater favour than ever and had made it a point of honour to take an interest in Count Egmont for his wife's sake. In actual fact the Count had become a Musketeer[1] in France during the lifetime of Charles II, his master, and during the period which his brother had spent at the Academy in Paris; there he had married Mlle de Conac, the niece of a sly and crafty bishop and a relative of the Princesse des Ursins, who accordingly hastened the advancement of Count Egmont.

1 A member of the *corps d'élite* of the *Maison du Roi*.

And so this gentleman, who had in the meantime purchased a French cavalry regiment in order to escape from the Musketeers, was to be made General of Horse in the Low Countries through Mme des Ursins's patronage; and, what is more, they were proposing to revive and re-establish this post (which was supposed to have been suppressed) for his benefit, and also in order to absorb the Spanish service within that of France.

I tore the signature off my letter and handed the text to Bergeyck for him to read. I told him I was pleased it had arrived so opportunely. He glanced through it, and then declared he could not credit the news, that it could not be true. I replied that it had come from a reliable source, and this being the case, he could assume *ipso facto* that I was no longer in the service of France and Spain. Nothing was further from my thoughts than to dictate to monarchs how they should comport themselves; they were the masters and might promote whomsoever they pleased. But I was also born a free man, and I would not serve a moment longer if such an injustice was done me, after my giving so much service, and that was for sure.

He sympathized, assuring me that he had nothing to do with it; he swore that he didn't even know anything about it, and I believe he spoke the truth. Indeed, I absolve both him and the Elector [*of Bavaria*] from any part in this matter. In the end I repeated to him that my resignation would not be put into effect if the invidious promotion never took place, but that it would stand as soon as it came into effect. All this took place in December 1704 or January 1705.

As spring approached, Marshal Villeroi was summoned to Paris towards the end of April to make plans and arrange dispositions for the coming campaign. He was duly consulted over this dispute, and to please Mme des Ursins, who had schemed the whole matter and whom he saw to be in high favour, he declared that we were all a pack of scoundrels and that he would not employ anyone who dared to grumble. With this declaration he came back from Paris.

As soon as I knew the appointment had been published I went to call on M. de Bergeyck, it happening to be a day on which he had plenty of company. As was his wont, he asked me to go into his study with him, but I replied that it was not necessary, as I had only come to tell him *quod dixi, dixi*, and thereupon made my way to the door. He ran after me to my coach and almost forcibly dragged me off to his office, pretending that he could not understand what I was talking about. I riposted that he ought certainly to be able to recollect what I had said to him in that very room. He then said 'Yes.' Thereupon I said that as the event had taken place, I was off. 'Where to?' 'To retire to my estates in Germany.' 'You won't be given leave.' 'A man of my rank does not require leave, and I won't ask for it. I give you my resignation.' 'When are you going?' 'Tomorrow.' 'I can obviously say nothing to you—but you must speak to the Elector.' 'I fully intend to do so, but as you are Minister of War I wished to tell you first; I shall now go to the Elector.' 'He won't let you go.' 'In no country in the world can an unwilling man be compelled to serve; if you want to put me under arrest you have twenty-four hours in which to do it in Brussels—or a further three days at Westerloo.' 'We can satisfy you and find some other suitable appointment.' 'It is impossible for you to promote me over the head of M. d'Egmont, but that is what I demand.'

I then left his house and went to court, where I found he had fore-stalled me and was already in conference with the Elector. After a quarter of an hour they allowed me to join them. I at once told the Elector that I could no longer serve with honour on account of what had transpired over M. d'Egmont, and that I had come to submit my resignation inasmuch as I could serve no longer, and that I was retiring from the service. The Elector replied that he could not accept the resignation of such as man as I, that he would write to the King and that he advised me not to act hastily. I told him I was very distressed to be unable to have the honour to continue to serve under his orders, and after some more conversation I took my leave.

Bergeyck came over to see me that same afternoon and said a great deal. 'You are out of your mind,' he said; 'I can tell you that as a friend; you are esteemed more than anybody else, so why do you want to throw away all your appointments and deserts so suddenly?' 'I am losing them in spite of myself,' I replied, seeking to console him. 'We will give you permanent command over our troops in Germany, with identical and even greater authority than before.' 'Nevertheless, some stroke of fate may ordain that the Flemish Army should march to join the troops in Germany, in which case M. d'Egmont, being in com-mand of one of the lines, will be in a position to give me an order. Do you want to see me compelled to answer him with a bullet?' 'Well, what are you going to do?' 'Plant cabbages.' 'A man of your quality cannot plant cabbages!' 'That is nevertheless my intention.' 'You will have to give your word that you will never serve the Emperor.' 'At least in his country one can do as one wishes—you are not forced to serve, as you are in France. All I will say to you is that if the Emperor offers me a position in his service, which I don't believe for a moment he will, I promise to anoint myself with Holy Water when the thought comes to me; but if the Holy Water fails to wash away the notion, I will quite happily do my best to make you all regret treating me so badly.'

All this was said laughingly, but I straight away ordered the preparation of my mules, coaches and wagons ready to leave the next day, and announced my decision to my wife.

[*After taking formal leave of Marshal Villeroi, the Elector and several friends, and returning to Bergeyck the warrant appointing him to his various appointments for the next six months, the Count set out with twenty-four mules, three six-horse coaches, twelve spare horses, six four-horse coaches and a large retinue, the populace lining the streets of Brussels to see his departure.*]

We spent three days at Westerloo, and eventually moved on to Petersheim with all our attendants at about the time that the Duke of Marlborough took his army up the Moselle. The Duke wished the Prince of Baden to join him there, but this was out of the question— partly on account of the shortage of supplies, and partly because the latter had no wish to do so on account of Marlborough. There is no doubt that Prince Louis was an experienced general, and the other much less so, for the country was stripped of everything, and Marshal Villars had taken up a good position at Sierck, where he enjoyed the good fortune of adding lustre to his reputation without being attacked.

M. de Overkirk was at this time entrenched to the teeth with the Dutch army on Mont St Pierre, close to Maastricht. When I reached Petersheim, I had no wish to unburden my troubles to anyone, so I contented myself with asking M. de Montagne, Chief Burgomaster of Maastricht—a truly honest man, one of my tenants at Petersheim and very devoted to my family—to go and greet him on my behalf and seek permission for my coaches to pass over the bridge at Maastricht. In due course I received permission to travel through the town, and so after three days' sojourn at Petersheim I set out for Aix-la-Chapelle. I had found my poor property at Petersheim truly ruined— as it had been the last time I visited it in 1702 on my way to Liège. This was due to the different encampments and comings and goings of armies, and above all to the camp at Lanaken.

[*The Count goes on to criticize the Allies for failing to act aggressively and the ill-effects this had on his property, and then describes his journey through Maastricht and the various acquaintances he met on his way to Aix-la-Chapelle.*]

While I was at Aix, the Elector Palatine (with whom I had been in correspondence since the death of the King),[1] wrote to me that he was delighted I had at last joined the just cause, and that he hoped I would go the whole way and serve the ancient House of Austria as I and my family had always done previously. He further exhorted me to make up my mind, and said that he would write to the Emperor, and, pending his reply, offered to restore to me my estate of Mérode which he was holding sequestered. I thanked him for his continued interest, and stressed how pleased I was to have returned my allegiance to the august House of Austria. However, I also told him that although I was quite certain that I had been honourably entitled to quit my former service on account of the injustices they had inflicted upon me, I was nevertheless determined to reside quietly on my estates and spend the rest of my life as a faithful servant of His Imperial Majesty.

The Elector replied that he was glad to see that I had made up my mind, but went on to say that he felt certain that a man of my character had not been born into this world in order to spend his life planting cabbages. . . . He would write to His Imperial Majesty and suggest that he should give me the post that his enemies had so unjustly refused me. . . . And in due course a courier arrived from Vienna bringing my commission as General of the Emperor's Horse together with a most flattering letter from His Imperial Majesty.

I had originally arrived at Aix [-la-Chapelle] in May 1705, and this happened the following August. I was both surprised and embarrassed by this development; on the one hand, in order to preserve my Westerloo property from harm I did not wish to adopt either party; on the other, my old leanings towards the House of Austria tempted me to take service. I began by sending Kessel to Brussels to rescue all my furnishings, but in his fear he quite needlessly burnt about 3,000 crowns' worth of my furniture and other possessions.

About this time I also learnt that the French *Maison du Roi* had pillaged my château at Westerloo on two separate occasions, and also cruelly despoiled all the villages. This angered me greatly, but I nevertheless wrote to the Elector Palatine telling him that although

---

[1] A rather obscure reference: probably refers to the Emperor Leopold I (who died in May 1705), whom Parker refers to as 'The King of the Romans' (the Emperor's secondary title) on p. 48 above; alternatively, it might refer to Charles II of Spain but this is less likely in the present context.

my desire was to enter His Imperial Majesty's service completely, I could not deem myself worthy of the honour until I had first observed all the preliminary forms that were expected of a man of my degree. So, before accepting the commission H.I.M. had done me the honour of sending, I begged his leave to write again to King Philip and the Most Christian King [*Louis XIV*] in spite of the fact that I had already submitted my resignation.

I awaited their replies, but received none. At length, after waiting a long time, with the Elector Palatine always telling me that it was time to come out into the open, I wrote to M. de Bergeyck and M. de Chamillart to the effect that owing to all the injustices I had suffered . . . [*here the Count once more catalogues all his grievances*] . . . I was accepting the offers and favours that His Imperial Majesty so earnestly wished to confer on me, and that I hoped to serve the Emperor sufficiently well to enable me to make them rue the day they had wronged me. I did not wait for replies to these letters—nor did I receive any.

While all this was going on, the Elector of Bavaria and M. de Villeroi besieged and captured Huy [*28 May–10 June 1705*] making the most of the absence of the Duke of Marlborough's army. They were on the point of meting out the same treatment to the citadel of Liège, while M. d'Overkirk lay snug within his entrenchments on Mont St Pierre, when the Duke of Marlborough returned by forced marches, after being obliged to abandon his Moselle design. He complained bitterly about the Prince of Baden. Perhaps the latter wished to be avenged for the slight he suffered at Hochstadt [*Blenheim*];[1] even more probably there were insufficient supplies and forage to support the army—or so some said. The English army accordingly passed on its way through my Mérode property, and a large number of English Officers came to Aix, where they danced with the ladies at La Fontaine every morning to the hautbois music of their army musicians. Every evening they danced, dined and supped at my house.[2]

At this time I committed two mistakes. The first was not to go straight to Vienna, but the difficulty of taking my wife there—or, alternatively, the double expense that would have been incurred in leaving her at Aix—dissuaded me. The second was not to go and see the Duke of Marlborough as he passed by to inform him of the

[1] See Parker, p. 51 above.

[2] See p. 52–3 n. above.

decision I had reached. Had I acted in this manner I would indubitably have been employed at once, and would probably have avoided all the annoyances which I suffered thereafter—and for that matter even to this day. However, my wish to protect my Westerloo property was one contributory factor, for even if they did not confiscate it they could still ruin it by laying it utterly waste. Then again there were the problems posed by my wife and children and the debts I had amassed during such a long period of misfortune, and these considerations also induced me to make the stupid blunder of staying on at Aix-la-Chapelle.

The Duke of Marlborough, after joining Marshal Overkirk while the foe were planning to attack the citadel at Liège, quickly made them drop this scheme, and soon they were falling back by forced marches to shelter within their lines near Tirlemont. These positions were so extensive that they were obliged to detach several corps to guard them, placing their men in a long line, closely spaced. The Duke surprised them there and broke through this famous scarecrow of a position. Thirty French squadrons hastened up after he had already passed the lines in force, and he charged and beat them so effectively that he was able to move his entire army into their lines [*17/18 July 1705*]. The enemy was so terror-stricken that they fled—rather than retired—without fighting, back beyond Louvain, placing the River Dyle before them. If the Duke had only listened to me, and had wished to follow my advice to follow the enemy up diligently instead of amusing himself capturing two battalions in the paltry fortress of Tirlemont [*18 July 1705*], he could have done everything during this year which he eventually achieved in the next.[1] As it was he afforded the enemy leisure to draw themselves up at their ease behind the Dyle and near Louvain; as a result, when the army had taken Tirlemont and at last marched to camp at Parck, they found it impossible to attack them. And so, after making various probing moves for several days, Louvain and the Dyle always separating the two armies, our troops marched off towards Aerschot and captured Diest.

The enemy army then set about raising new lines from the River Nethe to the River Demer while our army came back to camp on my property, leaving Aerschot and the Demer to its left and the Nethe to

1 Mérode-Westerloo makes no mention of Marlborough's attempts to force the French into a decisive battle near Waterloo (18 August). On this occasion—as on so many others —he was thwarted by the obstructive attitude of the Dutch Deputies attached to his army. (See p. 57 above.)

the right, razing the old lines which Verboom had made through my property at Ramsel, despite all I had said in 1702, before setting out for Italy. On that occasion I had dined with Marshal Boufflers and the Marquis de Bedmar, and had strongly represented that their lines would be better, shorter and far easier to defend if they placed them where, in fact, they did the second time. Nevertheless this same Verboom destroyed incalculable amounts of my timber and lands, and ruthlessly ravaged all my territory.

After the Duke of Marlborough had spent several days in his camp, during which time all my villages and even the château were pillaged and looted to the stunned surprise of my slow-witted tenantry, he established a garrison at Diest—a move that proved to be a great mistake. He then marched away through my marquisate to build another camp at the other end, still on my property, for although he moved his headquarters to Herenthals, the whole of his army was camped at Oolen. Thus, having been ruined on one side, I was now ruined on the other as well, and whatever excesses the French had not wrought to avenge themselves against me were now performed by these others—as the best of friends—and I suffered losses that would have ruined a lesser man. Then, having spent several days in this second camp, they at last marched away towards Antwerp, and went off to besiege Santvliet [or Santoliet, 23–29 October] which they burnt to the ground [31 October].

Next the enemy, making the most of the fault Marlborough had committed in leaving a garrison in Diest, made it prisoner of war and kept it to exchange for their troops at Santvliet and Tirlemont. And so this campaign ended almost where it had begun. It must be asserted that the Duke of Marlborough held his foes in excessively high esteem, and was too respectful towards the phantasmagoria of their lines—or else had some other motive that I do not know about.[1] All this time I spent at Aix, spending a great deal of money and growing very bored in spite of the new faces I saw from time to time.

[1] The obstructive attitude of the Dutch Deputies is the main factor that Mérode-Westerloo fails to take into account.

VI

The Campaign of 1706:
Ramillies and Turin

While still at Aix in 1706 we observed the famous eclipse that took place at the very moment that King Philip raised the siege of Barcelona [*12 May*]. This year proved almost fatal to France, for she also lost her formidable army besieging Turin [*7 September 1706*], the capture of which would have assured the French of the domination of Italy. She already enjoyed a preponderance of power through the influence of Pope Albani [*Clement XI*], who controlled the Duke of Parma, and through the power wielded by the French Crown over the Duchy of Mantua. Indeed, Italy was only saved by a very handful of men, thanks to the brains of the Duke of Savoy, Victor Amadeus II, and the victories of Prince Eugène, who, to his honour, recalled that he was more a Savoyard than a Mancini.[1] The Duke of Savoy, aware of the critical situation, did everything he could to save himself, and profited happily from the inexperience of the Austrian Minister, the young Count of Auersperg (who was under the spell of the Countess de la Trinité), by concluding a treaty which gave all the districts of Alessandria, Liniegiana, Tortona, Valenzia, Mortara and Vigevanso to Savoy.

This celebrated agreement made the Duke of Savoy master of the Milanese—and will perhaps render him master of all Italy in the near future, thanks to his cunning. This treaty also led directly to the happy outcome (the battle of Turin), which was the result of the combination of Prince Eugène's beneficent destiny and the great intelligence of the Duke of Savoy—his inspiration, lord and master. Had the numerous French only sallied out from their positions (as the Duc d'Orléans, the present Regent and possibly the future King of France, advised),[2] instead of standing fast within their lines in accordance with the orders

---

[1] His mother was a niece of Cardinal Mazarin, an Italian.

[2] It is evident that this part of the *Mémoires* was prepared before 1723, as that year saw the death of the Duc d'Orléans.

issued by that pedant M. de Chamillart to his relative the young Duc de Feuillade, they should have been able—with fortune on their side— to crush the bold Eugène; for he had exposed his whole army without reserves, and all the Emperor's interests in Italy into the bargain, in order to save his cousin. This episode illustrates how a fortunate bold- ness, indulged in without any knowledge of the outcome, can some- times succeed. Prince Eugène was inspired by a strong dynastic loyalty, which makes his performance even more impressive. With 22,000 men, joined by 6,000 more from the Duke of Savoy's army, he attacked and defeated an army of 70,000 troops, drawn up within strong entrenchments, who should have been capable of crushing double the force that had the temerity to attack them and the good fortune to overwhelm them, had they but come out from their positions.[1]

Thus the deliverance of Barcelona, the battle of Turin, and, most wonderful of all, the battle of Ramillies, all took place in this one year. Had we only known and decided to exploit our advantages in Spain and the Low Countries, we would not now be in the state we are. Whether through ignorance or malice, or because Destiny decreed it, we managed affairs so capably that we wasted our opportunities in both Spain and the Low Countries. However, in Italy the campaign ended with the treaty [*13 March 1707*] by which the French agreed to evacuate the whole area in a single day (in spite of the reverse suffered by the Prince of Hesse [*the battle of Castiglione, 9 September 1706*] under the eyes of his father the Landgrave, who was serving as a volunteer in his army), an outcome that was honourable for the Emperor, but still more profitable for the Duke of Savoy.

As for our campaign in Flanders, it opened when the enemy advanced before our army was fully concentrated. Learning that the Danish contingents were still some way off, the French believed them- selves to be the stronger army, and accordingly began to advance. They had no idea that the Allies were so close at hand. As a result the two armies met near Ramillies on the day of Pentecost [*23 May 1706*],

[1] Churchill (Book Two, p. 173) gives the following figures for the casualties sustained on both sides in this battle:

Allies—over 5,000 killed and wounded;
French—3,000 killed and wounded and 6,000 prisoners.

The historian Bodart places them as follows (p. 149):
Allies—4,300 (including 5 generals);
French—7,000.

just a few hours after the Duke of Württemberg and the Danes had joined the army. The French army protected its left behind some inaccessible places, and through overconfidence placed only the *Maison du Roi* on their right, believing this formation to be more valiant than Alexander the Great's phalanx. In fact this formation was soon broken up by a newly raised regiment of Danish dragoons, as the French failed to support it; in brief, our left wing cut this 'invincible' phantom dressed in gold and silver to pieces in a matter of minutes. Their centre soon followed them from the field, and their left wing did the same without being attacked.[1] We pursued them somewhat farther than the previous year. Because this battle was principally an artillery affair and we suffered only 1,500 casualties, and because we chased them closely without affording them any time to re-form, our forces drove them past the Dyle and Louvain and even across the Brussels canal. Still in dire confusion, the enemy fled for Ghent, and the victors followed them by forced marches, inducing them to abandon Bruges and almost all the Low Countries, apart from the very strongest places, in their eagerness to retire within their fortresses in the conquered areas.

The first siege we undertook was that of Ostend, a town that had become famous during the revolt of the Netherlands for withstanding a siege of three years and three months [*1601–04*], but on this occasion it surrendered in exactly three days [*in fact on 9 July*].[2] After this fortunate success, we proceeded to amuse ourselves besieging Menin for no really valid reason; this beautiful and well-fortified township fought it out with us, but was of no real significance, as it neither dominated any of our country nor uncovered any of the enemy's [*Menin surrendered on 22 August*]. Thereafter we finished the campaign by laying siege to Ath, which also held out a long time [*until 1 October*]. If, on the other hand, instead of amusing ourselves at Menin, we had undertaken the siege of Mons, which at that time would have offered no more resistance than Ostend, as there was only a single battalion in the town; and if, later, we had set out to capture Maubeuge, we could have reached Paris that same year, for we would have possessed a string of fortresses which could have protected our country and at

1 Although the Count was apparently present, he gives a very slight and misleading description of what was, probably, Marlborough's greatest victory. See above, p. 60–2, for Parker's fuller and more reliable account.

2 'Three *weeks*' would have been more accurate; possibly a slip of the quill. The siege of Ostend lasted from 19 June to 9 July.

the same time have opened up the enemy's. However, although I suggested this to the Duke of Marlborough and the Army Deputies they did nothing about it.[1] I don't believe that the Duke of Marlborough and Cadogan had any desire to make peace so soon; I even consider that my making so good a suggestion made them wish me ill, for not only did they want to dispense with my services thereafter they also set out to blacken my reputation with Prince Eugène.[2]

This was not the only mistake which this motive led them to commit; they also made weighty political errors by setting up a government of men expressly sent from Ghent by the French for this very purpose; they would have gone still further had not the clever M. de Bergeyck checked their misapplied zeal. Moreover, one of the Dutch Deputies [*probably the notorious Colonel Goslinga*] accompanying the army was very much in the French pocket.

As for me, I eventually left Aix after a fourteen-month sojourn, paying 14,000 crowns in promissory notes drawn upon my estates to settle all my debts—my bailiffs in due course producing every penny. At this time Aix was riddled with French sympathizers, and Maquinet, a friend of theirs in the Namur garrison, took it into his head to take me prisoner. To this end he laid an ambush with 500 men, dividing them into several detachments between Galoppe and Aix. The garrison of Maastricht was very sparse, being continuously called upon to provide escorts for convoys of all sorts on their way up to the front, and this obliged me to remain a further eight days at Aix before I could venture forth with my not inconsiderable baggage-train in safety. At length I was on the point of setting out following the arrival of 250 infantry and fifty cavalry sent by the Governor of Maastricht, when a courier from that same officer brought news warning me that the enemy was reputed to be considerably stronger than my escort, and that he would send off a further 300 men the next day to meet us at Galoppe or the Forest of Aix. Accordingly I set out at about seven o'clock, and on reaching the Forest of Aix we discovered the enemy in position. I descended from my coach and mounted a horse, divided my infantry into five platoons supported by

[1] The complete 'conquest' of the Spanish Netherlands was considered as the vital prerequisite for any future advance over the French frontier towards Paris.

[2] This sense of being slighted—whether true or false—soon developed into the most extreme jealousy and persecution-mania. The Count has hardly a single good word for the two greatest soldiers of the day in any part of his narrative. It would seem that the Count grossly overestimated their hostility (see above, p. xiv).

the cavalry, and then marched the first two platoons forward towards
the enemy. To our great surprise they turned and fled without waiting
for us, and we were even more astounded to see more troops moving
into sight behind them. This induced us to halt. At length I decided
to march towards the new-comers, having put everyone on the alert,
as they were advancing towards us. We then discovered that this was
the second escort coming from Maastricht to join us—the enemy
having spotted them first. We left our advanced guard with them,
and made our way peacefully on to Galoppe, where I refreshed my
household and escort—taking all necessary precautions. I ate some fine
trout there, I remember. Then I continued on my way, passing
Maastricht, and went to bed at Petersheim. I wished to stay there for
some time, but the very next evening the Commandant of Maastricht
advised me that it was not safe; he had heard that the foe was sending
out several more detachments from Namur, and on the basis of this
news begged me to come into the town as he would not be able to
come to my assistance speedily enough if I was attacked in my château,
whose garrison was very weak. Accordingly I set out at ten that night,
and entered the town with all my suite.

[*In due course the Count moved on to Westerloo and Malines, and
thence to Brussels, where for a time he was embroiled in political intrigues
with the pro-French ministry set up by the Allies.*]

A few days after my arrival there (at Brussels), I went to wait upon
the Duke of Marlborough. He was currently encamped at Helchin
while General Salin invested Menin. The Duke paid me a thousand
compliments. On my return to the city I went back to the ancient
Hôtel de Chimay, where I had previously stayed. As I had lost both
of my own town houses during the bombardment, I was particularly
eager to obtain an establishment in Brussels—at that time a very
significant matter for a man of family. And so I bought the ancient
Hôtel de Croy (in the year 1706). That same year I lost my younger
daughter, who had been born on 30 December 1704. She died aged
eighteen months—almost the precise age of her brother at the time of
his death.

VII

The Campaigns of 1707 and 1708

[*After describing the bad characteristics of the new Government set up by the Allies in Brussels in 1706, the Count goes on to outline the main events in Spain (omitted here, since the author was not an eyewitness) before returning to his main theme, the war in Flanders.*]

If only we had wished to be governed by the rules of common sense during 1706, we could have been masters of Spain, Italy and the Low Countries—and the following year might have seen us in Paris. Everything was lost, however, thanks to intrigue and errors, and France was given time to assume the guise of a fox, having had her original lion-skin badly rent! Selfish interests proved our undoing. It would not have cost much in terms of men, time or money to have captured Mons and Maubeuge instead of Menin and Ath—and our conquests would then have been consolidated in such a way that both the business of Ghent and the siege of Brussels could have been avoided. We would have been at Paris, forcing the foe to disgorge these places for nothing, although in actual fact their capture cost the lives of many men. When Marlborough said he wished to conquer Spain by way of France, he was on the right road; but it was a mistake to attack France on a sector where she possessed four or five lines of the finest fortresses in Europe, whereby we left all our own large towns and the very heart of the country completely exposed. These were such gross mistakes that the leaders must have been blind not to see them.[1]

[*The Count next turns to consider the Italian theatre (omitted here), acidly commenting that the Prince Eugène's private ambitions led to the ruin of the true Allied interests in Naples and Sicily—and ultimately to the fiasco before Toulon in 1707. See pp. 69n above and 251 below.*]

---

[1] Mérode-Westerloo doubtless had the French bombardment of Brussels (*22–27 November*) in mind when he penned this complaint. Perhaps there is a grain of truth in his criticism, however, when he asserts the Allies were blind to attack France on its strongest side. Marlborough himself was to advocate (in 1708, after Oudenarde) an advance along the coast to the River Somme—ignoring the complex fortress barrier and relying for supply on the Anglo-Dutch fleet—but this radical suggestion found no favour with his Allies.

In the Low Countries, however, the year 1707 passed without seeing any stirring events. It merely proved useful—like every other year—to the Duke of Marlborough's pocket. Matters were very different, however, the following year, when there were a whole series of prodigious efforts and equally enormous errors taking place on every side, the Allies emerging at the end with all the glory and advantage more by luck than judgement.

The campaign opened with a calculated advance by the Duke of Marlborough, who was awaiting the arrival of Prince Eugène and his army. The Elector of Bavaria and the Duke of Vendôme, kept fully informed of what was happening by Count Bergeyck at Ghent, made a move which appeared to threaten the camp at Louvain, hoping thereby to induce us to change our plans. This indeed made us take to 'burning the road' again, making a forced march in an attempt to place ourselves across their path. One column of our army passed round Brussels, and then proceeded down the canal to the bridge of Laeken and the small River Senne; the other marched through the covered way past Brussels, leaving the town to its left.

A few days earlier I had received news from a reliable source advising me to take good care of Ghent and Bruges, which were soon to be betrayed to the enemy. This information came to me from Lille, and from such a sure quarter that its validity could not be doubted. I hurried over to break the news to M. van den Bergh, the Dutch Deputy at Brussels. He asked me to pass it on to the Duke of Marlborough. This I did, but he treated my news as something of no account, telling me that it was impossible,[1] and I could say nothing to make him change his mind. I told this to van den Bergh, and sent a private warning to Colonel d'Audignies of my dragoons, who was at the time encamped with his four squadrons outside the gates of Ghent, alongside two battalions under the command of General Murray. The colonel showed this to General Murray, and two days later he received an almost identical warning which he forwarded to me, for he had more capability for intrigue than soldiering and was one of the best 'gifts' the Dutch ever gave us. I absolutely refused to speak further on the subject to Milord Duke, and Murray for his part dared do nothing about it, as his orders simply told him to stay where he

---

[1] If this story is true, it would seem to reveal that Marlborough was completely fooled by the French stratagems of early 1708. There is no doubt at all that the events of early July represented a considerable setback to the Allies, although the subsequent battle of Oudenarde more than redressed the balance.

was. At length, on the urgings of d'Audignies, he tried to make his way into the town to place a guard on the gates, but neither enterprise prospered. For the magistrates, on the pretext that they wished to economize on billets, fire and candles (and who had also given Cadogan [*Marlborough's Quartermaster-General*] 400 pistoles to ensure that troops would not enter the town), opposed his move, wishing, they said, to see an express order to this effect from the Duke of Marlborough, which they were quite sure he would not have received. All this happened two days before the enemy's arrival. General Murray's hands being effectively tied, he was forced to stay outside the gates right up to the time that La Faille, an enemy infantry brigadier-general and Grand Bailiff of Ghent, advanced up to the gates with between 1,200 and 1,500 men under cover of darkness, and took possession of them [*5/6 July*], finding only a couple of ancient burghermilitiamen on guard, who neither dared nor knew how to close the gates or raise the drawbridge. He then proceeded to occupy the gate facing the small camp, which was still closed, the keys being, as was the custom, in the town hall. Thereafter he easily took over all the others, and opened fire on General Murray, who was forced to fall back to Sas-le-Gand [*Sas-von-Ghent*] while the enemy reinforced their garrison. Instead of marching to Louvain, Murray hurried off as fast as possible to pass over the River Dendre.

This little contretemps again caused the Duke of Marlborough to begin marching with a vengeance, and he was soon crossing over the canal and heading for the Dendre. He could have fought and annihilated the larger part of the enemy army in its vicinity, for they still had not completed their crossing and were caught in the middle of the operation in a state of incredible haste and confusion; but instead of fighting he amused himself at the mill of Tomberg, leaving them undisputed masters of the Dendre to their front, enabling them to cover Ghent and at the same time go and take possession of Bruges as well [*in fact, 5 July*]. A single squadron of my regiment caused a complete panic to spread through their whole rearguard by getting in amongst their baggage trains, making a good booty the while. But all the time the English Duke stood passively by, apparently awaiting the arrival of Prince Eugène's army which his right wing under Cadogan had set off to meet near Maastricht. The enemy made a grave error by failing to send off a strong detachment to occupy Oudenarde, where there were no troops at that time. Although I personally stressed the need to send two or three regiments of dragoons post-haste to Oudenarde, the Duke chose to do nothing about it[1] until Cadogan arrived back, who at once understood the vital importance of such a step and had them sent off. As a result they reached Oudenarde so late that it was almost too late, but with their usual 'heroes' luck' our commanders managed to save everything.

During this time Prince Eugène reached Brussels, riding ahead of his army, and descended from his coach at Cadogan's quarters, the Hôtel de Coupignies. He paid a very short and cold visit to his mother, whom he had not seen since their journey to Spain. This lady, who was ambitious and expected to be adored and accorded the very best of treatment by everybody, was very offended by this extreme coolness, and her death was attributed to the chagrin she felt—and from which she never recovered, despite the fact that the Prince later stayed with her for several days in an attempt to make her forget the matter. . . .

Eugène all on his own joined the Duke of Marlborough at the time when the Imperial army was moving towards Dieghem by way of Louvain. Many people award him all the credit for making the crossing over the Scheldt at Oudenarde, as duly took place, at the only possible place; as it was the enemy was close enough to be both in view and within cannon range.[2] As a result our army crossed the river in haste through Oudenarde and over some bridges built below the town. While this was proceeding the army was busily fighting, and in the end, despite the position hastily taken up amongst hedges and ditches lined by the enemy, we emerged the victors of the famous and memorable day of Oudenarde, 11 July 1708.[3] This action was more of an encounter than a set-piece battle, but had it only been followed up as both should and could have been done, the destiny of not only

[1] There is considerable contemporary evidence that Marlborough was far from well over this period. Lediard claims that the Duke was 'much indisposed and feverish' (*Life of John, Duke of Marlborough*, vol. II, p. 155) the day after Prince Eugène's arrival, and Churchill (Book Two, p. 351) supports this assertion.

[2] Rather an exaggeration. The enemy was taken almost completely unawares by the Allied crossing, and their nearest positions were one and a half miles from the pontoon bridges laid over the Scheldt. Nevertheless, the operation did involve a considerable risk, as Marlborough himself freely admitted after the battle was over. In his dispatch he wrote: 'When I left England, I was positively resolved to endeavour by all means a battle, thinking nothing else would make the Queen's business go on well. This reason only made me venture the battle yesterday—otherwise I did give them [*the enemy*] too much advantage.' (Coxe, *Memoirs of John, Duke of Marlborough*, vol. IV, p. 154.)

[3] See above, p. 73–4 and n., for further details of this battle.

the Spanish monarchy—over which the whole war was being waged, or so they said—but that of France and Europe, might well have been decided. For the enemy, in full flight up the Ghent canal in all the customary disorder of a French defeat, shut themselves away between that waterway, the Dutch fortresses, an area of partially inundated countryside and the sea, except for a few battalions which retired towards Tournai. If only we had attacked them the next morning, they would have been faced with no alternative but to retreat into the sea or to lay down their arms. Accompanying their army, moreover, were two princes in the succession to the French throne, the Dukes of Burgundy and Berry. Although our victorious army could in any case have launched their blow, there were, of course, the completely fresh forces of Prince Eugène. By passing through our town of Dendermonde they could have turned the enemy's flank while the victorious main army maintained the frontal pressure. Instead of doing this, however, they stood by with their arms folded.[1]

Not only did we waste time, thus affording the enemy the chance to reorganize and fortify, but we also stayed fast in our camp, although it was known that at this time Lille was defended by only a single battalion. For no good reason we wished to besiege the place, but instead of doing so immediately we gave the foe time to throw into this strong place twenty-five battalions, some dragoons, cavalry, munitions—under Marshal Boufflers and a proportionate number of general officers. Only then did we undertake the investment [*from 11 August 1708*], heedless of where our convoys were to come from, what with the enemy possessing all the fortresses interposed between them [*the depots*] and the army they were expected to sustain. Had the generals only attacked Tournai, and not Lille, we would have opened up a safe line of communication with our bases,[2] and at the same time

[1] A complete travesty of the truth. In fact, the greater part of Eugène's army was fully engaged observing the Duke of Berwick's French army, which was operating from the direction of Namur in a threatening manner.

[2] There is scant evidence to support this assertion. Although the capture of Tournai would have opened up the waters of the Middle Scheldt to the Allies—and thus possibly have facilitated some of their communication problems—it is very unlikely that the large garrison of Lille (not more than ten miles away) would have stood idly by. In other words, Lille had to be dealt with before Tournai could be besieged.

Nevertheless, Marlborough was not very eager to undertake the siege of Lille. He preferred a more imaginative plan for a descent upon France along the Channel coast.

In any case, the continued French occupation of Bruges and Ghent farther up the Scheldt constituted the real problem concerning the Allied army's communications with

continued to protect our own country and opened up a sure road towards Lille, by taking up a position on the Scheldt. As it was, we left all of Brabant and Brussels exposed—the latter being without fortifications or garrison, wide open to attack on the Meuse side (where the Elector of Bavaria was situated) and surrounded by Charleroi, Namur, Ghent and an army totalling 80,000 men led by princes of the blood, the Elector of Bavaria (who also had plenty of sympathizers throughout the country) and Marshal the Duke of Vendôme. Even this was not enough—for we felt compelled to attack the strongest sector of the whole region—the fortress of Lille, King Louis XIV's favourite conquest, which had been fortified with infinite care and at huge expense [*by Vauban*].

Accordingly off we set to besiege this place, taking no care whence we would draw our convoys, never consulting a map, and leaving this large enemy army—which could have been completely crushed a little earlier—in unchallenged occupation of all the positions and river lines, supported by good towns on all sides. It certainly required an extraordinary degree of good fortune to enable the escort of one convoy to defeat a greatly superior adversary which attacked it at Wynendael [*28 September 1708*].[1] One result of this, following the capture of Lille on 23 October after an investment that only dated from 13 August, was to afford us with the chance to re-cross the Scheldt and put to flight the entire enemy army without recourse to a major battle, in spite of the fact that the foe was holding the strongest conceivable series of posts behind the river. Similarly, we were able to put the Elector of Bavaria to flight after he had attacked Brussels [*22–27 November 1708*], forcing him to abandon his guns there. Then we returned to besiege the citadel of Lille with our hands somewhat freer than formerly, but it only yielded on 8 [*some sources say 10*] December. Even then, despite the lateness of the season, we still had the good fortune to take possession of both Ghent and its garrison, which was made up of formations drawn from the enemy's complete army, and also Bruges on 1 January 1709—the eve of the worst frost and bitterest winter weather known to the memory of man. During

---

its bases. Marlborough might have been better advised to settle finally with the remains of Vendôme's forces before trying conclusions with Boufflers in Lille, but Mérode-Westerloo does not make this point.

1 See Parker, p. 79 above, for a fuller account of Major-General Webb's considerable success against long odds.

that winter you saw men and horses freeze to death on the march; this actually happened to my regiment, which lost two troopers and their horses frozen to death on the road between Vilvorde and Malines. They had marched with the regiment on 2 January 1709, wrapped up in their cloaks, but they were nevertheless frozen solid mounted on their horses, which also remained upright. This may seem incredible, but it really happened.

The combination of gross faults and blind good fortune of our two generals during this campaign truly beggars belief. For, besides the other errors I have already recounted, they only summoned a single middle-sized convoy from Brussels—albeit with great difficulty and risk—as if they considered Lille to be a fortress of scant significance. Then, short of everything, scattered in all directions and harassed by the enemy army, they had recourse to bringing convoys from Ostend for as long as the enemy held Bruges, the supplies having first arrived at Ostend from Zeeland and Holland by sea.[1]

I have not yet spoken about the affair of the gunpowder, which Prince Eugène has informed the world was the fault of Count Schlick, who as Commissary-General and an Imperial Field-Marshal was second in command (under Eugène) of the Imperial troops. Count Schlick was sent off with a detachment to cover the siege and observe the enemy. In spite of their fair-sized magazines, the French conducted their defence with so much determination and vigour that they soon ran short of powder. Lieutenant-General the Chevalier de Luxembourg (the present Prince of Tingry) accordingly mustered 3,000 cavalry, each trooper carrying a bag of gunpowder across his crupper, and managed to make his way close to Schlick's camp. That officer unfortunately permitted them to pass through, as they arrived by night and spoke German. When they came close to our vedettes— one of whom was a man from my regiment, the other being drawn from the Regiment of Palffy—they called out that they were friends. However, they went on their way in such a hasty and anxious fashion that the suspicions of my trooper were aroused, and he tried to investigate them further. As they none the less continued to spur past at high speed, he decided to fire at them and thus give the alarm and then save both himself and his comrade. During this time their parent

---

[1] There can be no denying that the Allied arrangments for supplying the troops besieging Lille were extremely perilous. Nevertheless, the use of shipping to supply Ostend is an interesting example of the advantages conferred by naval command of the Channel— and illustrates Marlborough's awareness of sea-power and its implications.

formations retired in another direction, and my horseman accordingly rode in himself to Prince Eugène's headquarters to give the alarm at a time when the enemy were actually still within our lines. One of their parties sped along the whole length of a regiment of dragoons, giving rise to suspicion. Our men seized their arms and opened fire; this made several sparks to set fire to some of the enemy's powder bags; in an instant several hundred of them were hurled into the air amidst a terrifying explosion which shook the earth. As it turned out between six and seven hundred of the men in the centre and van of the column reached the city, but those in the rear turned about and made for Douai. As their powder-bags were made of linen and not of leather, several sprung leaks, leaving a trail of powder along the road behind them. As they rode their horseshoes made the sparks fly up which set fire to the powder-trail and this in turn ignited the sacks, blowing up a number of men and horses with an infernal din. It was a horrible spectacle to see the remains of men and horses, whose legs, arms and torsos even had been flung into the trees. As for the Count of Schlick (the present Grand Chancellor of Bohemia), he returned very ill and discontented to Brussels. He never saw anyone while he remained there—and never even visited me—but gambled every evening. He left for Vienna a short time ahead of Prince Eugène, travelling by short stages with all his entourage. He was a man of spirit, but was hardly the friend of Prince Eugène.

Despite the presence of their Commissary-General and the General-issimo, this large force of Imperial troops were provided with hardly any money, and as a result many were soon dying of hunger, most particularly the infantry regiment of Trenck, which had achieved prodigies at the siege of Brussels under their brave and honest Lieuten-ant-Colonel Bettendorf. These poor fellows would have died of hunger and exposure in the open streets had not the charity of the citizens of Brussels induced them to take them into their houses and feed them, thus saving over half the regiment. As for the rest of our forces, we were obliged to pledge all our revenue for twelve years to the Dutch in return for bread, forage and the wherewithal to pay the troops and to fatten the commissaries and generals.

Recently I have only spoken of my regiment in passing. I must retrace my steps some little way to mention that immediately after the battle of Ramillies and the setting-up of the new government I worked hard to persuade the English and Dutch to raise a (Walloon) corps of troops for the King so as to enable them to occupy the country in his name. When I had at last convinced them—not without considerable trouble, I might add, on account of their unspoken prejudices—I found myself with an even greater obstacle to surmount, put in my way by our fine government. Thanks to the insinuations of Count Bergeyck, who wrote to the two powers four or five times declaring that it was impossible for the country to sustain a single regiment, our government became opposed to the scheme, at first secretly and later openly. Nevertheless the troops were raised, and although the ministers clung obstinately to their absurd attitude they never received the punishment they deserved, and consequently remained in power. I raised my regiment at Malines from amongst the expert and excellent horsemen who had formed the backbone of our old Spanish cavalry. No sooner was this regiment formed than it was ready to take the field—something very rarely seen. Indeed, it was so handsome and so good a unit that it was worthy to take the right of the line in the army.[1] I personally had the good fortune to retain this post and associated privileges over the heads of all the nations represented in the army, although we were only two regiments strong and despite the fact that our infantry, thanks to the ineptitude of Pascale, allowed itself to be employed as drafts for other formations.

It is true that this cost me a scandal, although it was all the fault of my Lieutenant-Colonel Lejeune. If only at that time the Allies had been willing to spend 200,000 crowns and had given me a free hand, they could have deprived the enemy of the services of that complete and fine corps of Walloon troops which by its valour has kept Spain for them—and we would have reaped the benefit of their services. But the good friends the enemy had in our midst made it their business to thwart this coup which I could certainly have brought off, and which would have been worth millions to us.

I think it was during this year that this same Pascale sought the distinction of being able to brag to the world that he was going to fight me. I took no notice of this bravado until a certain morning when Baron Dilher, an Austrian colonel in the Emperor's service, came to see me to report all the gossip from the army, which he had left the previous day. As it was either a Sunday or a Feast Day, I took him with me in my coach to hear Mass, as was my custom, at the Augustins, where they always reserve a seat for me high above the choir to save me the trouble of having to pay compliments to the ladies. As we were passing, as usual, towards the chapter-house in

[1] The post of honour in the line of battle.

order to enter, I saw Pascale with his crony General Wrangel in the street outside the church. These two were already surrounded by a considerable crowd in front of this place of worship where I invariably attend Mass on Sundays or Feast Days whenever I am in Brussels. It was almost the stroke of noon, and so my coach was in a hurry. Seeing these two gesticulating in the middle of the crowd, I did not know what was going on except that my coach had been stopped by the obstruction in the street; then I saw Pascale and his friend striding towards us, swearing foully the while. At that point the street is very narrow, and Pascale, blocking the way with his bulky body, made as if to catch hold of my coat. Noticing this, I raised my cane, and told him that if he was truly desirous of having the honour of measuring swords with me he should get straightway into my coach with no further noise or stupid ado in front of all these people. Then, pushing him along in front of me, I forced him into my coach, and sat him down on my left hand. Lieutenant-General Wrangel and Baron Dil-her also climbed in, and then I tugged the cord to make my coachman drive off fast. Pascale was armed with a long and heavy blade, but I had only a light court sword with a thin blade and tiny guard without branches.

We passed out of the River Gate, and after going through the barrier I led him on to the covered way between the River and Flanders Gates and thence on to a discreet spot close by some trees. I told him to draw. As he did so, I noticed that the ramparts were packed with people. I pointed this out to him, and urged him to hurry. This crowd which he had gathered about him while he was acting the enraged madman in the middle of the street prior to my arrival had followed behind my coach, growing larger every second. As I realized what was about to happen, I again urged him to hurry up, and put myself on guard, being determined not to spare him. After parrying three or four thrusts, I began to drive him back towards the road; but then, at the very moment I had him on the edge of the ditch and had just given him a blow on his wig which stunned him and all but made him fall into it, all the people came rushing up in a crowd after forcing their way through the barrier. They at once fell upon us and dragged me back from him. As these stupid hinds clung on to me but *not* him, he launched a furious blow at me that I somehow or other managed to parry, but his blade glanced my hand, cutting the skin. This caused my rage to redouble, but since I was being restrained by this whole mob who thought they were doing me a favour (for I am better loved by these people than some people think, although, in fact, on this occasion they had come close to costing me my life), I let Pascale make good his escape. Then I saw Wrangel and Dilher sheathe their swords which they came near drawn to exchange several blows. My adversary lost no time in entering his coach, and I climbed into mine. As it was by now too late to attend Mass, I drove off home, hoping to hear one from my own chaplain, taking Dilher with me.

I was particularly eager to forestall the rumourmongers who never miss this sort of opportunity, for at that time my wife was big with child. I found her in bed, and in a few words told her of my adventure, putting some Peruvian balm on my wound with Dilher's assistance. I then set out once more for the Great Carmelite church in another attempt to hear Mass, and whom should I find there but Pascale and M. Wrangel once again. I have never been able to find out what induced him to make this public scene, unless it was his absurd vanity in wishing to be seen measuring swords with me before a large crowd of strangers despite the wide gulf that existed between our respective stations in life. He would have wasted all his time had only the mob arrived a minute later.[1]

[*After a lengthy dissertation on the ignoble antecedents of Pascale, the son, according to our rather biased informant, of a Spanish non-commissioned officer who eventually obtained the position of* capitan reformado, *the irascible Count goes on to describe further quarrels with the Dutch Treasurer, General Hope and Lord Albemarle—all of them due to small points of precedence or imagined slights to our hero's overweening sense of pride—but these were resolved without recourse to gentlemanly satisfaction and do not directly concern the development of events in Flanders, and accordingly have been omitted here.*]

[1] These quarrels eventually reached the ears of Marlborough himself. On 8 July 1708 the Duke wrote to the Dutch Deputy, van den Bergh, acknowledging his letter 'touching upon the differences between the Marquis de Westerloo and M. Pascale', and informing him that he was sending General Cadogan to Brussels 'to attempt to reconcile these gentlemen'. (See *The Letters and Dispatches of John Churchill*, vol. IV, p. 99.)

Some seven weeks later we find Marlborough writing to our prickly friend in person (letter dated 26 August 1708), presumably shortly after the duel described above. For the courtly and restrained Marlborough the tone is harsh. 'I was very surprised, as you may well believe, to learn what recently took place between you and M. de Pascale; the Council of State has even written to me on the subject. . . . Without going into past history, I find myself obliged to require you, in the name of His Majesty [*i.e. Charles, Pretender to the Spanish throne*] to give your word of honour that you will go no further in the matter, and that this dispute will have no ulterior outcome' (ibid., vol. IV, pp. 191–2).

VIII

The Campaigns of 1709 and 1710

Next winter I was asked to visit the Hague when the campaign ended by Count Sinzendorff (the Emperor's Minister in Holland), and this I accordingly did. At that time there was a plan to send a corps of our Walloon soldiers to Spain, replacing them here by a similar number of newly raised troops. Such a decision would have had a good effect, and I had always advocated this course, for, besides the harm it would have done the enemy, this would have provided the King with some troops who would never have refused any useful enterprise for reasons of personal caprice, or have derided their monarch's authority. Such a body of men would, of course, have been Catholic, and this would have avoided the ill effects aroused by the word 'heretic' in Spanish breasts. They would also have observed a stricter discipline than the English, Dutch and other nationalities, whose generals permitted them to pillage and commit other atrocities in churches and other places which caused the Spanish people to nurture that horror for our cause, and they certainly would never have proved as expensive as the rest. Indeed, I might have taken command of this force of more than 6,000 men myself, but the whole matter—although agreed to—was countermanded by the Duke of Marlborough on the old pretext of taking Spain by way of France. This he did to prolong the war in order to further his own advantage.

[*For some time Mérode-Westerloo was seriously ill at the Hague, after being attacked by a fever while attending a dinner with Marlborough and other dignitaries. As soon as he was seemingly fit to travel, he had himself moved to Brussels, where he suffered a relapse and lay at death's door for a further six weeks. His improving health was typically accompanied by a blazing quarrel with the Earl of Albemarle over regimental precedence— Albemarle had dared to place the Count's regiment on the left of the battleline instead of the post of honour on the right!—but in the end Mérode-Westerloo apparently won his way. He then continues to chronicle the military events that befell in Flanders.*]

Some little time later, owing to his usual avarice and his failure to pay his own spies sufficiently, the Duke of Marlborough asked me to send out a party to gather news from Mons. I sent off Captain Camusel with thirty troopers, who should have proved sufficient for the task, taking some soldiers from both my regiments. However, he unfortunately fought a skirmish very maladroitly; he claimed that he was attacked by 300 cavalry (but other eyewitnesses said they saw but thirty). I was naturally very angry at this sorry outcome to our very first sortie, but my annoyance was soon surpassed by a second source of embarrassment that was sent to plague me. For the enemy wanted to hang two of my dragoons that they had taken prisoner, as sometime soldiers of the Spanish army. I at once sent off a trumpeter to claim their release on the grounds that they had changed their allegiance by due forms of law, but they were already in prison awaiting court-martial. The enemy returned me no satisfactory answer, but pressed ahead with their declared intention. I at once threatened reprisals, but to cap it all, Count Bergeyck informed me that the Allies had the right to hang deserters from amongst their troops, and that the King of Spain could doubtless deal accordingly with his. At this all the old generals and ministers believed that there was no answer I could return, but then I remembered a ruse once played by the great Prince de Condé. I sent my trumpeter back to Bergeyck with a message that if he had men hung who had been formally confirmed in their present allegiance by the legal powers of their legitimate sovereign, I would for my part hang all those who had *not* quitted the enemy's service as men who had failed to return to their proper duty. It so happened that a few days before we had captured a cornet of horse and two troopers. The cornet was dining at my table that particular day, and after I had risen from the table I said to him— very gravely—that I regretted I had some bad news for him: I was going to have him hanged on the morrow. This was not my personal wish, I hastened to assure him, but my generals would have it so. All I could do was furnish him with pen, ink and paper for writing a letter to his generals, and a drummer to deliver his message. If they strung up my dragoons, I would most assuredly hang him and his two troopers the very next day. He was then taken off to prison; the gibbet was erected in sight of his cell and some Jesuit Fathers were sent to visit him. The poor fellow lost no time in writing as we had hoped, good and strong, and the drummer duly set off for the enemy camp. His message made our foes put water in their wine! M. de Bergeyck wrote about my conduct to the Duke of Marlborough, who forwarded the letter (which was full of complaints against me) together with a copy of his reply. In this he wrote that he had only been sent over by his sovereign, the Queen, to support the interests of King Charles III of Spain against the insinuations of his enemies, and that consequently he had no power to instruct me on this matter, as I was one of King Charles's generals as well as one of the Emperor's—and that I knew my own business best. Thereupon M. de Bergeyck, knowing that I was determined and that there was nothing he could do against me, decided to return my two dragoons, but only after detaining my trumpeter for more than three weeks. He had clearly seen my letter in which I had given solemn assurances that if anybody was hung I would have a captain swing immediately after the cornet, and thereafter proceed rank by rank. From then on he was very polite to me for the duration of the war. Accordingly I let the wretched cornet go—the poor fellow had truly been scared stiff; so I had him to dinner again and released him on parole. The outcome of this incident was to give our Flemish troops a certain assurance they would otherwise have lacked.

Soon after my return to Brussels from Aix the Elector Palatine had sent me a very full *laissez-passer* and an escort, and a second passport, with a separate guard, for my wife, together with a copy countersigned by myself for my servants and escort. My desire at this time was to reside peacefully on my estates, for the Duke of Marlborough and Prince Eugène were busily scheming to drive me out of the service. I verily believe that one of the reasons that embroiled me with Prince Eugène—besides the tales told him by many members of Pascale's circle and the thousand other little men who had reason to fear me, and the embarrassments I had caused Cadogan and Milord Marlborough—was the occasion when I had been in conversation with the Prince and he had suggested that I might care to serve a campaign with him as a volunteer. To this I replied that I was rather too old to return to the humble status of volunteer.[1] This rejoinder plainly hurt his vanity a trifle, and he has never forgiven me, always doing his best to persecute me—particularly because he recognizes that I am a man excessively (to his mind) attached to the true service of King Charles.

It was in 1708 or the following year that our twin heroes served me

[1] It was the contemporary custom for great generals to surround themselves with friends and relatively senior colleagues for the period of a campaign; the idea was to allow them to understudy the commanders-in-chief. Prince Eugène had invited the Count to join him in this capacity as long ago as 1696, prior to the Zenta campaign. See 'The Career of Feld-Maréchal Comte de Mérode-Westerloo', p. 141.

another bad turn. At that time I possessed a very good contact at Charleroi, with whose assistance I could have introduced some troops into the town to carry out a surprise attack. I communicated this design to our two generalissimos, together with part of my plan, but retaining for myself the most important role for reasons of prudence and simple justice. They found my plan so good that they approved it in every respect—but they wanted to deprive me of the glory by giving it to Pascale to execute. They duly entrusted it to him, together with all the hints and instructions which I had passed on to them. That individual, of course, wrecked the whole project by making a hundred stupid mistakes and through lacking the main secret; although he followed the rest of my plan in every respect, he ended by really putting his foot in it—which made me laugh in my sleeve. Nevertheless I lost some of my own good money which I had invested in the project to arrange matters, and after this affair I felt completely justified in my prudent attitude of keeping large mental reservations about two such men who had so unworthily sacrificed me. At this time I was continuously engaged in disagreements with these gentlemen, and more than once I almost made up my mind to quit the country.[1]

[In the following pages the Count breaks off to describe how badly King Charles III was served by his ministers and advisers in Spain, not concealing his opinion that the use of his own services there would have caused a major improvement. After long descriptions of the foibles of the Spanish Pretender's ministers, and an account of the military and political errors committed in the Peninsula by selfish and double-dealing statesmen, he returns to describe the events that occurred in the Low Countries.]

Let us now turn to the campaign of 1709.

Our twin heroes did nothing with their formidable army until 27 June, when they invested Tournai—a step that they should have taken before besieging Lille, had they truly applied the principles of war. The town surrendered on 28 July [usually said to be the 30th], the citadel

---

[1] Probably the Count's reputation as a turncoat partially accounts for the Allied leaders' evident distrust of his opinions and advice. However, there is no evidence to prove the existence of any type of vendetta. It would seem that most fault lay with the Count. In a letter to the Archduke Charles, dated 31 July 1709, Marlborough reported that he had distributed honours and promotions on the former's behalf 'with the exception of that intended for M. le Marquis de Westerloo, who, having only been a maréchal-de-camp [or Major-General] in the enemy service, was nevertheless not prepared to accept your commission as lieutenant-general.' (The Letters and Dispatches of John Churchill, vol. IV, p. 559.)

on 3 September.[1] We would not have won it so cheaply had not the garrison been so short of powder and other necessaries—and there we might well have lost our entire army, no matter how formidable in appearance, had the place been properly provisioned. However, Fortune remained our friend and we became masters of the town for a cost out of all proportion to its importance. From there our generals proceeded to invest Mons [*from 9 September*], which fell on 21 [*in fact 20*] October, for there again the place was sadly lacking in the wherewithal to offer a stout resistance. In this way we at last began to safeguard Brabant and Flanders, after so long a period of inexcusable negligence.

That same year our generals' good fortune enabled us to win another battle [*Malplaquet*], which was risked in a very foolhardy fashion on 11 September, eight days after the investment of Mons.[2] This success nevertheless cost us dear, for I verily believe we lost 20,000 of our best infantry, which performed prodigies of valour, most particularly the Dutch, who were practically destroyed. Marshal Villars—the only French commander who had, despite his reputation for bravado, sustained his reputation as a general blessed with glory and good fortune—had chosen a sensible position near Blaregnies. It was a difficult position to approach on account of its situation, and was well placed to incommode our siege of Mons by intercepting our convoys on their way from Brussels. It was accordingly resolved that we should attack him there. All might have gone well had this been executed at the right moment, but in order to permit a reinforcement to reach us from Tournai we afforded M. Villars and Marshal Boufflers (who had come to join him) three whole days in which to entrench himself to the teeth in an almost impregnable position, thus enabling him to make the best dispositions and manoeuvres possible. This notwithstanding, by an amazing stroke of luck, we succeeded in driving him out of three successive lines of entrenchments, but only after a fearful blood-letting. Marshal Villars, wounded in the thigh [*in fact, the knee*], withdrew in very good order, and we were permitted to take Mons at our leisure—the sole fruit of our victory [*20 October 1709*].

As for me, at that time I saw myself being excluded from active service in perpetuity, and I spent my time enjoying life as best I might

---

[1] See p. 242 below.

[2] See Parker's account, p. 86 above, and the relevant footnotes regarding casualties, etc.

on my estates, though seething inwardly with rage and frustration; this I was able to do thanks to my arrangement with the Elector of Bavaria and the French, who provided me with renewed *laissez-passer* every six months in exchange for corresponding passports and concessions I obtained for Count d'Arco and the Elector himself, which I did twice. But this frustrating passivity was truly mortifying for a man of my age, for my only wish was to serve with honour and leave a memory or two behind me when I was dead and gone.

[*Amongst other activities, the Count used his leisure to supervise the building of a road to link Westerloo with the Abbey of Tongerloo, employing the free—and we may suspect enforced—labour or* corvée *of some 600 peasants, 'which cost me nothing for the work except some small beer, although on the first Sunday I provided them with strong beer to the music of violins in their villages'.*]

Soon after the completion of my road (in 1710) I went to dine for the very first time at Tongerloo. While I was still at table an officer of my regiment arrived bearing tidings of the surrender of Douai on 25 June, which had been invested on 23 April.

For the Allies this whole year was nothing but a succession of triumphs and captured towns, all gained without order or plan, thanks to sheer chance—at least that is the most charitable interpretation; otherwise we might say that all was done in order to prolong the war. Instead of being sensible, after taking Douai, and going on to Cambrai, our generals set off on 14 July for Béthune, which capitulated on 28 August. From there they proceeded to Saint-Venant, investing the town on 5 September and receiving its surrender on the 29th—*truly a fine way to set out to take Spain through France* [the Count's italics.] Lastly they besieged Aire on 5 [*in fact, 12*] September, at the same time as operations were proceeding against Saint-Venant, and the town fell on 8 November. All this time the French left us to acquire glory at our leisure, but we must not overlook the great number of men we lost at these five sieges which were so utterly useless for the prosecution of the overall design that our leaders claimed to be pursuing.[1]

[*This chapter concludes with a further survey of the war in Spain, describing King Charles III's victory at the cavalry battle of Almenara (27 July) and his second success at Saragossa (20 August). Thereafter, Mérode-Westerloo acidly points out, every advantage was thrown away*

---

[1] See Appendix II, p. 242–3, for a summary of these operations and their cost.

because of the fatal attraction asserted by Madrid, which eventually led to the enemy winning the battle of Brihuega (9 December)—a disaster that was, however, somewhat offset by General Starhemberg's limited success at Villaviciosa the following day.]

Here, then, in a few words, are all the faults committed in this year of grace 1710. They deserve a full volume to themselves.

IX

The Campaign of 1711 and the Coronation of the Emperor Charles VI

By this time I was beginning to forget about my troubles a trifle, and I busied myself throughout the following year, 1711, surveying those parts of my lands that I desired to enclose. Then, one day soon after noon, at the time when I was laying down the western boundary, to my great surprise I received a letter from Prince Eugène just as I was riding out to supervise the work. This informed me that the King [*i.e. Charles III*] had sent him instructions that I was to travel to join His Majesty at the end of the campaign, either in Spain or wherever he might be found. I was truly amazed to receive a letter from this source, and even more by its content. I replied that I would hasten to obey, and impatiently set myself to await the close of operations, passing the time continuing my improvements. When all was finished I made ready to leave, but before proceeding to say my *adieux* to the Duke of Marlborough I had a new road laid down towards Gheel, running behind the church there, buying up a considerable amount of land in its vicinity.

I took my leave of the Duke at Antwerp, at his suggestion,[1] and returned to Brussels, where I left my wife. Then I rode back to Westerloo, where I summoned six or seven hundred of my peasants. My intention was to set out the next afternoon, but I wished to ride

---

[1] Writing to Mérode-Westerloo on 19 August 1711, Marlborough stated: 'I am very obliged to you for the part you played in our passage of the lines [of *Ne Plus Ultra*, 4/5 August] and in my turn rejoice with you that the first effect of this achievement has been to thwart those enemy troops who were threatening the town of Brussels.' It is strange that the Count makes no mention of his part in this famous operation—implying, indeed, that he spent all his time on his estates! On 24 September the Duke again wrote to Mérode-Westerloo, approving his intention of joining King Charles, and stating that he would be 'enchanted to embrace you before your departure, either during my journey to Antwerp or at the Hague, whichever you find the most convenient.' (*The Letters and Dispatches of John Churchill*, vol. V, pp. 452 and 509). (See also p. xiv above.)

off down my new avenue, which could truly be called my very own road. I also wished to leave it in a sufficiently advanced state to prevent my tenants' sheer idleness and timorous lack of initiative, characteristics that typify the Fleming, from furnishing them with excuses for failing to complete it on account of any difficulties they might meet.

[*Leaving Westerloo on 9 November 1711, the Count made his way incognito towards Innsbruck, where he was summoned to attend the investiture of Charles VI as Count of the Tyrol. After several near brushes, he eventually met Prince Eugène, who was also travelling in disguise, and they finished the journey in company, reaching Innsbruck on about 17 November.*]

The very next day who should enter my room to embrace me while I was dressing than Lord Peterborough, newly arrived from Italy. I had known him in Flanders and Holland, and he already knew well enough that I was far from being an admirer of Marlborough's. This in itself was sufficient to assure me of his friendship.

As I continued my stay at Innsbruck, I witnessed the ceremony of *huldigung*—or the investiture of the Emperor as Count of the Tyrol. This was performed with great splendour in the great hall of the palace, where the Emperor dined with the Estates. It was a fine spectacle to watch. During the morning I attended mass there, dressed in a mantle [*of the Order of the Golden Fleece*] which I was forced to borrow from a member of the Regency Council. There were only the Prince of Lichtenstein, the Grand Master, and myself on the seats reserved for Knights of the Order, but I accorded him precedence, being uncertain whether or not he was my senior—preferring to claim less than my due rather than too much. Thereafter he invariably gave place to me, for he discovered that I was far his senior. The Bishop of Brixen officiated, assisted by four mitred abbots. He comes from the House of Künigh, the foremost in the land. . . .

When the time approached for the Emperor to leave for his coronation at Frankfurt, I discovered that I had been listed to travel in the fourth coach behind the Emperor, all expenses paid. However, I chose to travel on ahead at my own pace and comfort, and accordingly I left Innsbruck on 20 November, three or four days ahead of the Emperor.

The very next day Prince Eugène set off for England, and caught up with me on the road, two posting stages before Wertheim. He induced me to dine with him at the posting station, where to all external appearances we were good friends. He asked me what I thought about his voyage to England, and I told him that nothing would come of it, not knowing at that time that this was also his secret wish. While he was there he received some fine gifts, but otherwise carried out the behests of his cousin [*the Duke of Savoy*], who was his real master. After dining together he took his horses, and I my draught-oxen, making my way to Wertheim, where I embarked for Frankfurt. There again I was seriously ill—and even worse looked after by my servants—narrowly escaping death before the Emperor's arrival.

After reaching this point I must retrace my steps some little way. Never did I believe more surely that the Spanish inheritance would ultimately remain in our hands than when the young and virtuous Emperor Joseph died of smallpox on 17 April 1711, while awaiting his confessor—his demise being caused by youth and folly, or so the Austrians told us. Who could then have believed that a helpless Prince of his House, the Emperor Charles VI [*who was, of course, also the Pretender, Charles III of Spain*], who had suffered so much, seen and experimented on his own account, and bravely sustained so many contretemps, would not have sustained the cause which so closely involved both his glory and honour? This, nevertheless, is what eventually transpired, and contrary to all reasonable expectations this sad death proved to be our ultimate misfortune, even more so than the change of the Ministry in England in favour of the Tories, thanks to the intrigues and gold of France and, in part, to our own blunders.

During the autumn of 1710 that miserable wretch Pascale—having the Duke of Marlborough in his pocket—set out for the Hague to induce the Duke and the Dutch to give him half my regiment. Count Noyelles, my major, at once left the regiment and came with all haste to Westerloo, beseeching me to go there as well in order to forestall such an eventuality which my regiment was fearing worse than death itself, and which I hardly regarded more favourably myself. M. de Noyelles told me so many things that I decided to go despite my reluctance. We embarked at Moerdyck in the midst of a tempest which steadily grew as we sailed from Dorp towards Rotterdam. Indeed, the yacht's mast went overboard as we were passing over those stretches of water adjoining my lands at Ridderkerke, and we climbed into the small dinghy, over which the waves were breaking every moment. As I both understand and like the sea, I could do nothing but laugh, although the gale was worsening every minute, and I continued to sing away, although there was indeed some peril, as I well knew; but poor Noyelles and my valet Durieux looked half-dead. Nevertheless, in the end we safely reached Rotterdam, and thence travelled on to the Hague, where we arrived in time enough not only to confound the schemes of our enemies but also to give the Duke of Marlborough some cause for anxiety, for his power and prestige were on the wane in England.[1] Indeed, Count Sinzendorff came to my house on his account to beg me to appease my wrath. I agreed to do so—but out of consideration for the public weal and not for the Duke's own sake, as I made sure of pointing out. Thus the Duke reversed his original intention—though rather through fear than careful consideration. I thereupon returned to Westerloo.

[*On his return home our hero had another of his attacks of quarrelsomeness and pugnacity, conducting a lengthy and acrimonious dispute with the Abbot of Tongerloo which culminated in the Count pushing his road through the Abbey lands by a* coup de main *while the opposition was away complaining to the Council of Brabant at Brussels. After compulsory purchase of some of the Abbey's ground, Mérode-Westerloo organized a work force of 700 peasants, and by the time the Abbot returned was able to present him with a* fait accompli. *A reconciliation was eventually patched up between the parties, but the Count—needless to say—got his road!*]

I think it was at about this time that I went to see Prince Eugène at Brouck, meeting him at the posting station of la Vaert. I travelled from Westerloo by post, and was in time to see him. We supped together and he spent the night in my room. Everything went 'marvellously'—no more, no less. He departed for Vienna before dawn, and I returned home.

It will be remembered that I last left the Emperor on his way to Frankfurt, and as I arrived there ahead of the court for reasons of my own convenience, I was able to watch his ceremonial entry into the city. I had taken lodgings hard by the court in the house of a worthy merchant of the reformed religion named Bidel, whose father had been a French refugee [*doubtless after the Revocation of the Edict of Nantes in 1685*] and he had sought both safety and a new home at Frankfurt. The entry into the city was certainly magnificent. The escort and accoutrements of the Electors Palatine (those of Mainz and Trèves) certainly outshone the Emperor's in terms of showy magnificence, but his Imperial Majesty's entourage possessed a unique air of grandeur. His Majesty arrived in full mourning for his late elder brother, the Emperor Joseph; consequently, his coach was draped, and all his suite and horses were clad in black down to the very

[1] See Parker, pp. 113–16 above, for a description of some of the circumstances.

ground. He had hoped that the Electors and the entire procession would adopt similar tokens of respect, but they asserted that as they had a new Emperor they were not going to wear mourning for the old. All three Electors present in person and the ambassadors of the absentees (excepting those of Bavaria and Cologne, who were at this time under the Ban of the Empire)[1] went out to meet the Emperor half a league from the town. He passed through the gates after dinner, and first made a call at the church, where he swore the 'capitulation' [*an undertaking to protect the interests of the Princes of the Empire*]. There were hardly more than one hundred six-horse coaches, but the entry was nevertheless impressive, possessing something of regal splendour. The Imperial heralds led the procession, while the troops of the attendant Electors brought up the rear. After hearing a sermon, the Emperor was conducted to his apartments.

When I was dining a few days later at the house of Count Sinzendorff, the Court Chancellor, my host informed me that the Emperor wished to appoint me a Gentleman of the Bedchamber, and, as a special mark of favour, proposed to date my appointment prior to those he had felt bound to make in Milan and Catalonia at the time of his departure. Thus I became the senior of all thirty Gentlemen. At the same time he also dubbed twenty-two Knights of the Order of the Golden Fleece. Both these steps were well advised.

The Emperor had chosen 22 December 1711 for his coronation, and this was adhered to, although the Elector of Mainz wanted a postponement to enable him to produce a new altar frontal for the ceremony [*the period of Advent being regarded as a period of sober preparation for the feast of Christmas*]. He even petitioned the Emperor to this effect, and indeed this furnishing was the most magnificent of the many he owned—but to no avail. On the appointed day all the Electors rode out on horseback with their brilliant suites to fetch the Emperor from his apartments. All were dressed in their scarlet electoral robes, faced and lined with ermine, their caps of maintenance on their heads. The Emperor wore royal robes, with the king's crown all asparkle with diamonds on his head. He rode a horse whose saddlecloth, saddle, harness and other furnishings were covered with diamonds and pearls. The Electors and the representatives of the absentees carried the various symbols of royal majesty before the Emperor; one bore his sword, others the orb, sceptre, crown and the rest. The Crown of Charlemagne together with the imperial robes had already

1 On account of their close alliances with Louis XIV.

been borne to the church by the Grand Masters the previous day, and laid upon the high altar. All the Councillors of State, the Gentlemen of the Bedchamber, and the rest marched on foot before the Emperor. Only the Knights of the Golden Fleece waited in the church itself, seated in their allotted pew (the first directly facing the high altar). Behind us sat the Councillors of State; on one side the Counts of the Empire, and, somewhat higher than they, the Princes. The Electors stood nearest of all to the high altar, for each had some ceremonial to perform. The Knights of the Golden Fleece who were present were Count Harrach (formerly Ambassador to Spain), who was next after me in terms of seniority; next to him sat the Prince of Lichtenstein, the Grand Master, in continual attendance upon the throne, Count Philip of Dietrichstein, the Prince of Taxis and myself; we were all apparelled in our magnificent *costumes de campagne*.

The Elector of Mainz, attended by many a mitred bishop, awaited the arrival of the procession at the church porch. People of quality, two by two, supported by guards, had been posted at all the doors to restrict entry to only the well-known or necessary personages furnished with tickets by the Grand Marshal of the Court. At the back of the church was a raised amphitheatre for the ladies, who were guarded by the Noble Guard of the King of Poland (brought by the Ambassador of Saxony). The Emperor had two thrones, one as a King, the other as the Emperor. When he made his entrance he first mounted that of the King, but as the ceremony proceeded he was slowly divested of his regal regalia and invested instead with the imperial insignia. Towards the end he took his seat upon the imperial throne, where, after hearing mass, he received a sermon from the Elector who had anointed him, who spoke his piece wearing a mitre. Thereafter the Emperor dubbed the new Knights of the Empire, and left the church on foot, resplendent in all his imperial regalia, with the Electors of Mainz and Trèves bearing the train of his mantle, the rest moving off ahead of him from the dais which had been provided by the Magistrate of Frankfurt. His Imperial Majesty passed in procession over the wooden bridge, which was all bedecked in yellow, black and red [*the imperial colours*], to the town hall, preceded by the entire procession in strict order of precedence.

Count Harrach and myself, being the first out of church, as was our privilege, soon arrived in front of the town hall and were thus able to watch everything in comfort. First the Emperor went to take a rest, but in due course returned, preceded by the Electors, the crown upon his head, to take his seat on a throne placed near a small window. The three Electors assembled below this, and we were well placed to see the ceremonial duties they variously performed. One of them, the Elector of Saxony, mounted on horseback and carrying a silver measure, rode up at a gallop bearing a measure of oats, which he took to the Mews for the Emperor's horse. The Elector Palatine, also mounted, then rode off to carve a slice of beef from an ox being roasted whole in a wooden house, and returned with it to the Emperor's table. Then the oats and the beef were presented to the crowd —I believe it was the Court Chancellor, Count Sinzendorff, who performed this task, also on horseback. When the Emperor moved to his window he was acclaimed by all the people, who were swarming all over the roofs.

At supper all the Electors waited upon the Emperor according to their allotted functions, and then sat down at their own tables. Count Harrach, representing the King of Bohemia, carried the cup at His Imperial Majesty's request; Prince Alexander of Württemberg carved, and the Counts of the Empire carried the plates to and from the table. The Emperor returned very late to his apartments, taking the three Electors in his coach, two at the doors and one beside the coachman.

His Imperial Majesty paid me a signal honour which earned me much attention. I was standing on the second step of the throne while the people were regaling themselves with the beef, when the Emperor called me, and catching hold of my sleeve drew me towards him, talking the while, and pulled me after him as he stepped back in order to afford me a good view of the scene below —and all this despite the fact that he was wearing the regalia of Charlemagne with the crown upon his head. This mark of high favour, together with the compliment paid to me by the Elector Palatine when he approached to perform his duty, attracted the attentions of the other Electors to me as well as bringing me to the notice of a great number of people who did not know me.

[*All this pomp and ceremony clearly pleased Mérode-Westerloo's vanity, and he later followed the Emperor to Vienna, travelling along the Danube by road on account of the ice floes in the river. This delayed his journey, and to his chagrin he arrived at the capital too late to attend the formal* Te Deum *sung at St Stephen's Cathedral towards the end of January 1712. Then the Count reverts to the affairs of the Low Countries.*]

Two days after the Emperor's coronation my valet, Durieux,

arrived post-haste bringing me my clothes and with them the news that the magazines at Arras had been burnt down by our own side. I carried these tidings to the Emperor, who was at the time at dinner and knew nothing of the matter. This affair made more stir than the tale of the havoc done to the enemy, who, in fact, got off very lightly in the year 1711, losing only Le Quesnoy. This place was invested on 6 June [*usually put as the 8th*], and fell on 4 July.

[*A lengthy passage here deals with the intricacies of Imperial court politics; the Count soon tired of these, and received permission to make an extensive tour of Italy, where he saw most of the sights. On his return to Vienna, however, he was delighted to learn that he was promised a Governorship in the Low Countries. Happy in this further evidence of his preferment, he returns to his beloved Westerloo 'at three o'clock in the afternoon on 9 November, 1713'. Mérode-Westerloo was from first to last a lover of home. For his period, he was very much an 'improving' landowner.*]

Back at Westerloo, I found my wife in good health and my daughter much grown. I also discovered that my people had completed the avenue named 'de Diest' which I had ordered to be made during my absence, and which cost a great deal, both in trouble and money. I stayed there until Christmas, and then went off to visit the Duke of Marlborough at Antwerp, whither he had retired on account of his enemies in England. The new ministry wished him to render account for his actions, and this the Duke would have found it very hard to do. Yet although he had never done me anything but harm, I nevertheless wished to bestow some marks of my generosity upon him in his disgrace, and indeed to be numbered amongst his friends at a time when his power was gone—and this in spite of the fact that he had done me all the wrongs and malicious injuries in his power during the years of his greatness. And indeed we showed one another a deal of friendship, and this lasted until he returned to England. The Queen of England had died, and he was actually at sea at the moment she breathed her last [*31 July 1714*].

X

The Campaigns of 1712 and 1713:
The End of the War

It is salutary to consider the campaigns fought during the final years
of the war that ended with the Peace of Utrecht—which was so different from the preliminaries of Gertruydenberg [*this peace conference
was broken off by the French in late spring 1710*] and the offers made there
by the French. Despite all the losses she had suffered and continued to
suffer, France knew how to manage the Peace with the aid of gold and
intrigue, and even while the war was still being waged she proved
capable of influencing affairs in her favour, and in some ways even
continued to dictate the law to the rest of Europe.

The campaign of 1712 opened after the Duke of Marlborough had
been deprived of his command by the English; this had now been
entrusted to that High Tory and Jacobite, the Duke of Ormonde. All
arrangements had been completed long before, not just during the
previous year. Prince Eugène served under him, and had all the advantage of inside information, which suited him very well. Had he wished
to use it well, all the knowledge he possessed concerning the links
between the Ministry, the English general and France could have seen
them one and all utterly confounded, thereby bringing further lustre
to our glory and positive advantage to his sovereign. Instead he
committed fault after fault, and so gross were some of these that even
the dullest observer could hardly fail to realize that they were deliberate. He had never been the Emperor Charles's friend during the
lifetime of his predecessor, Joseph (who died, you will remember, on
17 April of smallpox), and was the friend of the Dauphin [*eldest son of
Louis XIV*], who died on the 14th of that very same month. He was
thus working towards the day when he could realize his ambition—
which both he and the Austrian ministry had always shared—of
compelling the House of Austria to relinquish the Spanish monarchy.
They worked at this as hard as the English Tories, and in the end they
got their wish.

At this time the Dutch were still inspired by the best intentions in the world, and the troops of the Empire were of the most helpful disposition; and despite the fact that the English soon withdrew from the struggle, they could have concerted some effective measures between them which would have stretched the French army on its back without any English assistance. This was not sufficient to induce them, however, to adopt the steps that a child would have taken, namely the sending of a battalion to Ghent and another to Bruges to close their gates. Instead, they had to allow the French free entry, thus depriving us at a blow of all our canal communications which we sorely needed for our convoys and necessaries. But even that was not enough; they had to go and leave all the magazines of Marchiennes intact for the use of the enemy, when, as the most junior officer was well aware, they could have evacuated every single item for the use of our own forces. We were too strong [*hence overconfident?*] and this led to the defeat of one of our corps at Denain [*24 July 1712*] which was kept detached from the main body for no better reason than to provide a command for Albemarle. In all this there were the most daunting and inexplicable circumstances that should have been clear to anybody else—but he had his head buried in the ground. On account of the enemy's march, conducted in our full view, and because of the total absence of any precautions, and through our very slowness in noticing the enemy's presence, and on account of all the trouble our hero [*Prince Eugène*] took to vindicate Albemarle after the event (when he should have been the first to denounce him), it was perfectly plain that all of Prince Eugène's conduct was inspired by a single aim—to see his cousin, the Duke of Savoy, made King of Sicily. This would never have been 'managed' without such gross behaviour.

This campaign was one of the most curious ever fought on account of its blatant and deliberate errors, and indeed this had to be the case if the Peace of Utrecht was to receive that particular slant required by the Tories of Vienna and England for their fell designs. And so it was that the tragi-comedy of Denain was played out on 26 [*in fact, 24*] July 1712. I was in Vienna at the time, and as a distant observer I was consequently only in a position to be lost in admiration for the way in which the setback was made complete. One after another I learnt of Prince Eugène's loss of the magazines at Marchiennes, the destruction of the corps at Denain, of the English splitting their forces, of the uncontested handing over of Bruges and Ghent to the enemy—and after all this, we heard that he had gone off to besiege Landrécies, which could well have been done two or three campaigns earlier. Nor was this all. He next proceeded to strip all our strong places of their garrisons in order to allow the foe to besiege Douai [*from 14 August*]— without having the least wish to foresee that this would happen. Then, having already invested Marchiennes [*25 July*], he refused to see it through lest the enemy should take Douai, and so abandoned the siege [*30 July*], exhausting his army with useless forced marches in order to make a show of giving assistance to Douai, but in reality merely to observe its fall. Last of all, to cap this string of disasters he had engineered, he insisted on massing all our heavy guns in Le Quesnoy (which we had managed to capture on 4 July), on the pretext of speeding the march of the army, which had the effect of forcing Douai to surrender on 8 September. Two days later, marvellous to relate, the foe undertook the siege of Le Quesnoy in its turn—taking it (with all our heavy pieces) on 4 October; this they did so much at their leisure that they were able to press on and besiege Bouchain, which duly fell on the 19th of the same month, thus capping a campaign which was to all external appearances glorious, and was, in fact, even more advantageous for their peace negotiations. This gloriously terminated a war which should have seen the defeat and even the destruction of France, had we so wished. More than six times we had that country's fate in our hands, despite all the advantages enjoyed by its proud monarch at the opening of the war. This truly shows how little stability there is in worldly affairs—even those that seem the most surely established and the most brilliant.

The preliminaries of peace, as signed on 8 October 1711 in England by M. Menager, included everything that Louis could desire, thanks to the Prince's conduct of the campaign, which did even more to this end than the suspension of hostilities between England and France (published at the head of their armies on 21 August 1712), which, after all, was certainly foreseeable. It required all this hard work on our side to produce the curious Peace of Utrecht, which was finally signed by France, England, Holland, Portugal, Prussia and the House of Savoy on 11 April 1713. Ever since the previous March it had been decided to abandon those unfortunate Catalans who had done so much for the Emperor and the common cause; on account of their staunchness, their efforts deserve to be compared to similar events in Antiquity.

Once this fine campaign was over, Prince Eugène returned to Vienna, happier at heart than anybody else, as he had at last acquired a throne (that of Sicily) for his cousin. He at once proceeded to reaffirm his belief in the all-powerfulness of Vienna, despite the mis-givings of those in the know. Following the death of his right arm—Count Wratislaw—he adopted another in the person of President of the Council Count Starhemberg, who was also a Gentleman of the Emperor's Bedchamber and a most casuistical Jesuit; between them, these two set out to betray Spain—the main sacrifice that was needed to put the seal on their complete success.

The Emperor, who would not even allow the Peace of Utrecht to be spoken of within his hearing, now desired to continue the war against France in isolation, displaying at this time a fine firmness of soul, which, along with all his other fine qualities, he has since lost.[1] Accordingly he drew up his dispositions for the campaign of 1713, placing a considerable army on the Rhine, consisting of his own [*i.e. Austrian*] as well as Imperial troops, which in my opinion could have performed wonders. However, Prince Eugène was given the com-mand. Had he but offered battle—and won—on a single occasion towards the beginning of the campaign he could have taken Stras-bourg and much more besides at his leisure. Even if he had lost it, he would only have forfeited Landau and Freiburg. But he chose to remain inactive, losing many good men to no purpose, in order to constrain the Empire to make peace. Had he risked a battle at the opening of the campaign he could under no circumstances have lost so much as he somehow managed to do by the time of its close, and this action would have obliged those Allies who had absconded from his side to reopen hostilities, or at the very least to intervene and pro-cure for the Emperor the type of peace he eventually concluded at Rastadt and ratified at Baden, for it was not in the public weal to see the Emperor and his Empire utterly destroyed.

I have no intention of describing the faults committed during the defence of Landau [*11 June–29 August*] and Freiburg [*22 September–16 November*]—nor will I talk about his [*Eugène's*] inaction during those two sieges, although he certainly should have been able to do some-thing with so fine and good an army, which, in fact, he permitted to

---

1 It was a fine, if hopeless, gesture for the Emperor to insist on continuing the struggle after all his former Allies had made separate peaces with France. In later years, however, Charles VI became completely obsessed with the need to have the Pragmatic Sanction—which would permit female succession to the Austrian Crown—ratified by the other European powers. To this end he was prepared to make considerable concessions of one sort or another, thereby earning Mérode-Westerloo's censure, and the final years of the reign proved both unsuccessful and unhappy for the last descendant of the male line of the Austrian House of Habsburg. Charles VI died in 1740.

waste away, although it lacked nothing. But, of course, he feared that if he saved the two towns and won some great battle this would result in his taking at least Strasbourg and all of Alsace, thus opening up a road into the very heart of France for the following campaign. This might have induced the Emperor—still a proud man—to order the reconquest of the Spanish monarchy as well, although the Austrians, the Tories, the Pope, the French and the Jesuits were all united in desiring him to renounce it once and for all.

However, after completing this last campaign both in Flanders and on the Rhine in so glorious a fashion, it was necessary for him [Eugène] to make peace, enjoying the status of sole plenipotentiary. To permit such a man to conclude the treaty was truly a horrible mistake and a great blindness on the part of the Emperor—who had been provided with warning of this when Eugène used him so scornfully in Catalonia. Surely the last two campaigns should have served to open the Emperor's eyes, but on the contrary Prince Eugène had now become the veritable master of the Emperor and his fate—and he still is, more so than ever, today. So off he went to conclude his peace treaty, all by himself, at the town of Rastadt, where he negotiated tête-à-tête with Marshal Villars in a novel fashion. When all had been agreed at the fine castle there (6 March 1714), the treaty was formally signed at Baden on 7 September following. Thus the Emperor made peace with Louis XIV, although he still refused to conclude it with Spain.

As for myself, I spent my time working on my projects at home, sad to see this poor prince as dependent on his ministers as had been that fine Spanish monarch, Charles II, before him. I travelled to Brussels and Antwerp to visit the disgraced Duke of Marlborough during his long sojourn in the latter city. He suggested a rendezvous for the purpose of seeing the Omegang at Malines [an annual folk festival of some importance]. We attended it at the city hall. Marlborough arrived with his Duchess from Antwerp, accompanied by the Governor, Don Louis de Borgia and his wife, the Princess d'Esquilalache. I travelled thence from Brussels, escorted by fifty horsemen of my regiment in order to preserve a little order at the request of the town magistrate. My poor wife also came on this excursion. We dined at the house of the Vicomte de Humbeeck, son of the current President of the Grand Council. Once the fête was over, the Duke returned to Antwerp with the Governor, and I set off for Westerloo with my wife and daughter.

That was how I spent the year 1714, during which the Queen of

England died. The next year, 1715, passed in much the same fashion, but during it there died the great king, Louis XIV, on 1 September, after so long and fine a reign. The 15 November following saw the signature of the fine Barrier Treaty between Count Königsegg, the Dutch Deputies and Cadogan, Minister of England, who had spent a spell at Vienna during the negotiations, serving as the 'oil' to the diplomatic wheels which, in fact, turned out to be 'Extreme Unction' for the Low Countries. When that was over he moved on to play a laughable role at the Council of State at Brussels, where he was surrounded by gullible and ignorant people. Everything worked as he desired, and the day after this comedy the treaty was finally signed.

[*Although the war was at long last well and truly a thing of the past, Mérode-Westerloo did not find life exactly dull in the months and years that followed. When, for instance, the Prince of Chimay was arrested for debt at Brussels, our peppery friend took five companies of his regiment and rescued his fellow Knight of the Order of the Golden Fleece by main force! In similar heavy-handed fashion he repressed a riot at Westerloo. The Count was clearly convinced of his feudal rights. Then, following the celebrations to mark the birth of the new Archduke (1716), there took place the last incidents that we have space to record before taking our leave of Mérode-Westerloo.*]

About that time [*1716*] something happened to me that I had long foreseen. Despite all the solemn promises made to me by the Emperor by word of mouth and by letter (which I am preserving like a Holy Relic), M. the Prince Eugène arranged for the Governorship of the province of Luxembourg to be given to Marshal the Count of Gronsfeld; not even content with that, he sent the Count of Vehlen to the Low Countries with some Imperial troops to take command there. Then Count Königsegg wrote to me that the needs of the service required me to hand over command of the troops I had originally raised and which were still under my orders. Although this was not the best way to deal with me—and certainly was not the wish of the Emperor—I decided to comply with this demand so as to avoid rousing tempers, and having little time for the current government. However, I did write to Vienna in no uncertain terms, though I knew it would have no effect.

These two setbacks, on top of all that had gone before by way of recompenses for my local services, made me resolve more firmly than ever to retire from public service and the affairs of the world. I had quite made up my mind to this when news arrived that Count Uhlfeld [*President of the Council of War*] had died; that the Vice-President of the Council of War, Field-Marshal Herberstein, had consequently succeeded to the superior post, and that it had been decided—wholly without my foreknowledge—to pass his old position on to me. A few days later, shortly after war had been declared on the Turks, I learnt that I had been promoted Field-Marshal and given seniority over the six others created at the same time.

I fully realized that this honour had been paid me in order to throw a veil over the eyes of the world, to conceal the breaking of the solemn undertaking that I was to be made Governor of Luxembourg, and also to put me firmly in the wrong if I were to decide to refuse such an opportunity and two such fine appointments. Furthermore, the effect would be to take me away from the Low Countries, where I was an embarrassment to them, and draw me into court circles, where my fortune would be dissipated. However, although I was fully aware of the trick being played, I could hardly refuse these offers without destroying myself and being condemned for it by all the world. Moreover, my wife would not hear a word against the project, not so much because she was incapable of understanding that the world is malevolent, but rather because she thought the Viennese court to be the finest place in the world. She had a great desire to go there, and was being encouraged all the time by her mother, the Countess d'Althan, who wrote to her continually. All the same, I made my excuses no less than half a dozen times—despite the fact that they promised to appoint me a Councillor of State into the bargain; but then, after having held out for more than a year and a half, I was obliged to give in, a decision based on sound reasoning, for my wife would have been the first to denounce me to the world had I decided otherwise.

[*And so we leave the Count on his way to Vienna to take up his new and important posts. In spite of his apparent reluctance, I think we can guess that he was secretly delighted at this outcome, for from first to last he was something of a snob and social climber, for all his many virtues. Many years of court life, rows, arguments, intrigues—even imprisonment—lay before him, but at this juncture in his affairs we must say our farewells.*]

Appendix I

Military Techniques in the War of the Spanish Succession

By the early years of the eighteenth century the general attitude of European opinion towards warfare had undergone a radical change. The religious partisanship that embittered the Wars of Religion had largely ebbed away, and the onset of the Age of Rationalism urged the virtues of military moderation on both rulers and generals. There was little trace at the time of aggressive 'national' spirit in its widest sense—although the desperate French war effort and partial recovery after 1708 was possibly an early indication of the force destined to increase the scale and horror of wars waged between peoples, as opposed to struggles between kings. Later in the century Dr Johnson could still maintain that 'Patriotism is the last refuge of the scoundrel.' In the years intervening between the eras of religious and national wars the conduct of military operations became 'limited' in the sense that the objectives were in certain respects restricted to dynastic or commercial ambitions; this did not mean that there were less wars, but it did imply that humanitarian interests were more to the fore in men's minds. All armies, however, still perpetrated the occasional excess.

Many factors contributed to the limitation of warfare at this time. There were the physical limitations—above all the appalling state of the roads and the shortage of fodder during the winter months—which had the effect of generally limiting active campaigning to the period between May and September. A second restraining influence was the social structure of the times—reflected in the military hierarchy—where high command was often the perquisite of the aristocracy—a class still imbued with some of the qualities of chivalry. The only officers who received any formal training for their profession were the gunners and engineers. The rank and file came from the lowest strata of society, kept in some form of order by the harsh discipline of the lash and fear of the noose, stake or firing squad. Conscription was as yet hardly heard of—and armies were mainly recruited from volunteers out of the depressed agrarian classes of society, with a minority of adventurers and freed convicts. Every army also contained a sizeable proportion of foreign troops serving on contract. These social factors had the effect of keeping military forces comparatively small, and the wars left the majority of the peoples of Europe relatively undisturbed.

The supply system of the age was a further check on the intensity of warfare. Most armies were dependent on magazines prepared in advance; troops could not be trusted to forage for themselves without the very real risk of mass desertions taking place; in consequence a field force was tied to the distance it could carry its bread. The low state of general agricultural productivity further restricted the size and activities of armies.

The Netherlands were the scene of many campaigns because of the comparatively high agricultural yield of the region, its strategical position, and its canal and river system which greatly facilitated military movement in the right season. However, the many towns and fortresses of the 'Cockpit of Europe' tended to make it a theatre of limited, defensive war. A general's first preoccupation in the area was often the security of his lines of communication, and this made inevitable the tedious operations of siege warfare. Certain advances in military science vastly encouraged the development of this form of defensive war. The artillery remained very cumbrous, and comparatively short-ranged and limited in effect, and its impact as an offensive weapon was very largely counteracted in the late seventeenth and early eighteenth centuries by the work of Vauban and his school of military engineers. The measure of impregnability that the three 'orders' of military defence works conferred on towns and fortresses compelled generals to concentrate on sieges and the operations in support or in relief of them. Vauban's system was—in the simplest terms—to make the widest possible use of enfilading fire, defence in depth, and the provision of sally-ports for sudden sorties by the defenders. At the same time, he perfected the techniques of the siege itself—with the laborious but almost mathematically certain 'sapping forward' by means of approach and parallel trenches and the clever siting of batteries, until the defending commander could either honourably yield up his fortress or face the prospect of a general assault with its far direr consequences.

These factors resulted in the definite limitation of war: the main attention of generals tended to be taken up with the disruption of the

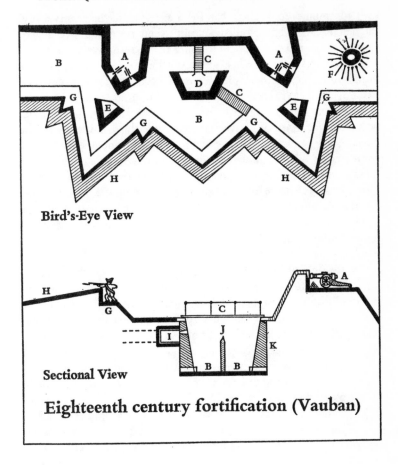

Bird's-Eye View

Sectional View

Eighteenth century fortification (Vauban)

A. Bastions—artillery positions situated to sweep the glacis.
B. Ditch—stone-faced.
C. Sally-port Bridges (temporary).
D. Demi-Lune—designed to cover the wall connecting two bastions (or curtain).
E. Ravelin—designed to cover the vulnerable angle of a bastion.
F. Tenaille—walls constructed to enclose a hill or other obstruction in the ditch.
G. Covered Way and Traverse—used to protect the ditch and enfilade the glacis.
H. Glacis—an area of levelled, sloping ground, affording a clear field of fire.
I. Counterscarp Gallery—designed to cover the ditch and for the opening of mining galleries.
J. Palisade—of sharpened stakes; used when the ditch was unflooded.
K. Scarp.

foe's communications rather than the destruction of the enemy army. Pitched battles were avoided (except when conditions were very favourable) as too expensive in irreplaceable man-power and material —although losses sustained in sieges were often proportionately greater[1] —and campaigns frequently hinged on elaborate manoeuvres designed to compel the foe's retirement from some important area.

The great French Marshal Turenne had taught fifty years before how to fight wars of movement and win small battles with the minimum expenditure of man-power, but in the hands of less talented commanders his teachings rapidly deteriorated into hide-bound methodicism and, in consequence, largely abortive forms of warfare. Only great leaders of the calibre of Marlborough, Prince Eugène, Charles XII and, on a slightly lower plane, Marshal Villars, were able to break away from the deadening military customs of the day and return some measure of activity, movement and decision to the conduct of war.

On the field of battle success or defeat rested on two chief factors: discipline and fire-power. By 1700, the standard infantry firearm in the English forces was the flintlock musket—the predecessor of the famed 'Brown Bess'—a far more reliable weapon than the ancient matchlock it replaced. The latter, however, lingered on in the French service for some years. A second important development was the growing employment of the ring bayonet: the English and the Dutch forces were among the first to be fully equipped with this refinement on the older plug bayonet; the French clung to the ancient pike as the defensive nucleus of some of their battalions until at least 1703. These two improvements in the weapons of the infantry soldier, when properly employed to exploit their advantages, were between them to account for a large measure of the success enjoyed by Allied arms.

The effect of the improved musket was a higher fire-power potential. The English Army was trained to make the fullest use of this factor on Marlborough's express direction. The line infantry fired by platoons, instead of by rank or even battalion volleys, as was the continued practice of the French and their allies. This innovation gave the English the advantage of a higher and more accurate rate of fire, based upon a far more effective direction of fire control by the sergeants and subordinate officers. An additional advantage lay in the fact that at any one time a third of the battalion was ready loaded. The true significance of the ring bayonet was that it enabled every infantry

[1] See Appendix II.

soldier to defend himself in close combat; once again, the English and Dutch made the fullest use of this development to encourage the more aggressive and mobile use of the infantry lines on the field of battle. Thus was born the modern method of 'fire and movement'. The French employment of infantry was generally less imaginative; its prime role was to provide a firm base for the cavalry and secondly to occupy and hold important positions—both basically static functions. This contrasted most strikingly, for instance, with the employment of Lord Cutts's battalions on the Allied left at Blenheim, which contained several times their own number of French infantry—including several 'crack' units—within the confines of Blenheim village: this made possible the deployment of the Allied cavalry (once again strongly supported by infantry brought well forward) across the marshes of the River Nebel in the centre against the weakest part of the enemy line. A revealing description of the British platoon-firing system in operation at Malplaquet is included in the Parker extract above.[1]

New weapons and tactics called into existence revised formations; the deep, phalanx-like formation did not survive the banishment of the pike from the battlefield. In its place gradually came formation in lines three to five deep, and the development of the hollow square to repel the charges of cavalry, although there was little uniformity at this period. Strict drill and firm fire discipline made a most redoubtable foe of the English infantry; the delayed volley, followed by the bayonet charge into the reeling enemy ranks, became the battle-winning formula. It was with very good reason that Louis XIV in 1706 ordered Marshal Villeroi 'to pay special attention to such part of the line as will endure the first shock of the English troops'—although in the event this advice substantially contributed to the loss of the battle of Ramillies. Linear tactics were wholly designed to exploit this new, far more deadly, fire-power of the infantry, although for many years there were few signs of real standardization of method. Armies still fought in elaborate battle arrays of two or more lines apiece which consumed much precious time to draw up, and as a result major engagements could often only take place by what amounted to the mutual consent of both commanders. Armies were very difficult to deploy, as no formation higher than brigade was then in existence. The heavier losses likely to be incurred further encouraged great caution, and no small part of Marlborough's success was his ability to

[1] See Parker, p. 88 above.

force action upon an unwilling foe by means of rapid marches under the cover of darkness into positions providing the enemy with no option but to accept battle. The rapid advance from Lessines to Oudenarde is one example: 'If they are there, the Devil must have carried them. Such marching is impossible', was Marshal Vendôme's reaction to reports of the Allied army's deployment over the River Scheldt.

The administration of most eighteenth-century European armies left much to be desired and nothing is more revealing than the contrast between the French and the English in this respect during 1704. In his march to reinforce the Elector of Bavaria in April, Marshal Tallard lost one-third of his effective force through desertion and men falling sick by the roadside; when, later in the year, he again joined the Elector, shortly before the battle of Blenheim, the greater part of his cavalry was smitten with glanders and had to be kept in quarantine. Very different was the tale of the Allied Army's far longer and more perilous march from the Netherlands to the Danube. By careful advance planning and vast preparations—including an alternative set of communications—the very last detail receiving attention, down to the provision of a new pair of boots for the infantry at Heidelberg— Marlborough executed an unprecedentedly rapid march down the flank of superior enemy forces, and brought his men to their objective fit enough to fight and win the bitter struggle for the Schellenberg Heights. Careful administration and care for both man and horse were the secrets of the high morale prevalent in Marlborough's forces, which in its turn enabled him to make calls on the endurance of his men that few other generals of the day would dare envisage. But the same high standard was not to be found in the English forces operating in Spain—Peterborough's and Galway's armies, for example, underwent terrible privations which seriously affected their battle-power.

Despite the increase in the role and importance of the infantry as a battle-winning arm, the cavalry retained much of its ancient importance and prestige. The tactical employment of l'arme blanche, however, varied quite significantly between the armies of the protagonists. The French regarded their cavalry as primarily a sophisticated weapon of fast-moving and manoeuvrable fire-power; Marlborough, in direct contrast, taught his to act as a shock force, using cold steel, and to this end would authorize the issue of only three rounds of pistol ammunition to his troops for each campaign. This was a return to the lessons of Gustavus Adolphus and Oliver Cromwell, but was far more effective than the French methods. Charging cavalry—properly supported by infantry—clinched each of Marlborough's victories; a large proportion of the allied horse was always kept back as a reserve for employment at the moment of crisis or decision.

The artillery on both sides was practically identical in type and range; once again it was not the question of equipment but of correct employment that distinguished the hostile batteries. On both sides the 'Train' was a vast and complex organization, embracing engineers, pioneers and supply services as well as the gunners. As Master-General of the Ordnance, Marlborough paid attention to the efficiency of all the component parts to the best of his ability. On the field of battle he frequently insisted on siting batteries personally; for easier and faster movement he introduced a form of light farm-cart, until recently called a 'Marlbrouck' in parts of central Europe. Of great tactical significance was the English practice of attaching two light guns to each infantry battalion to provide close fire support. This measure paid handsome dividends at Ramillies and again at Malplaquet; in the former case the Dutch infantry were able to capture the villages of Franquenay and Taviers, largely through the effect of their forward cannon, whilst in the latter Schulenburg's infantry managed to man-handle their guns through Taisnières Wood and this caused grievous losses to the French cavalry on the plain beyond. On the whole, the French made less effective use of their artillery arm—partly owing to the commonly held disrespect for the lowly-born professional gunner —but the terrible carnage inflicted on the Dutch Guards on the Allied left at Malplaquet was achieved by a cunningly sited concealed battery. Guns, however, made their greatest contribution to the conduct of war by their bulk and weight. The slow rate of progress they inflicted on any army on the march was fatal to most schemes of rapid or daring movement. The practice of harnessing horses in tandem to draw guns, and the use of civilian contractors to supply transport and drivers, did nothing to assist mobility or efficiency. In this respect the artillery arm reinforced methodicism and the unimaginative handling of field armies by reducing mobility to a minimum. A great commander such as Marlborough was prepared to leave his heavier field guns behind: only such a bold measure made his rule-defying march to the Danube possible.

On the whole, therefore, the armies of early eighteenth-century Europe were almost identical in weapons, grand tactics and methods of supply. Everything turned on the ability of the individual commander, still in personal control of every part of his army. Success was won by the ability of a general to overcome the many limitations of the time, and the adaptations he introduced or encouraged to make the uttermost use of the superior fire-power available from the improved musket.

In some respects the conduct of war was less barbaric than it had been in the immediate past, and by no means so extensive and total as it was to become in the future. The early eighteenth century was therefore a period of military transition and general mediocrity, enlivened by only a few men of genius; but it held the seeds of future developments in equipment and tactics, and, although all armies still committed the occasional atrocity, the period proved that the prosecution of war and the profession of arms could be both honourable and relatively civilized.

An Analysis of Selected Sieges in

Year	Place	Dates (*New Style*)	Duration	Defender (*and strength*)	
1702	Kaiserworth	18 Apr.–15 June	27 days	Comte de Blainville	(5,000)
	Luttich	13 June–17 Oct.	122 days	T'Serclaes de Tilly	(8,000)
	Venlo	29 Aug.–25 Sept.	28 days	Comte de Labadie	(1,100)
	Ruremonde	29 Sept.–7 Oct.	90 days	Prince of Hornes	(2,400)
	Liège	12–26 Oct.	14 days	Gen. Violaine	(7,200)
1703	Bonn	27 Apr.–15 May	18 days	Marquis d'Alègre	(3,600)
	Huy (1st)	14–26 Aug.	12 days	Gen. Millon	(7,500)
	Limburg	10–27 Sept.	17 days	Not known	(1,400)
1704	Trarbach	4 Nov.–20 Dec.	46 days	Not known	(? 600)
1705	Huy (2nd)	28 May–10 June	14 days	Baron de Trogne	
				(strength uncertain)	
	Huy (3rd)	6–11 July	6 days	Not known	
	St. Léau	29 Aug.–6 Sept.	8 days	Gen. Dumont	(? 400)
	Sandvliet (or Santoliet)	23–29 Oct.	6 days	Not known	
1706	Ostend	19 June–9 July	20 days	Comte de la Motte	(5,000)
	Menin	22 July–22 Aug.	31 days	Comte de Caraman	(5,500)
	Dendermond	27 Aug.–9 Sept.	13 days	Brig. de Valle	(2,000)
	Ath	16 Sept.–1 Oct.	15 days	Not known	(2,000)
1708	Lille (city and fortress)	12 Aug.–10 Dec.	120 days	Marshal Boufflers	(16,000)
	Ghent	18 Dec.–2 Jan.	15 days	Comte de la Motte	(15,000)
1709	Tournai	27 June–3 Sept.	69 days	Marquis de Surville	(7,000)
	Mons	9 Sept.–20 Oct.	41 days	Lt-Gen. Grimaldi	(4,000)
1710	Douai (1st)	23 Apr.–25 June	63 days	Lt-Gen. Albergotti	(8,000)
	Béthune	15 July–28 Aug.	44 days	Lt.-Gen Vauban	(4,000)
				(the younger)	
	St Venant	5–29 Sept.	17 days	Brig. de Seloe	(3,000)
	Aire	6 Sept.–8 Nov.	64 days	Marquis de Goësbriant	(7,000)
1711	Bouchain (1st)	9 Aug.–14 Sept.	36 days	Comte de Ravignau	(5,000)
1712	Le Quesnoy (1st)	8 June–4 July	26 days	Lt-Gen. de la Badie	(5,500)
	Landrécies	17 July–2 Aug.	16 days	Comte du Barail	(5,000)
	Marchiennes	25–30 July	5 days	Gen. Berckhofer	(7,000)
	Douai (2nd)	14 Aug.–8 Sept.	24 days	Gen. Hompesch	(3,200)
	Le Quesnoy (2nd)	8 Sept.–5 Oct.	25 days	Gen. d'Ivoy	(2,200)
	Bouchain (2nd)	1–19 Oct.	19 days	Gen. Grovenstein	(2,000)

[1] Casualty figures need treating with care; the main sources from which

the Flanders Region, 1702–12

Besieger (and strength)	Casualties (killed and wounded)[1]		Result
Prince of Nassau— Saarbrucken (38,000)	Allies— 2,900	French—1,000	Garrison capitulated
Duke of Marlborough (40,000)	Allies—not recorded	French—3,000	Garrison capitulated, on terms
Marlborough and Nassau (30,000)	Allies— 1,100	French— 839	Garrison allowed to evacuate to Antwerp
Duke of Marlborough (25,000)	Allies— 60	French—40–50	Garrison allowed to evacuate to Louvain
Duke of Marlborough (25,000)	Allies— 1,034	French—not recorded	Garrison capitulated and disarmed; a few allowed to evacuate to Namur
Duke of Marlborough (40,000)	Allies— c. 600	French— 860	Garrison allowed to evacuate
Duke of Marlborough (42,000)	Allies— c. 60	French—1,200	Garrison made prisoners of war
Prince of Hesse-Cassel (16,000)	Allies— 100	French —60	Garrison made prisoners of war
Prince of Hesse-Cassel (20,000)	Allies— 1,000	French— 350	Garrison made prisoners of war
Marshal Villeroi (strength uncertain)	Not known	Not known	Garrison made prisoners of war
Gen. Scholten (strength uncertain)	Not known	French— 700	Garrison made prisoners of war
Gen. Dedem (9,000)	Allies— 60	French— 40	Garrison made prisoners of war
Comte de Noyelles (strength uncertain)	Allies— 100	French— 50	French surrender
Duke of Marlborough (20,000)	Allies— 1,600 (naval included)	French— 800	French capitulated; Spaniards join Allies
Duke of Marlborough (30,000)	Allies— 2,620	French—1,101	Garrison allowed to evacuate to Douai
Duke of Marlborough (6,000)	Not known	Not known	Garrison made prisoners of war
Gen. Overkirk (21,000)	Allies— 800	French— 60	Garrison made prisoners of war
Prince Eugène (35,000)	Allies—16,000	French—7,000	Garrison allowed to evacuate to Douai
Marlborough and Eugène (40,000)	Allies— 4,800	French—4,000	Garrison allowed to evacuate to Dunkirk
Duke of Marlborough (40,000)	Allies— 5,400	French—3,183	Garrison repatriated for exchange
Prince Eugène (10,000)	Allies— 2,300	French— 980	Garrison allowed to evacuate, less cannon
Duke of Marlborough (60,000)	Allies— 8,009	French—2,860	Garrison allowed to evacuate to Cambrai
Gen. Schulenburg (31,000)	Allies— 3,365	French—1,200	Garrison allowed to evacuate to St Omer
Prince Nassau-Oranien (9,000)	Allies— 960	French— 400	Garrison allowed to evacuate to Arras
Prince Anhalt-Dessau (28,000)	Allies— 6,785	French—1,400	Garrison allowed to evacuate to St Omer
Duke of Marlborough (30,000)	Allies— 4,080	French—2,550	Garrison made prisoners of war
Prince Eugène (18,000)	Allies— 1,200	French— 600	Garrison made prisoners of war
Prince Anhalt-Dessau (20,000)	Not known	Not known	Allies abandon the siege on Villars's approach
Marshal Villars (22,000)	Allies— 200	French— 400	Garrison made prisoners of war
Marquis d'Albergotti (25,000)	Allies— 1,000	French— 500	Garrison made prisoners of war
Lt-Gen. St Frémont (28,000)	Allies— 700	French—1,000	Garrison made prisoners of war
Marshal Villars (20,000)	Allies— 700	French— 400	Garrison made prisoners of war

they have been drawn are Millner, Lediard, Bodart and Atkinson.

Biographical Notes

The following brief biographical notes relate to a selection of persons mentioned in the extracts from Parker and Mérode-Westerloo. The list is consolidated, and the characters are placed in alphabetical order. Sources of information are indicated at the end of each entry as follows:

Chambers's Encyclopaedia—Ch. Enc.
Dalton, C., *British Army Lists and Commission Registers,* (London, 1898–1904), 6 vols—Dalton.
Dictionary of National Biography—D.N.B.
Encyclopaedia Britannica—Enc. Br.
Larousse—Lar.
Pinard, *Chronologie Historique Militaire*—Pinard.
Biographie Nationale de Belgique—Biog. Belgique.
Raa, F. J. G. ten, *Het Staatsche Leger* (The Hague, 1950), vol. VII—H.S.L.

ALBANI (usually known as Clement XI), Pope 1700–21. Earned a reputation for being pro-French after recognizing Philip V as King of Spain. Published the famous Bull *Unigenitus* against the Jansenists in 1713. (*Enc. Br.*)

ALBEMARLE, Lord. See KEPPEL, Arnold Joost van.

ALBERGOTTI, François-Zénoble-Philippe, Comte (1654–1717). Distinguished soldier of Italian origin who became French by naturalization (1681); Brigadier-General (1691), wounded at siege of Mons (1692); present at battles of Steinkirk (1692), Luzzara (1705) and Denain (1712), *inter alia,* and at sieges of Turin (1706), Douai (1710) and Landau (1714). Lieutenant-General (1702). After 1714 employed on many diplomatic missions, especially to Parma. (Pinard.)

D'ALÈGRE (or de Alegar), Yves, Marquis (1653–1733). Experienced French cavalry soldier; wounded at Fleurus (1690); captured Bonn (1703); saw much service with the Elector of Bavaria (see under Wittelsbach below); prisoner of war (1705), but used as secret intermediary during period in the United Provinces. Marshal of France in 1724. (Pinard and *Lar.*)

ANHALT-DESSAU, Prince of. See LEOPOLD.

ANNE, Queen of Great Britain and Ireland, etc. (1665–1714). Second daughter of James II; married Prince George of Denmark (1683); many children, but all died young; succeeded William III to the throne (8 March 1702); strongly influenced by Sarah, Duchess of Marlborough, until 1710; thereafter by her enemy, Mrs Masham. Favoured the Tories and High Church party; greatest constitutional development of the reign was the Act of Union with Scotland (1707). (*D.N.B.*)

D'ARCO, Count (*fl.* 1704). Bavarian Marshal and unofficial Chief of Staff to the Elector; unsuccessful defender of the Schellenberg Heights (1704); at Blenheim commanded the Bavarian infantry near Lutzingen. (*Lar.*)

ARMSTRONG, Major-General John (1674–1742). Distinguished English engineer officer; Aide-de-Camp to Marlborough at Oudenarde and Malplaquet; Assistant Quartermaster-General in Flanders for several years; served with distinction at Wynendael (1708) and at the sieges of Menin (1706) and Bouchain (1711); Q.M.G. *vice* Cadogan (1712); Chief Engineer with rank of Colonel (1714); later Major-General and Q.M.G. in Ireland, and Surveyor-General of the Ordnance; F.R.S. (1723). (*D.N.B.* and Dalton.)

ATHLONE, Earl of. See GINKEL, Godart de, 1st Earl.

AUERSPERG, Count. Austrian diplomat of ancient and influential Carniolian family which held a princedom of the Empire from 1653. (*Lar.*)

BADEN, Prince Louis-Guillaume, Margrave of (1655–1707). Famous Imperialist commander, who served his military apprenticeship under Montecuccoli and the Duke of Lorraine. Served at the siege of Vienna (1683) and in many battles, including Nissa (1689), Salankamen (1691) and Belgrade (1688), but was defeated by Villars at Friedlingen (1702). During his career he served twenty-six campaigns, and took part in twenty-five sieges and thirteen battles. (*Enc. Br.*)

BAVARIA, Elector of. See WITTELSBACH.

BEDMAR, Isidore de la Cueba y Benavides, Duke of Villanova and Marquis of (1652–1723). After considerable service in Spanish armies in Italy and the Spanish Netherlands, he became Governor of Brussels (1681); he was promoted a Colonel-General (1692) and was present at Landen the next year. In 1700 he was promoted Commander-in-Chief of the Spanish Netherlands, and later became Governor of the country (1701–4). During this period he reconstituted the local forces and greatly expanded them. A great favourite of Louis XIV, he later became Viceroy of Sicily (1704), Vicar-General of Andalusia (1709), and President of the Council of War. (*Biog. Belgique.*)

BERGEYCK (or Bergheyck), Jean Armand de Brouchoven, Count (*fl.* 1700). An administrator of great ability, who served the Spanish Netherlands as *Surintendant-des-Finances* and later Minister of War (1702). He has been called 'the Belgian Colbert'. (*Biog. Belgique.*)

BERRY (or Berri), Charles de France, Duc de (1686–1714). The third son of the Grand Dauphin, and brother of Philip V of Spain, he married the eldest daughter of the Duc d'Orléans in 1710. He died after a horsefall. (*Lar.*)

BERWICK, Duke of. See FITZJAMES.

BLOOD, Brigadier-General Holcroft (1668(?)–1707). Son of Thomas Blood, the would-be thief of the Crown Jewels, he served as a young soldier in France. He returned to England in 1688, and was appointed Captain of Pioneers. After a very chequered career in the Trains and the infantry, he served as Chief Engineer at the siege of Namur (1695), and nine years later commanded Marlborough's artillery during the Blenheim campaign. Promoted Brigadier-General in 1704, he later served at both Ramillies and the siege of Menin (1706). (Dalton.)

BOUFFLERS, Louis-François, Chevalier, Marquis and Duc de (1644–1711). One of the most experienced French soldiers of his day, his variegated career took him to Africa (1664), Holland (1672) and Flanders (1667 and 1702–11). He was promoted Lieutenant-General in 1681, and Marshal of France in 1693. The stalwart defender of Lille (1708), he was second-in-command to Villars at Malplaquet (1709). (*Lar.* and Pinard.)

BRINGFIELD (or Bingfield), Lieutenant-Colonel James (d. 1706). First commissioned into the cavalry in 1685, he later became a Captain in the 1st Troop of Life Guards (1695), and was promoted Major of Horse in 1702. He served as Marlborough's Aide-de-Camp in 1706, and was killed at Ramillies. (Dalton.)

BURGUNDY (Bourgogne), Louis, Duc de, and later Dauphin of France, 1711 (1682–1712). Grandson of Louis XIV and eldest son of the Grand Dauphin; a willing and pious Prince of the Blood, but often indecisive. Married Marie-Adélaide of Savoy (1697); Generalissimo in Flanders and Germany (1700–3 and 1708), but of very moderate talents as a soldier. Joint Commander-in-Chief at Oudenarde (1708). (*Lar.*)

BYNG, Admiral Sir George, Viscount Torrington (1663–1733). English sailor of great distinction, who fought in the naval battles of Beachy Head (1690), Malaga (1704) and Cape Passaro (1718), and was also at the capture of Gibraltar (1704). Admiral of the Fleet in 1718, he held many important posts and commands, and became First Lord of the Admiralty (1727–33). (D.N.B.)

CADOGAN, General, William, 1st Earl (1675–1726). Served at the Boyne (1690), and later became Marlborough's great Quartermaster-General and unofficial Chief of Staff (1701–11). Promoted Brigadier-General after Blenheim, he became a Lieutenant-General in 1709. In that year he was wounded at the siege of Mons. He was instrumental in securing the fall of Bouchain (1711), but next year shared Marlborough's fall from favour. Restored to his positions in 1714, he conducted negotiations at the Hague (1714–18), and was second-in-command during the repression of the Jacobite Rebellion of 1715. He subsequently became Governor of the Isle of Wight (1716), a full General (1718) and Master-General of the Ordnance (1722), and was frequently employed on diplomatic missions. (D.N.B. and Dalton.)

CHAMILLART (or Chamillard), Michel de (1651–1721). Following a brilliant career in French regional administration, he became Controller-General (1699) and Minister of State the following year. In 1701 he was appointed Secretary of State for War, a post he held until 1709, when heavy criticism of his conduct of the war led to his resignation. (Lar.)

CHARLES II, King of Spain (1661–1700). From his accession to the throne in 1665, Charles II's feeble health and physical ailments caused him to be the puppet of a series of court factions. In the long wars with France his reign saw Spain lose French Flanders, Franche-Comté, Luxemburg and parts of Artois, and the state was soon crippled by bankruptcy. The intrigue over the succession reached its height from 1698, but on his death-bed Charles had the final word by leaving his possessions to Philip of Anjou. (Enc. Br.)

CHARLES VI, Holy Roman Emperor, formerly Archduke and Habsburg Pretender (as Charles III) to the Spanish throne (1685–1740). From 1703 to 1711 the Archduke Charles was deeply engaged in attempts to replace Philip V on the Spanish throne. Succeeding Joseph I as Emperor (1711), he continued the war with France and refused to accept the Peace of Utrecht (1713), but was forced to make peace at Rastadt (1714); the rest of his reign saw considerable successes against the Turks, but his later years were darkened by ceaseless intrigues over the Pragmatic Sanction and a series of unsuccessful wars. With his death the male line of the Austrian Habsburgs came to an end. (*Enc. Br.*)

CHARLES XII, King of Sweden (1682–1718). Succeeded to the Swedish throne in 1697, and the whole of his reign was occupied with bitter wars against the Poles, Danes and Russians. A commander of great talent, he won many battles (including Narva (1700) and Kissow (1703)), but his invasion of Russia came to final disaster at Poltava (1709); after a five-year sojourn in Turkey, he returned to Sweden and inspired a further continuation of the Northern War. He was killed at the siege of Frederickshall. (*Enc. Br.*)

CHURCHILL, General Charles (1656–1714). The third son of Sir Winston Churchill, he entered the household of Prince George of Denmark, and later saw much military service (including Sedgemoor (1685), Steinkirk (1692), Landen (1693) and Blenheim (1704)). He was promoted Major-General in 1694, Lieutenant-General (1702), General of Foot (1703) and full General in 1707. He was Governor of Guernsey (1706–10) and Lieutenant-Governor of the Tower of London. (*D.N.B.* and Dalton.)

CHURCHILL, John, 1st Duke of Marlborough (1650–1722). Eldest son of Sir Winston Churchill. Appointed a page in the Duke of York's household (1666), and commissioned as Ensign into the Foot Guards (1667). Saw considerable service with the fleet as a marine, and spent some time attached to Marshal Turenne in Flanders. Served as second-in-command during the Sedgemoor campaign (1685)—but three years later deserted James II for William III. Commanded the English contingent in Flanders (following service in Ireland at Cork and Kinsale), was present at battle of Walcourt (1690), but in disgrace 1691–1700 for supposedly betraying plans to the French. Close connections with Princess Anne eventually led to his being restored to favour, and he was subsequently deeply involved in negotiating the Grand Alliance and also appointed to command English troops in Holland (1700). Created Duke (1702) and made Captain-General of Anglo-Dutch forces shortly after Anne's accession. The following nine years held his greatest exploits as a soldier. Following his disgrace in 1712, he lived abroad in exile until the Queen's death in 1714. Restored to all his old offices by George I (1715), he spent his declining years between London and Holywell, watching the gradual building of Blenheim

Palace, and attempting to mediate in his family's quarrels. (*D.N.B.* and Dalton.)

CLÉREMBAULT, Philippe de Pallnau, Marquis de (d. 1704). The second son of Phillipe de Clérembault (1606–65), a former Marshal of France, he served in the armies of Louis XIV for considerable periods, and was ultimately promoted Lieutenant-General in 1702. He was drowned during the battle of Blenheim (1704). (Pinard.)

COEHORN (or Cohorn), Menno, Baron van (1641–1704). 'The Dutch Vauban' was famous for his work as a military engineer and as the inventor of the grenade-mortar that bears his name. He was also the author of several treatises on fortification. Major-General in 1692, he was promoted Lieutenant-General and appointed Director of Fortifications three years later. He ultimately became Master-General of the Ordnance of the United Provinces. (*H.S.L.*)

COLOGNE, Archbishop and Elector of. See WITTELSBACH, Charles.

CONDÉ, Louis II de Bourbon, Duc d'Enghien and the Great Prince of (1621–86). Probably the greatest French soldier of his day. The victor of Rocroi (1643) and several other battles, his career was somewhat chequered by divided loyalties and political disputes. Deeply involved in the Fronde plots, he transferred allegiance to the Spanish crown—and was defeated at the Dunes (1658) by Turenne. However, he returned to France in 1660, and led Louis XIV's armies to their greatest successes against the Spaniards (1668) and the Dutch (1672). His last victory was the battle of Senef (1674). (Pinard.)

COURTEBONNE, Jacques-Louis de Calonne, Marquis de (*fl.* 1700). A French soldier of some distinction, who became a Lieutenant-General in 1702. (Pinard.)

CRÉQUY (or Créquis), Marshal François de Bonne de Créquy d'Agoult, Marquis de (1624–87). This famous French commander saw much service in Flanders and Catalonia. He was appointed Marshal of France in 1668, and achieved his greatest fame as the stormer of Freiburg (1679). His less distinguished son served through most of the War of the Spanish Succession. (Pinard.)

CUTTS, General John, Baron Cutts of Gowran, Ireland (1661–1707). Cutts saw service in Hungary fighting the Turks (1686), and two years later he was a Colonel in the Dutch pay. He fought at the Boyne (1690), and was promoted Brigadier-General in 1695. After playing a prominent part in the siege of Namur (1695), he was promoted Major-General the next year, and assisted in the negotiations at Ryswick (1697). From 1701 he served in Flanders, led the storm of Fort St Michel (1702), and became a Lieutenant-General in 1703. He commanded the Allied left at Blenheim (1704), and next year was appointed Commander-in-Chief and Lord Justice for Ireland. He was also a Member of Parliament, representing Cambridgeshire (1689–1701) and then Newport (1702–7). (*D.N.B.* and Dalton.)

DAUN, General Philip Lorenz, Prince of Thiano, Marquis of Rivoli, and Count of (1668–1741). This Imperialist officer drove the French out of North Italy (1706) and conquered Naples (1708). He subsequently became Viceroy of Naples (1708–13). In later life he was appointed Field-Marshal and Governor of the Low Countries (1728), and from 1733 became Governor of the Milanese. (*Enc. Br.*)

DOHNA, Major-General, Count of Dohna-Schloditten (d. 1712). Distinguished Prussian soldier in the English and Dutch pay, who commanded the Allied centre at Almanza (1707) and was killed at the battle of Denain (1712).

DURELL (or Durel), Brigadier-General Henry (d. 1712). Served as Adjutant-General to the forces in 1704, and was present at both Blenheim and Ramillies. Promoted Brigadier-General (1710), he next year became Colonel of the 16th Foot. (Dalton.)

EARL (properly Erle), General Thomas (d. 1714(?)). Commenced his military career in the Dorsetshire Militia (1688); appointed Colonel of the 19th Foot (1691); he was promoted Brigadier-General (1695) and served as Governor of Portsmouth the following year. He became Major-General in 1696 and was promoted Lieutenant-General (1703). In 1707 he took part in the battle of Almanza, and was subsequently placed in command of an expedition against the French coast (1708). He eventually attained the rank of full General (1711). (Dalton.)

EGMONT, Procope-François, Comte de (d. 1707). A soldier-politician of scant achievement who was appointed General of Cavalry in the army of the Spanish Netherlands (1705). The male line of his family died with him. (*Lar.*)

EUGÈNE, François-Eugène de Savoie-Carignan, Prince of Savoy (1663–1736). The most distinguished Imperialist soldier of the period and one of the Great Captains of history. Following a rebuff from Louis XIV, he joined the Emperor's service (1683) and saw service at Vienna under Lorraine and Baden. Two years later he was made *Feld-Maréchal-Lieutenant* (aged 25). Defeated at Staffarda (1690), he later won the battle of Zenta against the Turks (1697). Following his services at Blenheim (1704), Turin (1706), Oudenarde (1708), Lille (1708) and Malplaquet (1709), and his failures at Toulon (1707) and Denain (1712), he negotiated the Peace of Rastadt (1714). Thereafter he again turned his attention eastwards, and defeated the Turks at Peterwardein (1716) and at the battle and siege of Belgrade (1717). His last campaign was on the Rhine in 1733. In all he sustained thirteen wounds. He was also a celebrated collector of works of art. (*Enc. Br.*)

FAGEL, Field-Marshal François-Nicholas (1655–1718). A distinguished soldier who fought in both the Dutch and Imperial forces. Served with distinction at Fleurus (1690), and was promoted Major-General in 1694 and Lieutenant-General in 1701. Present at Ramillies (1706) and Malplaquet (1709). Eventually appointed a Field-Marshal of the Empire. (*Lar.*)

FEUILLADE, Louis, Comte d'Aubusson, Duc de Roannais and de la Feuillade (1673–1725). French commander of medium talent. Heavily defeated at Turin by Prince Eugène (1706), he nevertheless eventually became a Peer of France (1716) and Marshal of France (1724). (Pinard.)

FITZJAMES, Marshal James, Duke of Berwick (1670–1734). The natural son of James II and Arabella Churchill, he was thus nephew to Marlborough. Educated in France, he received his Dukedom in 1687. His distinguished military career included service against the Turks, in Ireland against William III (1689–90), and later in Flanders as a French commander. He was taken prisoner at Landen (1695). In 1704 he commanded the French troops stationed in Spain, and after assisting in putting down the Camisard revolt in the Cevennes (1704–5), he was created Marshal of France (1706). Back in Spain, he was the victor of Almanza (1707), and later saw service on the Rhine front (1708) and the south-eastern frontiers (1709–10). Placed in command of the French army of the Rhine (1733), he was killed next year at the siege of Philippsburg. (*D.N.B.*)

FORBIN, Admiral le Chevalier Claude de (1656–1733). This famous French sailor—after a period as a soldier in Flanders (1676–7)—started his naval career as an Ensign, and was eventually promoted Lieutenant (1685). After travels in the Far East, he was taken prisoner with Jean Bart in the Channel (1689), but subsequently escaped. Promoted Captain (1702) and Commodore (1707), he enjoyed considerable success, and at the Lizard (1708) scattered a large English convoy in conjunction with Admiral Duguay-Trouin. The same year he commanded the abortive expedition to Scotland, and resigned from the service thereafter. (*Lar.*)

GEORGE, Prince of Denmark (1653–1708). Married Princess Anne (1683), and five years later joined the cause of William III. Shared his wife's fortunes, and in 1702 was appointed Generalissimo and Lord High Admiral, (*D.N.B.*)

GEORGE, Augustus, Electoral Prince of Hanover (and later King George II) (1683–1760). Placed in line of succession to the English throne (1701), he became a naturalized Englishman three years later. Served with the Allied army in Flanders, and was commended for his conduct at Oudenarde (1708). In 1727 he succeeded to the British throne. Later commanded the army at Dettingen (1743), the last British sovereign to do so in person. (*D.N.B.*)

GINKEL, Godart de, 1st Earl of Athlone (1630–1703). Experienced Dutch soldier; made Major-General in 1675, Lieutenant-General (1683), General (1692) and Field-Marshal (1702). Served William of Orange in Flanders and Ireland, and present at the battles of Senef (1674), the Boyne (1690), Aughrim (1691), Steinkirk (1692) and Landen (1693), besides the siege of Namur (1695). Appointed Marlborough's second-in-command in 1702. (*D.N.B.*)

GLOUCESTER, William, Prince of (1689–1700). Son of Queen Anne and George of Denmark; died as a child. His death led to the succession to the English throne passing to the House of Hanover. (*D.N.B.*)

GODOLPHIN, Sidney, Earl of Godolphin (1645–1712). English statesman of varied repute. Served James II, William III and Queen Anne in various capacities; Secretary of State (1684), First Lord of the Treasury (1700 and 1702–10), unofficial head of the Ministry (1702–10). Probably Marlborough's staunchest supporter, but quarrelled with the High Tories and hated by the Whigs. Dismissed in August 1710. A 'Trimmer', he kept in contact with James II in exile, and possibly betrayed the Brest Expedition to the French (1694). (*D.N.B.*)

HAMILTON, Lieutenant-General Frederick (d. (?) 1712). Lieutenant-Colonel (1690) and Colonel (1692) of the Earl of Meath's Regiment of Foot, recommissioned as Colonel of the Royal Regiment of Foot of Ireland after gallant conduct at the siege of Namur (1695). Promoted Brigadier-General in 1702, and Major-General two years later. Date of commission as Lieutenant-General uncertain. (Dalton.)

HANMER, Sir Thomas (1677–1746). A convinced Tory who persecuted Marlborough after his disgrace; Speaker of the House of Commons (1714); M.P. for Thetford and later for Suffolk until retirement from politics in 1727. (*D.N.B.*)

HARLEY, Robert, Earl of Oxford (1661–1724). A lawyer who rose to high ministerial rank under Queen Anne. A staunch Tory, he became secretary of State for the Northern Department (1704), and was a Commissioner for the Union with Scotland (1707). Gradually turned hostile to Marlborough, and was appointed Lord Chamberlain (1710) and a peer (1711). Persuaded Anne to dismiss Marlborough, and to leave the war (1712). Impeached by George I's Ministry (1715), but ultimately acquitted (1717), though never restored to favour. (*D.N.B.*)

HOMPESCH, Lieutenant-General Graf Reynard Vincent van (1660–1733). Dutch soldier of some ability. Promoted Major-General in 1701. Served in Marlborough's army at Blenheim (1704) and in most of the campaigns in Flanders. Surprised by Villars at Arleux in 1712, but subsequently played an important role in the passage of the lines of *Ne Plus Ultra* (*H.S.L.*)

HOP (sometimes, erroneously, Hope), Joseph. Distinguished Dutch statesman of vast experience in financial affairs. Served as ambassador to Berlin, Copenhagen, Vienna and London. Member of Council of State and Treasurer-General of the Republic before 1702. Fought with distinction at Eckeren (1703). Later proved very slow in producing money for Allied units in the Netherlands. (*Enc. Br.* and *H.S.L.*)

HORNES, Philippe Emmanuel, Prince of (*fl.* 1700). Sometime Governor of Upper Guelderland (1699–1702), who subsequently transferred his allegiance and commanded the Belgo-Spanish forces on the Rhine front (1703). (*Biog. Belgique.*)

HUMIÈRES, Louis-François d'Aumont, Marquis de Chappes and Duc d' (1671–1751). French soldier of distinction; promoted Lieutenant-General in 1704; served at Blenheim. (Pinard.)

INGOLDSBY, Lieutenant-General Richard (d. 1712). After service in Ireland (1689), he was appointed Adjutant-General of the expedition to the French coast (1692) and was later at the siege of Namur (1695). Promoted Major-General (1702) and Lieutenant-General (1704), he fought at Blenheim and in Flanders. In 1707 he became Commander-in-Chief in Ireland, a Lord Justice and M.P. for Limerick. (*D.N.B.* and Dalton.)

JAMES, the Old Pretender, or Chevalier de St George. See STUART.

JOSEPH I, Emperor of Austria, King of the Romans, etc. (1678–1711). Crowned King of Hungary (1687), and elected King of the Romans (1690), he became Holy Roman Emperor in 1705. His reign was dominated by the French and Turkish wars (he was present at the siege of Landau, 1704), by the Hungarian Revolt, and by contention with the Jesuits. He succumbed to smallpox. (*Enc. Br.*)

KANE, Brigadier-General Richard (1666–1736). Distinguished soldier and author; wounded at Namur (1695) and Blenheim (1704), he commanded the 18th Foot at Malplaquet (1709). Promoted full Colonel (1710), he later served as Governor of Minorca (1730–6), and was eventually promoted Brigadier-General (1734). (*D.N.B.* and Dalton.)

KEPPEL, Arnold Joost van, Earl of Albemarle (1669–1718). Dutch soldier who accompanied William III to England (1688); created an Earl (1695), he was promoted Major-General (1697) and Lieutenant-General (1701). Served in Flanders, being present at Ramillies (1706) and Oudenarde (1708); Governor of Tournai (1709) and of Denain (1712). (*D.N.B.*)

LA MOTTE (or Mothe), Louis-Jacques du Fosse, Comte de (*fl.* 1708). Eminent French soldier; promoted Major-General in 1702, he served several campaigns in Flanders. After capturing Bruges (1708), he was defeated at Wynendael; in early 1709 he unsuccessfully defended Ghent against the Allies. (Pinard.)

LEOPOLD I, Prince of Anhalt-Dessau (1676–1747). Notable Prussian soldier who served in the Flanders campaigns; he later rose to eminence under Frederick the Great, defending Brandenburg during the first Silesian campaign and being the victor of Kesselsdorf (1745). He eventually attained the rank of Field-Marshal. (*Lar.*)

LOUIS XIV, King of France. The most Christian King, *Le Roi Soleil*, etc. (1638–1715). Ascended the French throne as a minor in 1643; declared of age eight years later, but only really assumed power on the death of Mazarin (1661). His reign was dominated by a series of large expansionist wars, mainly directed against the Habsburgs of Austria and Spain. His reign probably reached its apogee in 1684 (following the capture of Luxemburg), but the brilliant domestic scene was darkened by religious disputes (Huguenots and Jansenists) and personal family tragedy. He was succeeded by his great-grandson aged five years. (*Enc. Br.*)

LUXEMBOURG, Lieutenant-General Christian-Louis de Montmorency, Chevalier and Duc de (1675–1746). Fourth son of the Great Luxembourg, he was a French soldier of some talent. Promoted Lieutenant-General in 1702, he later became Prince of Tingry and Marshal of France (1734). (*Lar.*)

MARSIN (or Marchin), Marshal Ferdinand, Comte de (1656–1706). Made a Marshal of France in 1703, he was a soldier of only moderate talent; replaced Villars in Bavaria (1703), fought at Blenheim (1704). Later transferred to Italy, where he was killed at the battle of Turin (1706).

MASHAM, Abigail, Lady (known as Mrs Hill) (d. 1734). Related to Harley and the Duchess of Marlborough; bedchamber woman to Queen Anne. Instrumental in causing the downfall of the Marlboroughs by supplanting Sarah as royal favourite (1711). (*Enc. Br.*)

MÉDAVI, Jacques-Léonor Rouxel de Grancey, Comte de (1655–1725). Experienced French soldier who was appointed Marshal of France in 1724. (Pinard.)

MURRAY, Lieutenant-General Robert (d. 1719). British soldier of note, who served at Landen (1693) and Namur (1695). Promoted Brigadier-General (1702) and Major-General (1704), he served in most of the Flanders campaigns. He became Lieutenant-General (1709) and was appointed Commandant of Tournai (1716–19). (Dalton.)

OPDAM (or Obdam), General Jacob van Wassenaer, Herr von Wassenaer en Obdam (1635–1714). Dutch soldier of fair distinction; promoted Major-General (1683), he became Lieutenant-General eight years later and ultimately full General (1702). Defeated at Eckeren (1703), he never received another field command. (*H.S.L.*)

ORKNEY, Field-Marshal Lord George Hamilton, Earl of (1666–1737). Highly experienced Scottish soldier who reputedly served at every battle and siege conducted by William III and Marlborough; after service in Ireland (the Boyne and Aughrim), he was wounded at Namur (1695) and promoted Brigadier-General. Promoted Major-General in 1702, he fought at Blenheim (1704) and saved Liège (1705). After Ramillies (1706) he headed the pursuit; played prominent parts at both Oudenarde and Malplaquet. Promoted General of Foot (1711), he became Lord of the Bedchamber (1714) and Governor of Virginia (1715). He was promoted Field-Marshal the year before his death. (*D.N.B.* and Dalton.)

ORLÉANS, Philippe, Duc de Chartres and Duc d' (1674–1723).

Nephew to Louis XIV, he first saw service at the siege of Mons (1691), and was present at both Steinkirk and Landen. His next military appointment was in 1706, but his command in Italy terminated with the battle of Turin. Sent to Spain (1707), he was soon implicated in plots against Louis, and lived in disgrace until 1715. On Louis's death he became Regent of France, and negotiated the Triple Alliance (1718). (*Lar.*)

ORMONDE, James Butler, 2nd Duke of (1665–1745). Soldier and statesman of varied reputation. Present at siege of Luxemburg (1684) and at Sedgemoor (1685), he later joined William III and fought at the Boyne, Steinkirk and Landen (where he was taken prisoner). Promoted General of Horse (1702), he was in command of the abortive Cadiz and Vigo expeditions. Appointed Lord Lieutenant of Ireland (1703–5, 1710–11 and 1713), he eventually replaced Marlborough as Captain-General (1712). Deeply implicated in the decision to withdraw Great Britain from the war, he was impeached in 1715 and became an ardent Jacobite. Died in Spain as an exile. (*D.N.B.* and Dalton.)

OVERKIRK (or d'Auverquerque), Field-Marshal Hendrik van Nassau-Ouwerkerk (1640–1708). Very distinguished Dutch officer who saved the life of the Prince of Orange at Mons (1678); appointed Major-General in 1683, he became Master of Horse to William III (1688) and a Lieutenant-General eight years later, and full General in 1701. One of Marlborough's trusted lieutenants, he served in most of the Flanders campaigns, and played an important role at both Ramillies (1706) and Oudenarde (1708). Died at the siege of Lille. (*H.S.L.*)

PALMES, Lieutenant-General Francis (d. 1719). A cavalry soldier of distinction; promoted Colonel in 1702, he led the charge that routed the *Gendarmerie* at Blenheim (1704). Earlier that year he had been promoted Brigadier-General, and 1707 saw him a Major-General and 1709 a Lieutenant-General. Sent as an envoy to Savoy in 1709. (Dalton.)

PETERBOROUGH, Charles Mordaunt, Lord and 3rd Earl of (1658–1735). A general and politician of great experience, but rather less good fortune. After much service in the Mediterranean area (including Tangier, 1680), he opposed James II. Favoured by William III, he spent some time in Flanders, but his hostility to Marlborough hampered his value. Jointly in command of the Allied expedition to Spain (1705), he captured Barcelona for Charles III, but was recalled in semi-disgrace to answer peculation charges in 1707. He was later employed as an envoy to Vienna, Frankfurt and Italy (1712). His last appointment was Governor of Minorca (1714). (*D.N.B.*)

RAVIGNAU (or Ravignan), Joseph de Mesmes, Marquis de (*fl.* 1710–18). As a Major-General defended Bouchain against the Allies, 1711. Became Lieutenant-General in 1718. (Pinard.)

ROWE (Rue or Row), Brigadier-General Charles (d. 1704). Gallant Marlburian soldier who became Colonel (1697) and Brigadier-General some time later. Killed at Blenheim. (Dalton.)

SABINE, General Joseph (1662 (?) –1739). Served at the Schellenberg (wounded) and Blenheim, Ramillies and Oudenarde. Promoted Brigadier-General (1707), Major-General (1710) and Lieutenant-General (1727), he became a full General in 1730, and the same year was appointed Governor of Gibraltar, a post he filled until his death. In 1727 he had also been M.P. for Berwick-on-Tweed. (*D.N.B.* and Dalton.)

SAINT-SÉGOND (or Sécond), Brigadier-General François de Rossi de Baville, Marquis de. French soldier; became a Brigadier-General in 1702. (*Pinard.*)

SALISCH, Lieutenant-General Ernst Willem van (*fl.* 1705). Dutch soldier of considerable experience. Promoted Major-General in 1694, he became a Lieutenant-General three years later and General of Foot in 1705. (*H.S.L.*)

SAVOY, Victor Amadeus, Duke of (1666–1732). Succeeded his father as Duke in 1684, and married Louis XIV's niece the same year. In 1690 he joined the First Grand Alliance against France, but withdrew from the war (1696) following a series of heavy defeats. In 1701 Savoy was the ally of France, but two years later Victor Amadeus changed sides. His position in Italy was secured by the battle of Turin (1706), in which he played a notable part. In 1713 he became King of Sicily, exchanging this throne for that of Sardinia in 1720. He abdicated in 1730, but subsequently tried to revoke his abdication. As a result he was imprisoned by his son for the rest of his life. (*Enc. Br.*)

SLANGENBERG, General Frederick van Baer van (d. 1713). A Dutch soldier of some note, he became a Major-General in 1683 and Lieutenant-General in 1692. He fought at both Walcourt (1689) and Eckeren (1703). Promoted Major-General (1683) and Lieutenant-General (1692), he later served as a Deputy attached to

Marlborough's headquarters for a considerable period of the Spanish Succession War, where he proved a thorn in the flesh. (*H.S.L.*)

STERNE (or Stearn), Brigadier-General Robert (d. 1732). An officer who distinguished himself at the sieges of Limerick and Namur, and who became Colonel of the 18th Foot, Parker's Regiment, in 1712. The previous year he had been promoted Brigadier-General. He ended his career as Governor of the Royal Hospital at Kilmainham. (Dalton.)

STUART, James Francis Edward, the Old Pretender (*alias* the Chevalier de St George) (1688–1766). The only son of James II and Mary of Modena, he was recognized as King of England by Louis XIV (1701). He spent part of his exile in France, and was present at both Oudenarde and Malplaquet. After a brief period in Scotland (1715–16), he later settled in Rome (1717) and in due course died there. (*D.N.B.*)

SUTTON, Lieutenant-General Richard (d. 1737). His first commissioned service was in 1689, and his career followed a successful course. Promoted a Brigadier-General in 1710, he was M.P. for Newark and Governor of Hull (1712). In 1713 he commanded the Bruges garrison, and at some subsequent date was promoted Major- and Lieutenant-General. (Dalton.)

TALLARD (or Tallart), Marshal Camille d'Hostun, Marquis de la Baume and Comte de (1652–1728). French soldier and diplomat. Promoted Lieutenant-General in 1693, he later negotiated both Partition Treaties (1698 and 1700) with William III. Served initially in the subsequent war with success, and was created a Marshal in 1703. Victor of the Battle of Speyer (1703), he was severely defeated and taken prisoner the following year at Blenheim. A prisoner in England until 1711. Later appointed a member of the Council of Regency (from 1717) and became a Minister of State (1726). (Pinard and *Lar.*)

TILLY, General Claude Frederick de T'Serclaes de Tilly, Count (d. 1723). Distinguished soldier in the service of the United Provinces who was promoted Major-General in 1691 and Lieutenant-General three years later. (*H.S.L.*)

URSINS, Princesse des (or Orsini), Anne-Marie de la Trémouille (1641–1722). The daughter of the Duke of Noirmoutier, she was twice married, and became highly influential at Madrid after arranging the marriage of Philip V to Marie-Louise of Savoy

(1701). Philip's second Queen, Elizabeth Farnese, drove her back to France. (*Lar.*)

VAUBAN, Marshal Sebastien le Prestre de (1633–1707). Very distinguished French soldier, engineer and economist. After a considerable amount of military experience, he was made Engineer to the King (1655), and served under Turenne. He carried out his greatest fortification work (1667–72) in Flanders and Artois. Promoted Brigadier-General in 1674, he became Commissioner-General of Fortifications (1678) and ultimately Marshal of France (1703). He built thirty-three fortresses, repaired 300 more, and conducted fifty-five sieges. He died in disgrace after publishing a volume criticizing the French economy, *Projet d'une Dime Royale*. (Pinard and *Lar.*)

VENDÔME, Marshal Louis-Joseph, Duc de Penthièvre and Duc de (1654–1712). Able French soldier. Promoted Lieutenant-General in 1688, he fought with distinction at Leuz and Steinkirk. Disliked by Louis XIV for his crude habits, he nevertheless obtained an independent command in 1695. Captured Barcelona (1697). In the Spanish Succession war he occupied North Italy, but was held to a draw at Luzzara (1702). Recalled to Flanders in 1706, he later lost the battle of Oudenarde (1708). After a year in disgrace, he returned to Spain, where he won the battles of Brihuega and Villaviciosa (1710). (Pinard and *Lar.*)

VILLARS, Marshal-General Claude Louis Hector, Duc de (1653–1734). Perhaps the ablest of Louis XIV's marshals. After a difficult early life, he became a Colonel of Cavalry (1674) and was repeatedly praised for his gallantry. Promoted Brigadier-General (1688) and Commissioner-General of Cavalry (1689), he rapidly became a Major-General (1690), and Lieutenant-General (1693). From 1697 he was ambassador at Vienna. In 1702 he won the battle of Friedlingen, and was appointed Marshal. In 1703 he resigned over differences with the Elector of Bavaria after winning the battle of Höchstadt, but in 1704 he successfully put down the Camisard Revolt. Created a Duke (1705), he captured Stollhofen in 1707, and in 1709 held the Allies to a draw at Malplaquet, where he was wounded. Subsequently he won the battle of Denain (1712) and recaptured many fortresses. Later a member of the Council of Regency, he became a Minister of State (1724), and was ultimately promoted Marshal-General in 1733 for his final campaign in North Italy. (Pinard and *Lar.*)

VILLEROI, Marshal François de Neufville, Duc de (1644–1730). A brave but somewhat undistinguished French soldier, who became a Lieutenant-General in 1677 and a Marshal of France (1693). Saw much service in Italy and Flanders, but was crushingly defeated at Ramillies in 1706. Never employed as a soldier again, but became a Minister of State in 1714 and a Member of the Council of Regency. (Pinard.)

WEBB, General John Richmond (1667–1724). First commissioned in 1687, he became Colonel of the 8th Foot in 1695. He later served with distinction at Venloo (1702), was a Brigadier-General at Blenheim (1704), a Major-General at Ramillies (1706), and was commended for his bravery at Oudenarde (1708). That same year he commanded the victorious force at the action of Wynendael. Promoted Lieutenant-General (1709), he was severely wounded at Malplaquet. In 1710 he became Governor of the Isle of Wight and M.P. for Newport. He was promoted General in 1712, but was forced to sell out after the fall of the Tory Ministry. (Dalton.)

WILLIAM III, King of England and Prince of Orange, etc. (1650–1702). Captain-General of the Dutch forces in 1672, he later became Stadtholder, and led his country's resistance to Louis XIV. Replaced James II as King of England (1688), and commanded the Allied forces in Ireland (1690) and then in Flanders until 1697. Defeated at Steinkirk and Landen, he nevertheless captured Namur (1695). Tried to find a peaceful settlement for the Spanish Succession problem, but failed. Created the Grand Alliance (1701). (D.N.B.)

WITTELSBACH, Maximilian Emmanuel, Elector of Bavaria (1679–1736). A gallant but impulsive character, who was a soldier by inclination. Joined the Franco-Spanish cause (1702) and seized Ulm. Joint victor of the battle of Höchstadt (1703) but quarrelled with Villars. Later captured Augsburg with aid of Marsin. His forces were defeated at the Schellenberg (1704), and at Blenheim, where the Elector commanded Tallard's left wing. The Emperor subsequently confiscated his lands and placed him under ban of Empire; lived in exile in France; saw service in Flanders. Restored to his possessions in 1714. (Lar.)

WITTELSBACH, Charles, Archbishop and Elector of Cologne (fl. 1700). Followed his brother in defecting from the Imperial to the French service in 1702, but almost immediately lost his lands to the Allies. Subsequently lived in France and Flanders.

WOOD, Lieutenant-General Cornelius (d. 1712). Distinguished British cavalry commander. First served soon after the Restoration, and was Lieutenant in the Life Guards by 1685. Became Colonel of Horse in 1693. Subsequently promoted Brigadier-General (1702) and Major-General (1704). Wounded at the Schellenberg that year. Promoted Lieutenant-General (1707). Present at Malplaquet (1709). (Dalton.)

WYNDHAM, Sir William, Secretary at War (1687–1740). Administrator and politician of some ability. M.P. for Somerset (1710), and Secretary at War (1712); deeply involved in decision to take Great Britain out of the war. Later Chancellor of the Exchequer (1713–14), but driven out of office; accused of complicity in the Rebellion of 1715, but never tried for it. Staunch supporter of Bolingbroke. (D.N.B.)

ZURLAUBEN, Lieutenant-General Béat-Jacques de la Tour-Châtillon, Comte de (d. 1704). Distinguished French soldier of Swiss origin who became a Lieutenant-General in 1702. He commanded Tallard's centre at the battle of Blenheim, but was mortally wounded. (Pinard.)

Glossary of Military Terms

APPROACHES—all earthworks, trenches, etc., constructed by a besieger to approach a besieged town or fortress.

BASTION—stone or brick-faced fortification of large size, usually built at the corners or other important points of a town's main defences.

BRIGADIER—(1) the lowest grade of general officer (eighteenth century); (2) the French equivalent to a Corporal of Horse.

BROWN MUSKET—smoothbore, muzzle-loading flintlock firearm, probably called 'brown' on account of the practice of painting the barrel to prevent rusting.

CASEMATE—a platform, frequently supporting cannon, placed inside the curtain wall.

CHAMADE—a signal made by drum or trumpet to communicate a wish to parley.

CIRCUMVALLATION (lines of)—fortifications built by a besieging army to protect its camp and siegeworks from any attempted attack by a relieving force.

CITADEL—a fort with between four and six bastions, usually placed at the best available place to dominate a town's defences.

COHORN—a type of trench-mortar invented by the Dutch Engineer-General, Cohorn, for throwing grenades and small bombs.

CONTRAVALLATION (lines of)—the trenches and fortifications constructed by a besieging army to isolate, and approach, a beleaguered town or fortress.

CONTRIBUTION—imposition or tax in specie or kind levied by an army from the area under occupation in return for promises not to plunder the region.

COUNTERSCARP—the outer side of a city's moat or ditch.

COVERT (or COVERED) WAY—area of fortifications placed on the outer edge of a moat or ditch, often protected by a parapet or palisade.

CURTAIN—a length of wall linking two bastions, and covered by their fire.

DRAGOON—a mounted musketeer, capable of fighting either mounted or on foot.

FAUSSE-BRAYE—area of ground at the foot of a rampart, protected

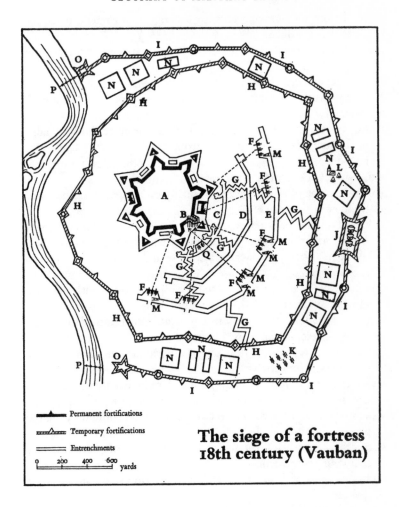

**The siege of a fortress
18th century (Vauban)**

▲———— Permanent fortifications

▵═══ Temporary fortifications

════ Entrenchments

0   200   400   600
⊢————————————⊣ yards

A. Invested fortress.
B. Breach.
C. Third Parallel.
D. Second Parallel.
E. First Parallel.
F. Ricochet batteries.
G. Communication trenches.
H. Lines of Contravallation.

I. Lines of Circumvallation.
J. Supply park.
K. Artillery park.
L. Headquarters.
M. Mortar batteries.
N. Camping areas.
O. Terminal forts.
P. River barrier.
Q. Final breaching battery.

on the outward-looking edge by a parapet, and intended for the defence of the ditch.

FIRELOCK—smoothbore, flintlock musket, discharged by sparks from flint on steel.

FOOT—generic term for the infantry.

GENDARMERIE—part of the crack Household troops of the French monarchy.

GLACIS—area of gently sloping ground leading up to the outer edge or a ditch, and swept by fire from the bastions, curtains, etc., beyond.

HORSE—generic term for the cavalry.

HUSSAR—type of light cavalry, originally of Hungarian origin; used for scouting, pursuit etc.

LINES—(1) areas of extensive field fortifications; (2) the customary battle formation of an army, usually two in number.

MAISON DU ROI—part of the crack Household troops of the French monarchy.

MINES—tunnels and chambers dug beneath the ground with a view to blowing up an enemy's defences or positions.

PALISADE—line of defence consisting of large stakes lashed together.

PARADE—parade-ground, used by troops for assembly, etc.

PARALLEL—large trench dug by a besieger to run parallel to the defenders' fortification.

RAMPART—large bank of earth raised to resist enemy cannon-balls and provide a firing platform for the garrison.

RAVELIN—a defence-work with two faces or sides commonly used to protect curtain walls, bridges, gates, etc.

REDOUBT—usually a small, square fort, used as an outwork; often of temporary construction.

TATTOO—beat of drum at nightfall warning troops to return to their quarters.

TRACE—the general configuration of a system of fortifications.

VAN—the advance guard or forward part of an army on the march or in battle.

Select Bibliography

CONTEMPORARY MEMOIRS

In addition to Parker and Mérode-Westerloo, the following authors wrote contemporary accounts of value (alphabetical order):

English Sources

BISHOP, MATTHEW. *The Life and Adventures of Matthew Bishop . . . from 1701–11,* etc. London, 1744.

CANNON, R. *Historical Records of the British Army.* London, 1835. Contains copious quotations from Brigadier-General Sterne.

CRICHTON, ANDREW. *The Life and Diary of Lieutenant-Colonel John Blackader,* etc. Edinburgh, 1824.

DEANE, PRIVATE JOHN. *A Journal of the campaign in Flanders AD MDCCVIII,* etc. London, 1846.

KANE, BRIGADIER-GENERAL RICHARD. *Campaigns of King William and Queen Anne. Also a new System of Military Discipline,* etc. London, 1745.

MILLNER, SERGEANT JOHN. *A Compendious Journal . . . begun in AD 1701 and ended in 1712.* London, 1733.

ORKNEY, EARL OF. 'Letters of the first Lord Orkney during Marlborough's campaigns', *English Historical Review,* April 1904.

STERNE, BRIGADIER-GENERAL ROBERT. *See* CANNON.

SWIFT, JONATHAN. *The Conduct of the Allies.* 1st pub. 1712. Included in *Works* (edited by Sir Walter Scott, London, 1883, 19 vols).

Continental Sources

GOSLINGA, SICCO VAN. *Mémoires.* 1857.

LA COLONIE, JEAN-MARTIN DE. *The Chronicles of an Old Campaigner.* Tr. and ed. W. C. Horsley. London, 1904.

PUYSÉGUR, M. LE MARÉCHAL DE. *Art de la Guerre,* Paris 1748. 2 vols.

SAINT-SIMON, DUC DE. *Mémoires.* Ed. Chéruel and Regnier. Paris, 1881–1907. 40 vols.

SCHULENBURG, J. M. *Leben und Denkwürdigkeiten.* Vienna, 1834. 2 vols.

VILLARS, CLAUDE-LOUIS-HECTOR, DUC DE. *Mémoires.* Paris, 1887.

GENERAL HISTORIES, DOCUMENTATION AND LIVES OF MARLBOROUGH

General Histories and Documentation
BURNET, GILBERT. *History of his own Time*. London, 1823.
EUGÈNE, PRINCE OF SAVOY. *Feldzüge*. Series One and Two. Vienna, 1876–81.
MARLBOROUGH, JOHN CHURCHILL, DUKE OF. *The Letters and Dispatches of John Churchill*. Ed. Sir George Murray. London, 1845. 5 vols.
PELET, J. J. G., and VAULT, F. E. DE. *Mémoires militaires relatifs à la succession d'Espagne sous Louis XIV*. Paris, 1836–42.
TREVELYAN, G. M. *England under Queen Anne*, London, 1930–4. 3 vols.

Lives and Historical Studies of Marlborough
ASHLEY, MAURICE. *Marlborough*. London, 1939.
ALISON, SIR A. *Life of John, Duke of Marlborough*. London, 1852.
ATKINSON, C. T. *Marlborough and the Rise of the British Army*. London, 1921. New edition, 1924.
—'Marlborough's Sieges', *Journal of the Society for Army Historical Research*, vol. XIII, pp. 201–5.
BELLOC, H. *The Tactics and Strategy of the Great Duke of Marlborough*. London, 1933.
CHURCHILL, W. S. *Marlborough, His Life and Times*. London, 1933–8. 4 vols. Also: London, 1947, 2 books.
COXE, ARCHDEACON W. C. *Memoirs of John, Duke of Marlborough*. London, 1820.
DUTEMS, J. F. H. *Histoire de Jean, Duc de Marlborough*. Revised by Duclos. Paris, 1806.
LEDIARD, THOMAS. *Life of John, Duke of Marlborough,* London, 1736. 3 vols.
TAYLOR, F. *The Wars of Marlborough, 1702–1709*. Oxford, 1921.
WOLSELEY, G. J. *Life of Marlborough*. London, 1894.

WORKS OF REFERENCE

BODART, G. *Militär-historisches Kriegs-Lexicon 1618–1905*. Vienna and Leipzig, 1908.
DALTON, C. *English Army Lists and Commission Registers 1661–1714*. London, 1898–1904. 6 vols.

Index of Persons

The following conventions have been adopted. Page entries relating to passages in the Mérode-Westerloo extracts are printed in bold to distinguish them from references in Parker (set in roman). When a page number is given in italics, this refers to a biographical summary of the subject; fuller information concerning names, dates and career will in these cases be found at the reference. The ranks of individuals given in the main body of the index are the highest they attained during their careers, and not necessarily those they held during the period covered by these books.

120, 122, 124, 125, 126, 127, **190**, **215**, **230**, 236, *259*

Villeroi, Maréchal François Duc de, 26, 27, 30, 34, 52, 53, 54, 59, 60, 62, **155**, **182**n., **183**, **185**, **186**, **188**, **192**, 237, *260*

Vitzthum, Mlle de, **157**

Waha, M. de, **162**
Wallis, Major-General, 122
Webb, General John, 79, *260*
William III, King of England, xv, 6, 11, 94, 113, **140**, **142**, *260*
Wittelsbach, Maximilian, Elector of Bavaria, 15, 29, 33, 34, 35, 37, 42, 47, 52, 54, 59, 60, 62, 64, 70, 81, 82, 96, 127, **141**, **143**, **156**, **160**, **162**, **164**, **169**, **172**, **173**, **177**, **178**, **179**, **181**, **182**, **183**, **184**, **186**, **189**,

192, **201**, **205**, **216**, **222**, 238, *245*, *260*

Wittelsbach, Charles, Archbishop of Cologne, 15, 26, **145**, **222**, *249*, *260*
Wolfenbüttel, Duke of, **168**
Wood, Lieutenant-General Cornelius, 39, *261*
Wrangel, Lieutenant-General, **209**, **210**
Wratislaw, Johann, Count, **229**
Württemberg, General Prince Charles Alexander, Duke of, 31, 35, 58, 61, **197**, **224**
Wyndham, Sir William, 130, *261*

Ximenes, Count, **142**

Zurlauben, Lieutenant Général Béat-Jacques, Comte de, **169**, **171**, **176**, *261*

General Index

This Index contains the names of places, rivers, and Allied and French regiments mentioned in the text. When a placename relates to a battle, siege, or other military operation, it has been printed in italics (although some textual references in such cases will only relate to geographical location). As in the Index of Persons, the differentiation between the two texts is indicated by the use of bold type for references in Mérode-Westerloo.

Aerschot, **193**
Aire, 92, **216**, 242
Aislingen, 162
Aix-la-Chapelle, 52, **190**, **191**, **193**, **198**
Alost, 63
Anchin, **123**, **124**, **125**, **129**
Anderlecht, 71
Antwerp, 9, 27, **146**, **147**, **153**, **154**, **194**

Arleux, 97, 98, 99, 101, 103
Arras, 91, 97, 99, 103, **225**
Ath, 64, **197**, 242
Augsburg, 33, 34, **161**, **162**, **179**, **183**
Autre Église, 59
Avoinlesecq, 107, **122**

Bachablan, 97
Baden, **229**, **230**
Berchem, **147**